THE SMITH AND
WORLD
ATLAS

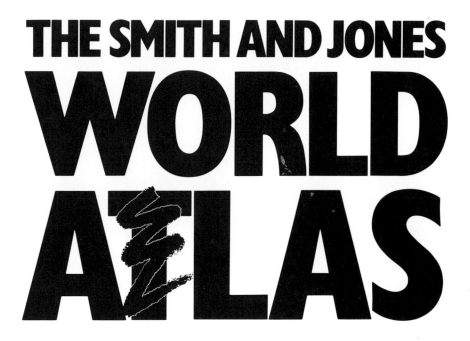

THE SMITH AND JONES
WORLD ATLAS

Conceived, researched, written and edited by
Griff Rhys Jones, Mel Smith
Simon Bell, Hilary Coffman and David Seymour

Designed by
Jo Harris

MITCHELL
ARTISTS
HOUSE
BEAZLEY

Published in 1983 by
Mitchell Beazley London Limited
Mill House, 87-89 Shaftesbury Avenue
London, W1V 7AD.

Designed and produced by
TalkBack, 76 Brewer Street, London W1R 3PH

Typeset by
APT Photoset Ltd.

© 1983 by Not Any Old Radio Commercials Ltd.

ISBN 0 86134 073 4

Printed in Spain by
Printer Industria Grafica S.A.
Sant Vicenc dels Horts, Barcelona, 1983
Depósito Legal 26827 – 1983

Just hold this splendid volume in your hand! Feel its weight! Riffle through these pages packed with facts and information from the four corners of the globe! Finger the glossy photographs and thumb through the range of contents! Now you've covered it with your grubby paw marks you'll have to buy it won't you?

But you won't regret it. Here, for the first time, in one book, is all you need to know about each and every country in the world. No country, however small and insignificant on the world stage, is omitted. The United Kingdom, for example, has a whole page donated to it.

This book has a hundred uses. Have you ever found yourself in that embarrassing situation at a cocktail party when the subject of industrial output in Djibouti comes up and you have nothing to say? Well now you can sit at home and read this wonderful book instead of going out to these boring, pretentious parties.

Thinking of travelling to Chad? Simply pick up this volume and you will think again. You will prefer to stay in England, until you read about England. Yes! Here at last, the ideal book for the xenophobe, the stay-at-home and particularly the lazy — short paragraphs, one page at a time reading, no long words, lots of pictures. And all this in handy paper-back size, bound in long-lasting cardboard.

We offer here the result of painstaking research, in depth analysis and laborious study. We should know, we have actually read it.

We sincerely hope that you agree that this volume will grace any library, in any home. With this book by your side you need never stir from the safety of your lavatory.

Griff Rhys Jones
Mel Smith

The World

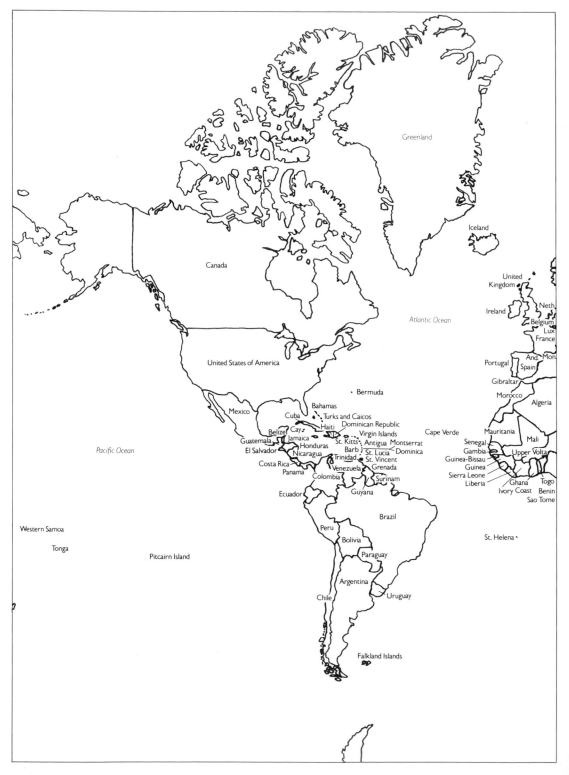

Greenland

Iceland

Canada

United
Kingdom

Ireland

Neth.

Belgium

Lux.

France

Portugal

And. Mon.

Spain

Atlantic Ocean

Gibraltar

Morocco

Algeria

United States of America

Bermuda

Bahamas

Cuba

Turks and Caicos

Mexico

Belize

Cay.

Haiti

Dominican Republic

Virgin Islands

Cape Verde

Mauritania

Mali

Guatemala

Jamaica

St. Kitts

Antigua

Montserrat

Senegal

El Salvador

Honduras

Dominica

Gambia

Upper Volta

Pacific Ocean

Nicaragua

Barb.

St. Lucia

Guinea-Bissau

Guinea

Costa Rica

Trinidad

St. Vincent

Sierra Leone

Panama

Venezuela

Grenada

Liberia

Ghana

Togo

Colombia

Surinam

Ivory Coast

Benin

Ecuador

Guyana

Sao Tome

Brazil

Western Samoa

Peru

St. Helena

Tonga

Bolivia

Pitcairn Island

Paraguay

Argentina

Uruguay

Chile

Falkland Islands

6

Arctic Ocean

Norway
Sweden
Finland
Denmark
Poland
Germany
Czechoslovakia
Liech.
Aus.
Switz.
Hungary
S.M.
Yug.
Romania
Italy
Bulgaria
Albania
Greece
Turkey
Malta
Cyprus
Syria
Leb.
Israel
Jordan
Iran
Tunisia
Libya
Egypt
Kuwait
Bahrain
Qatar
U.A.E.
Saudi
Arabia
Oman
Niger
Chad
Sudan
Yemen
Nigeria
Cameroon
Central
Africa
Djibouti
Ethiopia
Eq. Guinea
Uganda
Congo
Somalia
Gabon
Burundi
Rwanda
Kenya
Zaire
Tanzania
Angola
Comoros
Zambia
Malawi
Mozambique
Namibia
Zimbabwe
Mauritius
Botswana
Madagascar
S Africa
Lesotho
Swaziland

Union of Soviet Socialist Republics

Mongolia

China

Afghanistan
Pakistan
Nepal
Bhutan
Bangladesh
Burma
India
Laos
Thailand
Vietnam
Cambodia
Sri Lanka
Maldives
Singapore
Brunei
Malaysia
Indonesia

N Korea
S Korea
Japan

Taiwan
Hong Kong
Philippines

Pacific Ocean

Nauru
Kiribati

Papua
New Guinea
Solomon
Islands
Tuvalu

Vanuatu
Fiji

Seychelles

Indian Ocean

Australia

New Zealand

Antarctica

7

Contents

188	*Aden*
11	Afghanistan
12	Albania
13	Algeria
178	*America*
14	Andorra
15	Angola
16	Anguilla
17	Antigua and Barbuda
18	Argentina
19	Australia
20	Austria
21	Bahamas
22	Bahrain
23	Bangladesh
24	Barbados
25	Belgium
26	Belize
27	Benin
28	Bermuda
29	Bhutan
30	Bolivia
31	Botswana
32	Brazil
177	*Britain*
33	Brunei
34	Bulgaria
35	Burma
36	Burundi
37	Cambodia
38	Cameroon
39	Canada
40	Cape Verde
41	Cayman Islands
42	Central African Republic
43	Chad
44	Chile
45	China
46	Colombia
47	Comoros
48	Congo
49	Costa Rica
50	Cuba
51	Cyprus
52	Czechoslovakia
53	Denmark
54	Djibouti
55	Dominica
56	Dominican Republic
68	*East Germany*
57	Ecuador
58	Egypt
59	El Salvador
60	Equatorial Guinea
61	Ethiopia
62	Falkland Islands
63	Fiji
64	Finland
65	France
66	Gabon
67	Gambia
68	East Germany
69	West Germany
70	Ghana
71	Gibraltar
177	*Great Britain*
72	Greece
73	Grenada
74	Guatemala
75	Guinea
76	Guinea-Bissau
77	Guyana
78	Haiti
123	*Holland*
79	Honduras
80	Hong Kong
81	Hungary
82	Iceland
83	India
84	Indonesia
85	Iran
86	Iraq
87	Ireland
88	Israel
89	Italy
90	Ivory Coast
91	Jamaica
92	Japan
93	Jordan
37	*Kampuchea*
94	Kenya
95	Kiribati
96	North Korea
97	South Korea
98	Kuwait
99	Laos
100	Lebanon
101	Lesotho
102	Liberia
103	Libya
104	Liechtenstein
105	Luxembourg
106	Madagascar
107	Malawi
108	Malaysia
109	Maldives, Republic of
110	Mali
111	Malta
62	*Malvinas*
112	Mauritania
113	Mauritius
114	Mexico
115	Monaco
116	Mongolia
117	Montserrat
118	Morocco
119	Mozambique
120	Namibia
121	Nauru
122	Nepal
123	Netherlands
124	New Zealand
125	Nicaragua
126	Niger
127	Nigeria
96	*North Korea*

128 Norway
129 Oman
130 Pakistan
131 Panama
132 Papua New Guinea
133 Paraguay
188 People's Democratic Republic of Yemen
134 Peru
135 Philippines
136 Pitcairn
137 Poland
138 Portugal
139 Qatar
164 Republic of China
109 Republic of Maldives
140 Romania
140 Rumania
175 Russia
141 Rwanda
143 St. Christopher-Nevis
142 St. Helena
143 St. Kitts-Nevis
144 St. Lucia
145 St. Vincent
186 Samoa
146 San Marino
147 Sao Tome
148 Saudi Arabia
149 Senegal
150 Seychelles
151 Sierra Leone
152 Singapore
153 Solomon Islands
154 Somalia
155 South Africa
97 South Korea
156 Spain
157 Sri Lanka
158 Sudan
159 Surinam
160 Swaziland
161 Sweden
162 Switzerland
163 Syria
164 Taiwan
165 Tanzania
166 Thailand
167 Togo
168 Tonga
169 Trinidad and Tobago
170 Tunisia
171 Turkey
172 Turks and Caicos Islands
173 Tuvalu
174 Uganda
175 Union of Soviet Socialist Republics
176 United Arab Emirates
177 United Kingdom
178 United States of America
179 Upper Volta
180 Uruguay
181 Vanuatu

182 Vatican City State
183 Venezuela
184 Vietnam
185 Virgin Islands, British
69 West Germany
186 Western Samoa
187 Yemen Arab Republic
188 People's Democratic Republic of Yemen
189 Yugoslavia
190 Zaire
191 Zambia
192 Zimbabwe

Dependencies etc.

Aleutian Islands *Territory of USA*
American Samoa *Unincorporated territory (USA)*
Andaman and Nicobar Islands *Territory of India*
Aruba *Division of the Netherlands Antilles*
Ascension *Dependency of St. Helena (UK)*
Azores *Part of Portugal*
Bear Island *Island of Svalbard, Norway*
Bonaire *Self-governing island of Netherlands Antilles*
Borneo *Part of Indonesia*
British Indian Ocean Territory *Colony (UK)*
Canary Island *Part of Spain*
Celebes *Part of Indonesia*
Channel Islands *Part of UK*
Christmas Island *External territory (Australia)*
Cocos Islands *External territory (Australia)*
Cook Islands *Self-governing territory (New Zealand protection)*
Coral Sea Islands *External territory (Australia)*
Corsica *Part of France*
Curacao *Division of Netherlands Antilles*
England *Part of the United Kingdom*
Faeroe Islands *Part of Danish Realm*
French Guiana *Overseas department (France)*
French Polynesia *Overseas territory (France)*
Greenland *Part of Danish Realm*
Guadeloupe *Overseas department (France)*
Guam *Unincorporated territory (US)*
Guernsey *Bailiwick (UK)*
Heard and McDonald Islands *External Territory of Australia*
Isle of Man *Self-governing territory (UK protection)*
Java *Part of Indonesia*
Jersey *Bailiwick (UK)*
Macao *Overseas province (Portugal)*
Marquesa Islands *French Polynesia*
Marshall Islands *Part of Trust Territory of the Pacific Islands (US)*
Martinique *Overseas department (France)*
Mayotte *Overseas department (France)*
Micronesia *Part of Trust Territory of the Pacific Islands (US)*
Midway Islands *Unincorporated territory (US)*
Netherlands Antilles *Self-governing territory (Netherlands protection)*
New Caledonia *Overseas territory (France)*
Niue *Self-governing territory (New Zealand)*
Norfolk Island *External territory (Australia)*
Northern Ireland *Part of the United Kingdom*
Northern Mariana Islands *Part of Trust Territory of the Pacific Islands (US)*
Palau *Part of the Trust Territory of the Pacific Islands (US)*
Reunion *Overseas department (France)*
St. Pierre and Miquelon *Overseas department (France)*
Scotland *Part of the United Kingdom*
Society Islands *French Polynesia*
South Georgia *Dependency of Falkland Islands (UK)*
Tibet *Autonomous region (China)*
Tokelau *Island territory (New Zealand)*
Tristan da Cunha *Dependency of St. Helena (UK)*
Tuamotu — Gambies Archipelago *French Polynesia*
Tubuai Islands *French Polynesia*
Virgin Islands *Unincorporated territory (US)*
Wales *Part of the United Kingdom*
Wallis and Futuna Islands *Overseas territory of France*

Afghanistan
Democratic Republic of Afghanistan

RUSSIAN
• Herat   Kabul •
AFGHANISTAN
Kandahar •   PAKISTAN

If a soap opera were made about Afghanistan it would be called *Crossroads*. It has been that for centuries. A crossroads for trade, culture, invading armies and human migration. The latest episode is in Russian. Their troops rolled in late in 1979.

History

Invasion is nothing new to this landlocked, isolated, barren, mountainous country. During the past 2,500 years it has been taken over by a succession of foreign powers including the Greeks, Persians, Indians, Turks, Arabs and Mongols. Even when it emerged as an independent nation in the 19th Century, Britain and Russia could not keep away.

There were three wars between Britain and Afghanistan. The series was won 2-1 by the Afghans — to be expected, really, considering they were playing at home. Their prize was independence. Of a sort.

From 1919 until 1973, the country was ruled by a king who had no faddish notions of democracy. He was overthrown by his brother-in-law who was, in turn, killed during a further coup in 1978. The following year yet another coup paved the way for a pro-Soviet government 'inviting' the Russians in.

Politics

The king ruled absolutely until 1964 when he allowed a Parliament to be set up. This was dominated by the clergy and land-owning nobility, who opposed all reforms. No wonder fewer than 20 per cent of the people voted in elections.

There is only one political party: *The People's Democratic Party of Afghanistan.* The Russians help out with this democratic process. There is a government monopoly on petrol, sugar, cigarettes and cars. The few industries are mainly equipped by the Russians.

Transport

Afghanistan has the world's shortest railway — less than half a mile long. It has no navigable rivers. There are few roads but in any case, much of the country is only passable by camel and donkey. However, there are two airports. One built by the Russians and one by the Americans. This result of East-West rivalry was also responsible for the building of the roads — the Americans and Russians providing the cash and know-how in roughly equal proportions.

Communication

Afghanistan has 16 daily newspapers but they only manage to sell 100,000 copies a day between them. This is not surprising. More than 90 per cent of the people are illiterate. The Russians have recently helped to introduce television. In exchange, the Afghans are providing the Soviets with *natural* gas.

Wild life

The wild life in Afghanistan is very wild. It includes wolves, hyenas, foxes, jackals, wild dogs, wild cats, leopards, bats, bears and vultures.

The plant life isn't much more welcoming. It includes camel thorn, locoweed, poison vetch and spicy restharrow, the root of which may be used as a toothbrush.

Population: 15 and a half million

Size: Three times that of Britain, 245,000 sq. miles

Government: Communist

Language: Pushtu and Dari (Persian)

Main religion: Islam

Capital: Kabul

Currency: Afghani and puls

Tips for tourists

Eat your bread dry. The natives don't use butter but a substitute made out of the grease from the tail of the fat-tailed sheep.

If you go for a long stay, take a change of clothing. Temperatures vary from over 100 degrees Fahrenheit to 30 below freezing.

Be careful whom you make friends with in the western region. Syphilis is widespread there.

Take your own roughage — the Afghans eat fewer potatoes and nuts than any other race.

Afghanis display captured Russian troops in Kabul market.

Albania
Republika Popullore Socialiste e Shqiperise

Tips for tourists

Don't bother trying to sing the national anthem. It is called *Rreth Flamurit te per bashkuar* (The flag that united us in the struggle).

Don't bother looking for wild life. Most of it has been killed due to the Albanian tradition of carrying guns everywhere and shooting anything that moves.

Don't join the Albanian League of the Working Youth (although half of the 7 to 18 year olds have). You will spend your holidays doing things like building railroads.

Question: Take a tiny country, subject it to foreign oppression for 500 years, then set it free. What have you got?
Answer: Albania.

It is the most primitive country in Europe and the smallest socialist state in the world. It has fallen out with every friend it ever had.

Politics

Since Albanian independence in 1946 there have been six constitutions. The latest (in 1976) decrees that the country is a Socialist People's Republic. There is a Parliament of sorts but it only meets twice a year. For the rest of the time the president and a few close comrades run the shop.

There is only one political party, the Albanian Democratic Front (ADF). This does not mean that elections are never held. They are. The result in the last one, in November 1978, was:
Number entitled to vote: 1,436,288
Number voting: 1,436,287
Number voting for ADF: 1,436,284
Spoilt papers: 3

The Albanian government has Stalinist and pro-Chinese (anti-Stalinist) attitudes. It was much influenced by Chairman Mao's Cultural Revolution and it sent many of its top civil servants from the cities to eke out a living in remote villages. They were replaced by enthusiastic youngsters.

Labour pains

Albania has the highest birth rate in Europe. This is not surprising as its government forbids birth control — not for religious reasons (Albania is constitutionally an atheist state. All mosques and churches were closed in 1967) but because the country needs lots of people to work, particularly on farms. This is also why the government has halted migration to the cities. And office workers must provide a minimum of physical labour or they are shunted off to the fields.

Other pains

Blood vengeance still exists. Albanians will kill someone who murders a relative. But the rules of hospitality take precedence. They won't kill a guest in their house.

History

For 500 years Albania was ruled by Turkey. Independence was declared in 1912 and a conference in London decided to set up Prince William of

A government official checks that spelling is kept to a minimum in this repressive country.

Weid as ruler. He arrived to take up the post on March 7th. He didn't seem to like the job much. He left again on September 3rd.

In 1925 a republic was declared and Ahmed Beg Zogu became president. Three years later he turned the country into a monarchy and proclaimed himself King Zog. He ruled until the outbreak of World War Two, when the Italians invaded and Zog fled. After liberation in 1945 elections were held and a Communist-controlled Assembly was returned. It promptly declared the country a republic.

The Government formed close ties with the Russians but fell out with them in 1961 and withdrew from the Warsaw Pact in 1968 over the invasion of Czechoslovakia. It then forged links with China but in 1977 it attacked the ideology of Mao's successors and China cut off all aid.

Geography and travel

This is a wild place. The word *Shqiperise* in its title means 'Eagle's country'. Three quarters of the land is mountainous and nearly half is covered in forests. The north is mainly inaccessible except by pack-pony or donkey. There are just 2,000 miles of roads, 135 miles of railways and one airport, which only has flights when the weather is good.

Famous Albanians

Gjergi Kastrioti Skenderbeu, the national hero. He died in 1468, which shows how long it is since the Albanians had anything to celebrate. *Fan Noli.* A priest who was rocketed into the Premiership in 1924 after translating the Bible into Albanian.

Place to visit

Albania has the only town in the world which has recently been named after Stalin. It is Qytet Stalin (formerly Kucove).

Algeria

El Djemhouria El Djazairia Eddemokratia Echaabia

Geography

Algeria is the second biggest country in Africa and the tenth largest in the world. Most of its people live in a comparatively small part in the North. The rest of the country, 80 per cent, is the Sahara which is usually deserted.

History

Depending on whom you believe, the history of Algeria began in:
a) 1830
b) Time immemorial

Archaeologists believe the latter, having found some of the earliest evidence of human life here. The French support the date 1830 because that is when they invaded the country and started their colonial rule.

That began in the Kasbah in Algiers with an argument between the Dey (the Governor) and the French consul over a bill which had remained unpaid for 30 years. The Dey struck the consul with a fly whisk. The French promptly invaded. Thus began 162 years of oppression.

Many prosperous French people emigrated to Algeria to make money and exploit the Algerians. They were called 'colons'. The natives were so badly treated that they could not even justify the title of 'semi-colons'. They worked under slave-like conditions and were forced to pay heavy taxes to France. They were even relegated to the status of foreigners in their own land.

A number of resistance movements arose, notably the *League of Peasants and Proletarians* in 1870. But it was the *National Liberation Front (FLN)* which ultimately won independence. They were not popular with the 'colons', who wanted to remain French.

To do this, they set up the *Secret Army Organisation (OAS)*, to which they openly recruited deserters from the Foreign Legion who publicly assassinated 2,000 people.

Only one man could solve the problem: General Charles de Gaulle, a man famous for only saying 'Non'. He held a referendum in both countries which resulted in a big 'Oui' for independence.

Politics

A junta of army officers led a coup in 1965 and set the country on the path of socialism. The constitution says there can be only one political party (the FLN). All Algeria's considerable natural resources have been nationalised but it keeps a mixed economy.

The country is run by a president. There is a National Assembly with infrequent elections.

Industry

Times have changed since the 17th Century, when the main industry was playing host to the Barbary pirates. Today Algeria is one of the world's ten most important oil-producing nations. It is the largest exporter of liquefied natural gas and of bulk wine (no connection). It is also a big producer of cork and dates (the only one Algerians remember is 3rd July 1962 Independence Day).

The people

Algeria has the highest literacy rate in Africa. This is entirely due to its brilliant women. Only half the men can read, but for women the figure is 80 per cent. The country has a very high birth rate.

Population: 19 and a quarter million

Size: Ten times that of Britain, 900,000 sq. miles

Government: Socialist republic

Language: Arabic and French

Main religion: Islam

Capital: Algiers

Currency: Dinar

Tips for tourists

Don't bother to go canoeing. There are few rivers — and those are dry.

Do go to the pictures. Algeria is reputedly Africa's top film maker.

High life: Visit the highest sand dunes in the world — 1,410 feet.

Don't worry if you get an embarrassing complaint. Although there are only 300 health centres there are 50 VD clinics.

VAT on theatre is a problem here too.

Population: 40,000

Size: 179 sq. miles

Government: Independent co-principality

Language: Catalan

Religion: Roman Catholic

Capital: Andorra la Vella

Currency: Both francs and pesetas

Tips for tourists

Andorra has *no* railway, *no* air transport, *no* daily papers. But then, it has *no* income tax and *no* poverty.

So what does it have? Winter sports. Sixty-two miles of roads. Two privately owned radio stations. And TV beamed in from France and Spain.

Andorra

Principat d'Andorra

Industry

There are two industries in Andorra:
Tourism
Smuggling

Don't think these aren't connected. Day trippers from France and Spain take the winding, narrow road up the mountains to Andorra to stock up with cheap, duty-free booze and other goods. Then they try to smuggle them back — which is why the border roads are usually jammed in summer with cars being stripped by the Customs. Professional smugglers avoid the border posts. Andorra has the world's highest population growth — but this is not believed to be caused by smuggling.

Geography

Andorra is the largest of Europe's small states. It is a tiny principality (19 miles by 13) high up in the Pyrenees between France and Spain. It consists of seven villages surrounded by gorges, narrow valleys, high peaks and defiles.

History/Politics

Andorra has been a separate principality for 1,100 years. Since 1278 sovereignty has been exercised jointly by the President of France and the Spanish Bishop of Urgel. They are known as the co-princes.

Once every two years Andorra pays the President 960 francs (about £9) and the Bishop gets 460 pesetas (about £2.50). In exchange the Andorrans get free defence, free schooling, free social services and so on. Over the years, they seem to have got the best of the deal.

Andorrans are not allowed to vote until they are 25, the highest voting age in the world.

Alcohol is so cheap in Andorra that even the cows are muzzled.

Angola

Republica Popular de Angola

Dependence

Five hundred years ago this land was ruled by King Ngola. Then came the Portuguese. They took over Ngola's kingdom and renamed it Portuguese West Africa. That was typical arrogant colonialism. Their new territory, 14 times the size of Portugal, was used as a base for slave trading. The Portuguese refused to mix with the natives. Except a few tribal chiefs whom they converted to Christianity...and slave trading.

It couldn't last, of course. The struggle for independence grew throughout this century, culminating in a civil war which was bloody and brutal on both sides. When the Portuguese dictator Caetano was overthrown at home in 1974, freedom for Angola was not far off. It became independent the following year.

Independence

Before the people had time to celebrate, though, they were pitched into another battle. The Americans and South Africans were terrified that the newly independent state would fall into the hands of the Communists. To prevent this they drove Angola into the Communists' Arms.

After a few drinks the CIA opened a base in Luanda from which their agents carried out subversive operations under the codename *Puff the Magic Dragon.* Then South African forces invaded. So Angola called on Cuba to help. Their cavalry came riding over the hill, drove out the South Africans and forced the Yanks to go home.

Politics

This is a socialist state with a National People's Assembly. It has only one legal party. Its name is so long there wouldn't be room on a ballot form for others: *Movimento Popular de Libertacao de Angola — Partido de Trabalho.*

The current president, Jose Eduardo Dos Santos, is a busy man. He is also Foreign Minister, Vice-President and the minister for Economic Development.

Industry

Angola is rich in natural resources. Its main crops are coffee and bananas. But its reserves of oil and diamonds are worth far more.

The full effects of living under Portuguese rule for hundreds of years are only just emerging.

The people

About one-third of children in rural areas die in infancy. Those who survive can look forward to a long life — the major cause of death for adults is senility.

The most important tribes are the *Ovimbundu, Kimbundu, Bakongo, Ovambo, Koi Koi* and *San.*

There is widespread malnutrition. This is not believed to have anything to do with the best-known Angolan delicacy, a yellow coconut pudding in which the colour comes from the mass of eggs in it.

Culture

Drumming is popular. So is the playing of a type of portable piano. There are ritual dances for the coming of rain, harvesting, births, marriages, hunting and fishing.

On a more formal level there is a National Council for Culture which establishes People's Houses of Culture. There is also a Union of Angolan Writers and a National Union of Artists.

Population: 7 million

Size: Five times that of Britain, half a million sq. miles

Government: Socialist Republic

Language: Bantu and Portuguese

Main religion: Tribal beliefs

Capital: Luanda

Currency: Kwanza and Iwe

Tips for tourists

If you want to merge with the locals, get tattoed. Both men and women like to cover their bodies with them.

If you've got problems, see one of the tribal sorcerers. They not only practice medicine but interpret dreams and advise on personal worries.

Anguilla

Population: 6,500

Size: 35 sq. miles

Government: British dependency

Language: English

Religion: Christianity

Capital: The Valley

Currency: East Caribbean dollars

Tips for tourists

Avoid the rush hour. This is in the afternoon, when local fishermen saunter down to the beach.

If you forget your passport, don't worry. Immigration procedures are extremely casual.

Don't go to Anguilla if you dislike fish or hate water sports. There is little else to do — except lie in the sun.

The people of Anguilla are not keen on brash, noisy outsiders spoiling the tranquillity of their beautiful Caribbean island.

Unfortunately, they need the money. A few years ago they hit on the perfect solution. An advertisement was placed in US newspapers asking tourists to stay away — but to send donations.

Geography

Anguilla is 16 miles long and nowhere more than three and a half miles wide. That is how it gets its name — from the French *anguille* meaning 'eel'. The island is fringed with brilliant white beaches.

History

Columbus discovered this island in 1493. It became a British colony in 1650 but was lumped in with various other islands. It took the Anguillans 300 years to object. In 1967 they complained that St. Kitts was dominating them and threw out the St. Kitts police before declaring their island's freedom. Britain would not have this. Troops were sent in. Ten years later the Anguillans got their wish when their island was split off from those of St. Kitts and Nevis.

Politics

Anguilla is a separate dependency of Britain. It has a legislative assembly which has seven elected members, two nominated by the British Commissioner and three who are on automatically. Executive authority is still exercised by the Commissioner.

The island's ponds have been nationalised.

Industry

There is not much of this. A little phosphate of lime. A Board of Trade lighthouse. And some fishing. So the Anguillans have to fall back on the hated tourists.

Boredom induces mass suicide on Anguilla.

Antigua and Barbuda

Industry

The economy of this Caribbean island has had its ups and downs:

17th Century: *Down* — the main occupations were smuggling and charcoal burning.

18th Century: *Up* — Horatio (later Admiral Lord) Nelson opened a dockyard.

19th Century: *Down* — The economy was damaged by the emancipation of slaves.

20th Century: *Up* and *Up* — Rich Americans opened the Mill Reef Club, since when tourism has flourished.

Geography

There are three islands in this group.

Redonda is a cartoonist's desert island — 1 km square and uninhabited.

Barbuda is larger but it still has only one settlement — Codrington, named after an English family.

Antigua is the big one — big enough to have 600 miles of roads (even if it doesn't have a railway). It also has a few trees. But they are the tallest things on the island.

History

Discovered by Columbus in 1493 and named by him after a church in Seville, Spain.

    1632: The English colonised Antigua.

    1662: The English colonisers of Antigua colonised Barbuda. Over the years the islands have been part of the

In Antigua, native women are prepared to do anything in order not to grow taller than their husbands.

Leewards, part of the West Indies, a separate Crown colony and an associate state of the UK.

    1st November 1981: Triumph! Antigua and Barbuda achieve independence. The Premier is the Hon. Vere C. Bird, senior.

Population: 74,000

Size: 171 sq. miles

Government: Independent Commonwealth member

Language: English

Religion: Christianity

Capital: St. John's

Currency: East Caribbean dollars

Tips for tourists

Drive on the left

Drink rum, the local tipple

Eat lobster, the local delight

Listen to the steel bands

See their theatre: the Little Theatre Group and the Community Players (even littler)

Buy a warri board — used for the seed game which Antiguans play infuriatingly at taxi stands.

A monument to the female islanders' memory of British seamen through the ages.

Argentina
Republica Argentina

Population: 28 million

Size: Ten times that of Britain, 1 million sq. miles

Government: Federal republic

Language: Spanish

Religion: Roman Catholic

Capital: Buenos Aires

Currency: Argentine peso

Tips for tourists

If you want to get oiled, try sunflower seed oil. It is Argentina's most popular since sunflower seeds were first planted early this century by Russian immigrants.

Most exciting festival: *Misachicos Valleros*, which combines elements of Christianity and paganism.

Most boring festival: *Fiesta del Poncho*, in which woven ponchos are displayed. It is in Catamarca — but don't bother.

Politics

Since 1912 voting has been free, secret and compulsory for everyone over 18 (except clergymen). The generals who have mainly run the country since that time have found a way to get round this. They don't hold elections.

Of the last 19 presidents, 11 were military men. Nine of these were deposed — usually by other military men. The biggest political figure in the past 40 years was one Juan Peron who ruled from 1946 to 1955 and in 1973 and 1974. The Peronists are still the biggest national movement. The biggest international movement has been led by Andrew Lloyd Webber and Tim Rice on behalf of Peron's first wife, Eva. His second wife, Isabel, was distinguished by being this century's only Argentinian President (1974-76) without either of the titles General or Dr.

Since Isabel was kicked out, a military junta has ruled, drawn from the heads of the armed services. There are political parties apart from Peronism. Two of the less well-known ones are:
The Christian Revolutionary Party
The Intransigent Party

Power is still where it has always been — with the big landowners who control a third of the country.

Top and bottom

Argentina is among the top dozen countries in the world for education, literacy, health care and number of phones, TVs, radios and cars. But it is still backward in one way — it likes going back to the bad old ways. For example:
1947: Death penalty abolished
1976: Death penalty re-introduced
1949: New constitution adopted
1957: Government goes back to constitution of 1853
1954: Divorce made legal
1956: Divorce banned
1870: Free health service founded
1977: Free health service abolished

Boasts

Highest world inflation since World War Two: 350 per cent in 1976.

Biggest fall in the value of money: to one two-hundredth of its value over 20 years.

Trial by jury is enshrined in the constitution. (Unfortunately, it is never practised).

The world's holiest government department: The Department of Worship, which operates under the Foreign Ministry.

The highest increase in bankruptcies: rising from 700,000 dollars-worth in 1976 to 610 million dollars-worth four years later.

Winning the World Cup in 1978 (but they were at home).

The world's biggest Bovril estate.

More railways than anywhere else in Latin America. In fact, Argentina has more miles of railways than of roads.

The highest extinct, dormant and active volcanoes and the highest mountain in the Western Hemisphere.

Biggest average size of farms in the world.

The Disappeared Ones. These sheep have been hidden at the top of a multi-storey car park.

Australia

The aborigines of Australia have an imagination the size of the country in which they live. To be initiated into a tribe, you had to jump out of a tree, drink blood and have your two front teeth knocked out — in any order.

Dreamtime

Their myths about the world and their arrival in Australia defy the modern mind. These myths, legends and stories which comprise the aborigine culture are called *dreamtime*.

One story tells of a whale and a starfish, who are the best of friends. The whale is the only member of the community to possess a canoe. The other creatures want to go to Australia, and induce the starfish to trick the whale out of his canoe. This the starfish does by lulling the whale to sleep, picking gnats off his head. When the whale wakes up and sees the others heading off in his canoe, he beats up the starfish (accounting for the starfish's misshapen appearance) and suffers a head injury himself (whales have a hole in the head).

The aborigines thought the world was once silent and dark and that in a cave slept a beautiful woman, the sun. Women should not look at the moon in case they got pregnant or the moon got angry. They got fire from the rainbow bird who swooped down and stole it from the crocodile, thrusting the fire sticks up its bottom (which accounts for the rainbow birds' fiery tail-feathers). The rainbird, on the other hand, originates from *Bougoodoogahdah* — an old woman who lived with 400 dingoes. When she died, the bird was found in her heart and, whenever it sings '*Bougoodoogahdah*' today, the aborigines believe it will rain.

A new design for Liz Taylor's brassiere is tested in Sydney harbour.

Nightmare time

The whites have left their own immortal marks on Australian culture. The song:
Click go the shears boys, click click click,
Why do his hands and heart go click?
The poem:
Here is the wattle, the symbol of our land.
You can shove it in a bottle or hold it in your hand.
The expressions:
To have a full hand — having syphilis and gonorrhea simultaneously.
Cock-tax — alimony.
Gunga Din and squatter's daughter — gin and water.
Hand warmers — female breasts.
Rolf Harris' national self parody: *Tie me kangaroo down sport.*

Long time

Australia has been around for 50 million years and is the world's oldest continent. The north is tropical and Antarctica is a day-trip by plane from the south.

When the British landed in 'luscious Victoria', they found an area the size of England and Wales covered in prickly pears and 'the miserablest people on earth' instead of the 50 million potential trading partners they expected. The interior consisted of heat, drought, dust, scorpions, ants, centipedes, termites, 10 per cent of the world's reptiles — and willy willies. They called mountains Hopeless and Disappointment. But soon, with the best will in the world, they were producing the best wool in the world.

Serving time

Early arrivals consisted of convicts. They were transported for breaking up hop binding or impersonating Egyptians (among other things). Hatred of the English was expressed in the *Sydney Bulletin*, 1884:
'Australians will never consent to be spat upon by dirty little cads whose soap-boiling, nigger-murdering grandfathers left enough money to get the cad's fathers ennobled and to enable the cad himself to live without working'.
In 1933 they came closest to leaving the British Empire over an argument about bodyline bowling.

Population: 15 million

Size: Ten times that of Texas, 3 million sq. miles

Government: Independent Commonwealth member

Language: English

Main Religion: Christianity

Capital: Canberra

Currency: Australian dollar, cent

Tips for tourists

Think before you go. Convicts used to beg to be executed rather than exiled to Australia.

The tiles outside Australian pubs are there to make it easier to clear up the vomit.

Watch the company you keep. Australia has the worst record for rape and sex crimes.

Population: 7 and a half million

Size: One third that of Britain, 32,000 sq. miles

Government: Republic

Language: Austrian

Religion: Roman Catholic

Capital: Vienna

Currency: Schilling, groschen

Tips for tourists

Wear: Tyrolean hats, leather shorts (lederhosen), dirndls
Eat: Weiner schnitzel, strudel
Drink: Gspritzte (wine and soda). Or, failing that, just try to pronounce it.

Austria
Republik Osterreich

War

From 1000 AD until 1945 there has been hardly a moment to take a breather from internal and, mostly, external wars. The problem with Austria has been that it lies slap-bang in the middle of Europe. How do you tell where it begins and ends? (There is *this* merit in being an island race). From the days of Henry the Quarrelsome, nearly 1,000 years ago through countless Leopolds and Henrys, to Frederick the Warlike and the rise of the Hapsburgs in 1278, there was no more than three weeks annual holiday and then back to war. Even the Hapsburgs could not control the situation although they were in charge for more than 600 years.

It was all about territory, balance of power in Europe and succession. Philip the Handsome tried to add Spain to the Austrian Empire by marrying Joan the Mad. That didn't work. Subsequent emperors tried fighting France, Turkey, Hungary, Prussia and the Balkan States. Still they could not decide what Austria consisted of. Hundred Years Wars, Thirty Years Wars, Seven Years Wars. Every conceivable combination was attempted. They simply couldn't get it together.

A 'new initiative'

In 1918 the Hapsburgs threw the towel in. The mighty Austro-Hungarian Empire, which in 1800 had controlled most of Central Europe, tried to settle down. The result was that Austria provided the incentive behind the two most destructive wars in history. In the first — or First World War — the assassination of their Franz Ferdinand gave the Germans the opportunity to 'have a go'. Having made ludicrously outrageous demands of Serbia, which the Serbians somehow accepted, these accepted demands were ignored by Austria and the war began. The second — or Second World War — was started by Austria's most famous citizen, Adolf Hitler. Between the wars Austria was crippled by depression in the 30's, suffered two civil wars in 1934, a dictatorship until 1938, the Nazis until 1945 and, after the war, a ten year occupation by the Four Powers.

Another new initiative

After World War Two with half the road and rail system destroyed and the country in utter ruin, Austria tried democracy. They had given it a whirl for two or three years in the late 20's but it

had failed. Elections were supposed to be every six years. There wasn't one from 1929 to 1950. There are now three major parties, the *People's Party* and the *Socialist Party* (who have their own national newspapers) and the *Freedom Party* which started out as the *Liberal Party* (presumably because its early members were ex-Nazis). The Socialist Party is now in power with 'Freedom' pulling in only 11 seats out of the 183.

With democracy has come prosperity not seen since the days of the Empire. The most dense forests in Central Europe provide a thriving lumber trade. Austria is the leading producer of magnesite in the world, its tourist industry has increased ten-fold and car production eight-fold. There is virtually full employment. Austria must be the only land-locked country in the world which has a ship-building industry.

National game: jumping up and down in leather shorts (the audience gets drunk).

Harmony

Against the continuous background of war Austria was somehow inspired to produce Haydn, Mozart, Schubert, Strauss and Gluck and provided a home for countless others including Beethoven. There was a court orchestra as early as 1498 and a man called Fux was responsible for developing opera as a distinct musical form.

Music is still as important, with major international festivals in Vienna and Salzburg and the living conductors, Herbert von Karajan and Karl Bohm, carrying on with the pianist Alfred Brendel. Austria got *its* National Theatre in 1776.

Stress

Austria now has the world's worst record for deaths from cancer and is third in cirrhosis deaths. It has the highest proportion of elderly people in the world.

Bahamas
The Commonwealth of the Bahamas

Industry

The chief local industry used to be sponging. So it is quite logical that when the inhabitants of these beautiful islands wanted to extend their natural gifts they should turn to tourism. Several attempts were made in the last century but it failed to catch on until the invention of the plane put the islands within a couple of hours of mainland America.

In the last century their most successful year was 1873 when there were 500 visitors. Now the group of 700 islands, with only 22 occupied, proves too tempting a holiday for city-rich Americans.

Tourism is *the* industry. It provides 70 per cent of the national income. Two-thirds of the population is employed in tourism. Every year the tourists outnumber the population by ten to one. The Bahamas have more exports and imports than any other country and are the world's top salt producers.

The six no's

No.1: Capital Gains tax
No 2: Real Estate tax
No 3: Personal Property tax
No 4: Excise tax
No 5: Customs duty
No 6: Income tax
Otherwise you can do what you like.

So what's wrong?

In the old days nothing worse happened than the constant war between Great Britain and Spain. Now the horrors that have to be faced include plagues of beetles which destroy the trees. There are no streams so that fresh water has to be got from bores — the most boring occupation. Ominously, a leading manufacturing industry is the production of pills for birth control and diseases of the joints. Alcoholism is the chief cause of mental illness.

The Bahamas also have the second highest murder rate in the world, second highest theft rate and ranks fifth highest in drug offences.

History

Columbus made the first landfall on the island of San Salvador. He wrote to Ferdinand and Isabella "The natives love their neighbours as themselves. There is not a better people in the world." Within 25 years of his landing all the Indians had been taken into slavery or slaughtered. So much for loving thy neighbour.

The islands' most famous occupant was the pirate Edward Teach, commonly known as Blackbeard, until piracy was eliminated by the Eleutheran Adventurers. But twice more the Bahamas acted as a haven for smugglers. In the American revolution loyalists fled there, doubling the white population and tripling the black. The blockade-running resulted in imports increasing 25 times between 1860 and 1864. During Prohibition in America the islands acted as a smugglers' paradise.

A relaxed moment on the beach as they wonder whose baby it is.

Greatest optimist

The Spanish explorer *Juan Ponce de Leon* — a sort of international Larry Grayson — who looked on the Bahamas for the Fountain of Youth.

Politics

Until tourism the Bahamas were a classic lack-of-success story. The attempts at production of cotton, pineapples, citrus fruit, tobacco, tomatoes and sisal all failed. So no one really cared who ran the country. When tourism became profitable the (black) *Progressive Liberal Party* and the (white) *United Bahamanian Party* were born. Independence came in 1973 since when the Governor General has been appointed by the British monarch. He in turn appoints the Prime Minister who must nevertheless command a majority in the Assembly.

Population: 210,000

Size: 5,300 sq. miles

Government: Independent Commonwealth member

Language: English

Religion: Anglican

Capital: Nassau

Currency: Bahamian dollar, cent

Tips for tourists

Watch out for:
The Junkanoo Parade on Boxing Day
Goomboy rhythm dances
A three-toed human-faced creature called the *Chickcharney* (believed to be mythical)
The smallest lizard in the world, *Sphaerodacyllus*, or inagua.
The biggest underwater dredge in the world (for *Aragonite*)
Lack of pavements

The Biminis are the big game fishing capital of the world. Five hundred records have been set there.

Al Muharraq

Manama

BAHRAIN

Gulf of Bahrain

Population: 400,000

Size: 256 sq. miles

Government: Constitutional monarchy

Language: Arabic and English

Religion: Islam

Capital: Manama

Currency: Bahrain dinar and fils

Tips for tourists

Don't bother hiring a car. There are only 20 miles of roads.

Don't bother waiting for a train. There aren't any.

Don't bother trying to take part in the local sports of falconry, gazelle and hare coursing, and horse and camel racing. Only wealthy Bahrainis can join in.

Don't bother taking an umbrella. Only three inches of rain fall a year.

Bahrain

Industry

This is the poor little rich country of the Arab world. It has oil and booming industrial development but is nothing compared with its oil-rich neighbours. Generously, they are helping out by starting still more industry.

They weren't the first. That honour went to a British banker, Mrs. Tyndale, who happened to be sitting next to a Bahraini Minister at a conference in 1967. *He said* his country was looking for industries to replace the dwindling oil resources. *She said* she knew a firm with nowhere to put its latest aluminium smelter. *The consequence was* the Bahraini aluminium project, now the largest non-oil industry in the Gulf.

That and oil have taken over from the traditional, and far more glamourous, occupations: building dhows (Arab sailing boats), fishing, making reed mats, and pearling — where once 1,000 boats looked for them, now there are less than a dozen. They may return, however, as Bahrain is expected to be the first Persian Gulf nation to run out of oil.

Bahrainis cannot make enough pots for their money.

History

Since 1783 this land has been ruled by the sheiks of the Al Khalifah family. From the middle of the last century Britain had a 'special relationship' with them. The sheiks agreed to 'refrain from the prosecution of war, piracy and slavery'. In exchange Britain agreed to look after their foreign affairs and defence. In 1956 and 65 this included using British troops to put down popular uprisings.

In 1971 Bahrain declared itself independent. And its 'special relationship' with Britain became a platonic 'special friendship'.

Politics

In centuries-old authoritarian tribal fashion Bahrain is ruled by an Emir. He allowed a parliament to be formed in 1973 (only the second in the region, the first being in Kuwait). Two years later he abolished it. Now once again the Emir rules supreme, aided by his Cabinet, half the members of which are his relatives (they can be spotted by their surname, Al-Khalifah).

Yet Bahrain is practically a welfare state. Medical care and education are free; and housing and transport are subsidised.

Geography

Bahrain consists of 33 islands, the largest of which is 30 miles long and 10 miles wide.

Bangladesh
People's Republic of Bangladesh

History

When Britain granted independence to its Indian Empire in 1947 the separate nation of Pakistan was created for the Muslim minority. But that meant Pakistan was in two bits, East and West, separated by 1,100 miles of India. More than half the population of Pakistan lived in the East. But all the power was in the West. Such are the legacies of Empire.

Naturally enough the people of East Pakistan didn't much care for this arrangement. They showed it in the general election of 1970 by voting for a majority of candidates who wanted a separate state in the East. The West replied by declaring martial law. The East responded by starting a civil war and proclaiming themselves the new nation of Bangladesh. India joined in on their side. So did George Harrison. Against such opposition, West Pakistan surrendered.

The first president of Bangladesh, Sheikh Mujibur Rahman, showed his devotion to this hard-won freedom by banning all political parties. In 1975 he was killed and martial law imposed. The new rulers banned all political parties, apparently not realising they were already proscribed. Since then:

1979: Martial law ends. Six months later, a new president is elected.

1981: President is murdered by army officers. Six months later, a new president is elected.

1982: Another military coup.

Politics

The constitution has been suspended — even the part that pledges 'absolute trust and faith in Allah'. Parliament has ceased to function.

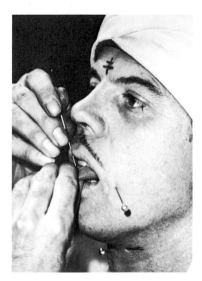

The only work available for this young Bangladeshi is as a *Sasco Year Planner*.

Geography

Bangladesh is a vast, low, flat plain, packed with people. Although it is the most densely populated place on earth (apart from some tiny states) it has only three cities, being one of the least urbanised parts of southern Asia. Large areas are covered with thick greenery with many villages seemingly buried in groves of mango, jackfruit, bamboo and date palm. No wonder there are only 2,500 miles of made-up roads.

Industry

This is an overwhelmingly agricultural country. Eighty per cent of the population work in farming, except during the monsoon. The main crops are rice and jute (half the world's jute cloth and gunny bags come from Bangladesh).

The people

Less than one in four adults can read. There is a very high birth rate. There are fewer nurses for the size of population than anywhere else in the world.

Population: 92 million

Size: Just over half that of Britain, 55,000 sq. miles

Government: Republic

Main Language: Bengali

Religion: Islam

Capital: Dhaka

Currency: Taka

Tips for tourists

Try listening to some Bangladeshi music. There are five kinds — classical, light classical, devotional, George Harrison and popular.

If the music grabs you, don't dance. The natives like snake dancing.

Remember to take an umbrella. They were introduced by English colonists and the locals still treat them as prized possessions.

Population: A quarter of a million

Size: 166 sq. miles

Government: Independent Commonwealth member

Language: English

Religion: Anglican

Capital: Bridgetown

Currency: Barbados dollar

Tips for tourists

Take several extremely long novels with you. *Great Expectations* would be inappropriate.

If you are determined to get some excitement on Barbados, choose the season you go carefully. With luck you might be hit by a hurricane — or even an earthquake.

Take care. The rate of deaths from syphilis is the second highest in the world.

Barbados

For 350 years Barbados had to contend with nothing but wonderful weather, beautiful beaches and benevolent British rule. And it shows. It is an utterly boring place.

Boring history

The British arrived in 1627, one hundred years after the Portuguese discovered this island (21 miles by 14) and named it after the bearded fig trees which dotted the landscape. ('Barbados' means 'bearded' in Portuguese).

As the years went by nothing interrupted the calm. The island was missed by pirates, ignored by adventurers and shunned by foreign powers which were trying to seize other Caribbean lands.

Frantic preparations to build palm trees for the tourist season.

Boring politics

Barbados became self-governing in 1966 without ever really complaining about its colonial status. It still has a Governor-General, appointed by the British, and he appoints members of the Senate. No one seems unduly upset about this arrangement. Barbados is reckoned to be the most stable of all Caribbean countries. It has the lowest defence expenditure in the world.

Boring culture

English culture has been transferred wholesale to Barbados. And the locals love it. They are crazy about cricket, delirious about drinking tea, utterly delighted over the uniforms worn by the

police and horse guards, and pleased with the parliamentary system.

The island is littered with place names like Windsor, Yorkshire and Hastings.

Bored people

Barbados has the highest literacy rate of any country in the Americas outside the United States. This is a terrible indictment of a place where people should be spending all their time having fun.

Three-fifths of the population is women. It is said that the men leave as the islands are over-crowded. Women stay because the men leave? It is the most unequal country in the world. Ten per cent of landowners own 95 per cent of the land.

Belgium
Royaume de Belgique

Belgians have a reputation for stupidity, gluttony and self-indulgence. They seem to take whatever no other country wants, including the headquarters of the European Common Market. They are best summed up by the phrase *Give it to the Belgians*, which is advice to someone complaining about food or clothing.

They pinched their language from the Dutch, French and Germans, consume more food than almost any other people, and are the only nation which established a monarchy *after* a successful revolution.

The only example of them giving anything away was during World War Two, when King Leopold III gave his country to the Germans.

Monarchy

The state of Belgium was formed in 1830 after a revolution against the Dutch rulers. Queen Victoria's uncle was set up as the first king, Leopold I.

Leopold II suffered the double indignity of being forced to hand over his Congo interests (he had been treating the Congo's mineral wealth as his own) *and* being sued by his daughters for trying to make off with their mother's fortune. The next king, Albert, died falling off a mountain.

Leopold III killed his first wife in a car crash, offended his Catholic subjects by remarrying, led the Belgian army to disaster at the start of World War Two (nearly destroying the British and French forces in the process) and then spent the rest of the war with Hitler while his people suffered at home. He abdicated eventually and his son, Baudouin took over. He is still king.

The memorial to the king who defended Flanders in World War Two. The entire German army is just left of the picture.

Politics

There are so many political parties in Belgium that most governments are coalitions. Senators and Deputies get 900,000 francs (about £12,000) a year plus free rail passes. This is probably because the Belgians are very proud of their railway, which has been state-owned since its foundation in 1834. They have the most rail track for the size of the country.

People

The people of this small country (only half as big again as Wales) are among the richest and best-fed in the world (they have the highest calorie intake of any nation). Yet they have an identity crisis, being split between Walloons, Flems and foreigners. More than one in ten of the population comes from other lands.

The language

If Belgians had run the Tower of Babel there would have been no problem there. They have three official languages — French, Dutch and German. To avoid confusion official language frontiers have been set: Dutch-speaking in the North, French in the South and German in the East.

There are two TV stations, one in French, the other in Dutch. German speakers have to make do with the radio (three stations). Belgium has the shortest surname — O. There are 18 of them in the phone book.

Industry

Belgium has huge coal and steel industries. It produces a lot of sugar and has a thriving tobacco industry. Being the organised place it is, it also produces matches — 45 billion a year.

Art

Remember Jan Van Eyck, the inventor of oil painting.
See The Virgin with a Parrot, painted by Rubens, in the Antwerp Gallery.
Keep your granny away from *Mannekin Pis*, the statue of a small boy pissing (in Brussels). It was commissioned by a distraught father who promised the city a statue of his missing son in whatever position he was found.

Population: 9 and three-quarter million

Size: A tenth that of Britain, 12,000 sq. miles

Government: Constitutional Monarchy

Language: Dutch, French, German

Religion: Roman Catholic

Capital: Brussels

Currency: Franc

Tips for tourists

Do go to Bruges, the most beautiful place in the country, known as *The Venice of the North*.

Don't go anywhere else if you have to ask the way. With place names like *Borgerhout*, *Wilruyck* and *Kortrijk*, you won't be able to.

Festivals:
In Ostend — The Dead Rat Ball
In Aalst — the Procession Day of Dirty Aunties *and* the Day of Onion Throwing.
In Ypres — The Cats' Festival in which cats (devils) are thrown from town hall towers to show they are human. Replicas are used nowadays (presumably because of a shortage of cats).

Belize

Population: 160,000

Size: 8,866 sq. miles

Government: Independent Commonwealth member

Main language: English

Religion: Christian

Capital: Belmopan

Currency: Belize dollar

Tips for tourists

Visit the Maya ruins. They are on the border with Guatemala and are used to spot a Guatemalan invasion.

Visit the Great Barrier Reef — the second largest barrier reef in the world.

There are occasional outbreaks of yellow fever and cholera.

Caribbean paradise?

Through the centre of Belize City runs Belize River which is a massive open sewer. All the filth of the 50,000 population is chucked in. There are no other sewage arrangements in the entire country. The government, therefore, encourages an indigenous fish, the catfish, which relishes a hotch-potch of human excrement. These fish are like piranhas. Throw a piece of shit in the river and the water will literally boil with their frenzied attempts to eat it — up to two foot high. If *you* should fall in with an open cut, they'll devour you in about two minutes.

Otherwise there are invisible flies that inflict three inch gashes, an insect that digs out your toenails and a termite which destroys small parts of the body, noses and ears a speciality.

The coastline is called the Mosquito Coast. Somehow, though, the population are very healthy. The Canadians have lent some money to make a sewer.

Murky past

In 1638 a former British seacaptain by the name of Wallace, who had set out with Walter Raleigh to purge the area of buccaneers, became a pirate himself and was shipwrecked on the coast of Belize where he made a living selling mahogany.

The Spaniards had previously — and rather ambitiously — claimed the entire new world as their own — North and South America. They were ungenerous about British support for the new settlement and warred against it, unsuccessfully.

Shadowy origins

The name 'Belize' some think to be an Indian corruption of *Wallace*. Others say it comes from the French word *balisse* meaning 'beacon', and that it was a safe haven for sailors. The most likely explanation is that it derives from the Indian word for 'muddy water'. Certainly the modern Belize is as great a mixture of cultures as you'll find anywhere.

Muddy water

It is made up of English settlers, Creole Indians, Maya Indians, Indians from St. Vincent, Indians from the Honduras, Mestizos, Carib Indians, Asians, Mideasterners, black former slaves from the West Indies/Africa, and a strange sect of German speakers from Mexico called Mennonites. These races have now all inter-related and produced a sort of muddy hotch-potch.

Independence

Gained in 1981, the Queen is still Head of State but is represented by a Governor General who is appointed by the Crown and the Prime Minister of Belize. Between them they rule a country 70 per cent of which is impenetrable jungle, and agriculture the main occupation. Sugar is the chief export. Belize's industrial development consists of:

A citrus processor
A sawmill
A sugar refinery.

It was a precondition of governorship to be able to balance a cheese souffle on your head.

Benin

Republique Populaire du Benin

The Belly

Formerly the French Colony of Dahomey, Benin gained its independence in 1958. 'Dahomey' means *In the belly of the Da,* the Da being a neighbouring king who was beheaded by King Ougbadja in 1660 and buried under Ougbadja's palace. 'Benin' probably dates from Ougbadja's son's conquest of the coastal area to which the name was subsequently attached. The country was split into several kingdoms of which the Great Oyo Empire and the Kings of Abomey, who defeated it, were the greatest.

The guts

Dahomey is the home of voodoo which comes from the Fon word *vodun.* Practices such as human sacrifice have largely died out — or, at any rate, they are kept to the less violent forms. The explorer Sir Richard Burton recorded cases in which more than 500 people were sacrificed at a time. Common methods were crucifixion and being thrown from a high place to be torn to pieces by the tribe below. On the death of the king his wives would attack and murder each other until order was restored by the incoming sovereign.

Racial discrimination

Dahomey was the world's largest exporter of slaves due to its predominance over the Western Coastal States. This trade reached its peak in the 1840's with about 30,000 slaves a year. The British involvement in the area was largely due to its desire to prevent the slave trade (it was alleged). To this end it began to colonise Nigeria next door. The inhospitable nature of Benin found its way into verse:
Beware, beware, the blight of Benin,
One comes out though forty go in.

Sexual discrimination

Apart from voodoo the most singular Dahomean institution was its female army of Amazons. When this first attacked the Oyo Empire it was on the point of winning when someone on the other side noticed they were women. Instilled with new courage, the Oyo boyos won. Eventually, though, the Amazon army helped Dahomey to conquer the surrounding kingdoms.

Lack of discrimination

This is one of the most politically troubled states in Africa. In the first 10 years after independence Benin had eight changes of government and four military coups. The president of the Military Revolutionary Government since 1972 is Lt.-Col. Mathieu Kerekou who, on assuming office, rejected communism, capitalism and socialism. Two years later, he declared: *"The new society in which each Dahomean will find happiness is a socialist one".* He changed the country's name to Benin and announced a Marxist-Leninist state. Kerekou has had his problems. In 1975 his Minister for Interior and Security was shot dead by the gendarmerie while escaping after allegedly making love to the president's wife. A plot is, however, suspected. In the reshuffle that followed, Kerekou made his Minister for Tourism into commander of the Parachute Commando.

Other discrimination

In pre-colonial days a citizen could be stopped on sus. and required to recite the list of ancestral kings off by heart. Penalty for failure: death.

Population: 3 and a half million

Size: Half that of Britain, 45,000 sq. miles

Government: Republic

Official Language: French

Main Religion: Traditional beliefs

Capital: Porto Novo

Currency: CFA franc, centime

Tips for tourists

Contract only exotic diseases. There are more leprosy clinics than hospitals.

Don't try Benin for a holiday job. There are only 50,000 wage earners.

The bulk of the military failed to back this attempted coup in 1979.

27

Tips for tourists

Please do not ask taxi drivers: *"Why is the sea so blue?"* All the tourists do, and the taxi drivers are getting mad.

Recommended dress to blend with the locals:
Winter: tartans and tweeds
Summer: Bermuda shorts

On Mondays: go to St. George where the mayor personally greets visitors (ll a.m.).
On Tuesdays: visit City Hall where the Minister of Tourism will conduct you round the display of local crafts.
On Wednesdays: don't go to Fort Hamilton unless you like the sound of bagpipes. Kilted pipers parade up and down while playing.

Bermuda

Geography

Bermuda consists of 300 coral islands — only 20 of which are inhabited — bathing in the Atlantic just 700 miles from New York. It covers an oval area 22 miles long and 5 miles wide. The largest island in the group, Great Bermuda, is 14 miles long and one and a half miles wide.

This is one of the world's most densely populated places, even without counting the hundreds of thousands of tourists. Two thirds of Bermudans are descendants of African slaves. The locals are known as *onions* after the local vegetable they used to grow.

History

This was Britain's first colony although it was discovered (in 1503) by a Spaniard, Juan Bermudez (hence the name). The lazy Latins couldn't be bothered to settle it. Then in 1609 Sir George Somers and 150 true Englishmen (including women) were shipwrecked here. Their exploits led to (a) the British settling on Bermuda; and (b) Shakespeare cribbing their story for his play *The Tempest*.

Politics

Since 1968 Bermuda has enjoyed some measure of self-government. But there is still a Governor, appointed by the British, who in turn appoints the Prime Minister and looks after foreign affairs, defence and the police. There is a Cabinet (appointed by the Governor) and a small Parliament (the Senate is partially appointed by the Governor).

Trade unions were legalised in 1946. This does not herald a sharp break with Bermuda's colonial history. The Governor still collects, in a grand ceremony, an annual rent for the old State House of one peppercorn on a velvet pillow.

Travel

Cars were banned here until 1946. The Motor Car Act of that year legalised them. But they must not travel faster than 20 miles an hour (15 in towns). The rail service was discontinued in 1948. There are more motorbikes for the size of population than in any other country.

Industry

Despite its limited resources (if you exclude sun, sand and warm seas) Bermuda is prosperous. Its climate — plus tax concessions — make it a haven

Special police are drafted in for community policing in Bermuda's gay areas.

for rich tourists and foreign investment. Other industry: Bacardi

Most industrious period: the Second World War, when 1,200 British intelligence experts packed into the cellars of the pink Hamilton Princess Hotel to intercept mail and messages between the U.S. and Europe.

Sport

Bermuda is a great sporting nation. It has won more Olympic medals for the size of population than any other nation. It has more golf courses for its size than any country. It boasts that one of its citizens, Mary Outerbridge, introduced tennis to the United States. The world's first tennis tournament was held here in 1877.

Apart from sport, Bermudans spend their time watching TV, phoning each other and going to museums. They spend more on advertising per head than anywhere apart from the U.S.A. This life style has the inevitable effects. Bermudans go mad and get divorced at a greater rate than almost any other people.

Bhutan
Druk-yul

Ancient and modern

If the people of Bhutan could read (only 2 per cent of them can) they would have found plenty of good news lately in their country's only newspaper (weekly circulation: 5,000). Slavery has been abolished and schools established. A major campaign was launched to eradicate venereal disease. Money has been introduced to replace the barter system (although few people can pronounce the unit of currency, the the *ngultrum*).

It no longer takes six days to travel to the capital, Thimphu, from the border, as it did when the only way to get there was by mule. Tourists have been allowed in and Bhutan has started to produce postage stamps — progressive moves which have earned swift rewards. Tourism and philately have become Bhutan's biggest foreign-currency earners.

But being the country which has been least affected by 20th Century progress has its advantages. There is no income tax, no lawyers and no political parties.

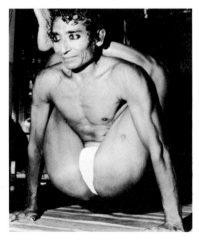

Someone trying to pronounce *ngultrum*.

Topography and bottomography

Bhutan is a land of steaming jungles and snow-covered mountains inhabited by a million hardy people who still stick to the tribal prejudices of their forefathers (foremothers aren't recognised in this patriarchal society). It is bigger than Switzerland but seems much smaller, tucked in, as it is, between the giants of India and China — a strategic position which it would exploit far more if it wasn't for its Buddhist purity.

Britain moved into Bhutan in 1865 while extending its domination of India, but it never really had a chance of seriously influencing this isolated land which is three-quarters covered with forests and where elephants, wild boar and bears still roam.

After Indian independence Bhutan formed a special relationship under which India controls its little neighbour's foreign affairs, provides finance for modernisation and most of its trade and public servants.

Putting the Bhutan

This closeness to India has not pleased the Chinese. They make sporadic incursions into Bhutan in border disputes. To combat this Bhutan now has an army of 4,000 men. The Chinese army has 3,900,000.

Politics

The king is supreme in Bhutan although the monarchy was only established in 1907. The present king, Jigme Singye Wangchuck — meaning *Fearless Thunderbolt Master of the Cosmic Powers* — is the great grandson of the first monarch, Sir Ugyen Wangchuck.

There is a national council, the Tsongdu, which advises the king. But he appoints a third of its members and it only meets twice a year anyway. It does have a unique power, though — it can vote to depose the monarch. This is not likely to happen, as democracy is not one of Bhutan's strong points. When the present king's father, Jigme Dorji Wangchuck, had to choose a prime minister he picked his brother-in-law, who had the same name. This was convenient when the Prime Minister was assassinated — the king took over and did not have to change the letter headings. There is a five-strong council of Ministers, three of whom share the king's name.

Industry

Bhutan has factories which produce whisky, gin and marmalade. A higher proportion of people work on the land than in any other country.

Language

Bhutan has five different and mutually incomprehensible languages — Dzongka, Ngalong, Tsang, Bumthang and Mon. Names are utterly unpronounceable. Examples: *gsang-sngags Zab don rDzong,* and *mGar-sar Bdra-shis Mthong-smon rDzong,* and *Spa-groo dpon-Slob Brug don-grub.*

Population: One and a quarter million

Size: One-fifth that of Britain, 18,000 sq. miles

Government: Monarchy

Main language: Dzongka

Religion: Buddhist

Capital: Thimphu

Currency: Ngultrum and tikchung

Tips for tourists

Do your best not to fall ill. There are only ten general hospitals and three just treat leprosy. There are 15 centres for malaria sufferers.

Take five friends. Tourists may only enter in groups of six.

Don't bother trying to get a job, the average national income is less than a pound a week, the lowest published income of any nation.

Visit a *dzong*. These are fortified monasteries and are the homes of the monk-governors. You might have to stay there. Bhutan has only one hotel.

Take your bows and arrows — archery is the most popular sport.

Listen to the ten radio stations, eight of which transmit nothing but flood warnings.

Tips for tourists

Avoid called Indians 'Indios'. Call them 'Campesinos'. This means peasants

Avoid ambulances. They are used to pick up people for torture.

While visiting the Presidential Palace, have a look at the 'Lynching lampost' outside.

Bolivia
Republica de Bolivia

Industry

There are three main industries in Bolivia:
Tin mining
Drug trafficking
Corruption
The second and third of these are closely connected and are now far more important to the Bolivian economy than tin. Thanks to cocaine the country is reaching a new high. This is partly due to the oddest union in the world, *the Union of Commercial Smugglers.*

Geography

It has some other highs, too. Like:
The highest navigable lake in the world — Lake Titicaca
The highest capital in the world — La Paz
The highest forest in the world — Parce Nacional Sajama
The highest airport in the world — La Paz
The highest railway station in the world — Condor
The highest ski run in the world — Mt. Chacaltaya
This isn't all due to cocaine, of course. The Andes mountains, some of the tallest in America, are responsible.

Bolivia is a large country but used to be more than twice the size. It lost huge tracts of land to its neighbours in a series of disastrous wars at the end of the last century and early years of this one. It even managed to lose the bit that connected it to the sea, making it the only land-locked country in the Americas.

Diplomacy

When a British diplomat was run out of the capital naked on a donkey Queen Victoria ordered gunboat vengeance. On learning that the country was land-locked she erased it from her atlas and declared: *"Bolivia no longer exists."*

To this day the remnants of the Bolivian navy chug endlessly around Lakes Titicaca and Poopo — the rudest lakes in the world.

Politics

The army has been considerably more active. Since Bolivian independence in 1825 there have been 378 revolutions/uprisings/coups. Military governments outweigh civilian by 58 to 32. The record is three different presidents on a single day, October 3rd 1970.

The standard of government, not surprisingly, is rotten. Natural gas was discovered — then sold off to Argentina for half the usual price in exchange for junta support. Tin is sold cheap for the same reason. And the railway to the sea has never been finished.

In keeping with such a disorganised political structure, there are a large number of disorganised-sounding political parties. These include:
The Social Democratic Movement of the Revolutionary Left.
Siles Suazos Historical National Revolutionary Movement.
The Marxist Leninist Communist Party.
The Bolivian Section of the Fourth International.
Guevara Arces Authentic Revolutionary Party.
The Nationalist Revolutionary Party of the Left.
The Socialist Party — One.
The Workers Vanguard.

This should not imply a high turnout at elections. Sixty per cent of the population is illiterate. Before 1952 the only people allowed to vote were those who could sign their names in Spanish. Even the literate 40 per cent are largely non-Spanish speaking.

There has been a recent change for the better. Since late in 1982 there has been a civilian government which has introduced a major new export — Nazi war criminals.

Pleasure

The only pleasure for the impoverished, downtrodden, serf-like population is chewing coca leaves, from which cocaine is made. They numb the senses and ward off hunger and cold.

No pleasure

Life expectancy is just 46.
There is only one doctor for every 2,127 people. It has the world's second highest maternal mortality rate.

A member of the Smugglers' Union goes through the *Green* exit at La Paz airport.

Botswana

Language

There are 18 different languages in Botswana (because of the arbitrary boundaries of colonial rule) although Tswana is the main one. Early British missionaries committed it to writing for the first time. But the innate wisdom of the population comes through the language in proverbs.

The fool does not return to the virgin twice.

This is either because she is no longer a virgin or because there's no point in asking the same girl twice.

Man is like the melon. The interior ripeness is invisible.

The man is meat, while the woman is a vegetable.

The President has sensibly named the country's new currency the pula which means 'giver of life'.

Useful word: *Mokgabana* — Hernia of the navel.

History

Formerly the British colony of Bechuanaland, Botswana developed in the opposite way to most other African countries. Whereas others were disturbed from their tropical lethargy by the colonial powers and thrust into internecine strife post-independence, Botswana had a pretty tough time from the start. The Zulus attacked under their great war-leader Chaka.

The Boers forcibly encroached onto their territory, and a mad European circus operator called Fandini kept insisting that there was a non-existent lost city in the Kalahari Desert and dragging their tribesmen off around the world as exhibits from it. By contrast, after independence Botswana has had one of the most consistent political systems in Africa and is just about the only parliamentary democracy left. This is largely due to one man, Sir Seretse Khama.

Khama after the storm

In 1948, while studying as a student in England, Chief Seretse Khama married a Lloyds underwriter, Miss Ruth Williams, in Kensington Register Office.

Frowned on by Britain and the family alike, Seretse, Chief of Bechuanaland, stuck to his guns. For five years Britain refused to let him re-enter his own country.

In 1962 he formed the Bechuanaland Democratic Party, became the first Prime Minister and President in 1966 and has been re-elected by a large

Women store food in their bottoms and men have permanent erections in this tourist paradise.

majority ever since. His policy of Racial Harmony is symbolised by the National Flag and Coat of Arms, both of which have adjacent black and white designs.

Papier machinations

All four political parties have their own newspapers. The Government's is the *Daily News*. The others are *Dawn, Straight Talk* and *Consultation*.

Who's game

An example to other African countries in a lot of ways, Botswana also looks after its wild life better and has been rewarded with probably the best collection on the continent.

It has several large game reserves and the quantities of certain species are phenomenal. Herds of 50,000 wildebeest are not uncommon and in 1967 a flock of flamingoes 10 miles long was seen over the northern lakes.

Perhaps this is due to the fact that flamingoes have first call on the fish in the country. The Tswana tribe do not eat fish because of their respect for the crocodile.

Sexual problems

The Bushmen (and women) have rather a lot of these. The nipples of pubertal girls look like bright orange balls loosely attached to their breasts. When they get older, the inner lips of their genitalia will hang down 3 or 4 inches through the vaginal entrance due to a deficiency growth in the labia majora. Most Bushmen males have penises which protrude forward even when not in erection and they suffer from monorchy — they only have one testicle.

Population: I million

Size: More than twice that of Britain, 222,000 sq. miles

Government: Republic

Language: English and Tswana

Main religion: Traditional beliefs

Capital: Gaborone

Currency: Pula

Tips for tourists

Visit David Livingstone's house in the north.

Do not drink *Kgadi* — it is illegal. In fact, Botswana is a good place to dry out anonymously. The two great shortages of the country are water and people.

Population: 125 million

Size: 34 times that of Britain, 3 and a half million sq. miles

Government: Republic

Language: Portuguese

Religion: Roman Catholic

Capital: Brasilia

Currency: Cruzeiro, centavo

Tips for tourists

Don't fly to Sao Paulo airport — it is farther from the city it serves than any other in the world (60 miles).

The best Carnival Ball is *Hawaiian Night* at the Rio Yacht Club.

Brazil

Republica Federativa do Brasil

Brazil is a massive country: huge by any standard. It is not far behind Canada, the second biggest country in the world. It is as big as the whole of the rest of South America put together and contains half its population. What dwarfs even these statistics is the Amazon Basin.

A basin full

The Amazon Basin covers 45 per cent of the country and contains 5 per cent of the population. The Amazon River itself is 4,000 miles long with thousands of tributaries. The effect of so large an area containing just jungle and water is that the Basin provides the world with 40 per cent of its oxygen and a quarter of its fresh water. Of the 22,000 known species of plants found in the world 18,000 exist here. Of the 2,000 types of fish there are 1,600 that could make up the biggest fish pie in the world. The island of Marajao (in the river) is bigger than Denmark.

Other big things

The Maracana Municipal Stadium in Rio is the biggest stadium in the world. The world's widest street — in the capital of Brasilia — is 273 yards wide and, not surprisingly, called the *Monumental Axis.*

The world's heaviest spider would have had difficulty crawling out of domestic plugholes, fortunately. It weighs in at 3 oz.

Brazilians eat more nuts than any other people.

Fixed nuts

The population consists of Portuguese, German, Dutch, English, Negro and Indian elements. What has largely saved Brazil from the vicissitudes of Spanish-American politics is that they are Portuguese. Columbus, for all the propaganda in his favour, missed the biggest country and landed at El Salvador, leaving Brazil for the Portuguese.

They set about chopping down the hard wood called 'Brazil', with the help of the local Indians. They called the Indians *Bugres* — or *Buggers* — because they didn't work hard enough. So slaves were imported from Africa — about 15 million of them in 300 years.

Nuts about Brazil

Birthplace of the Samba and Bossa Nova, Brazil's hip-swinging African rhythm and *manana* attitude dictate

their lifestyle. Apart from the world's most famous carnival at Rio, on New Year's Eve you can see four miles of voodoo worshippers on the Rio beach rushing into the sea with sacrificial offerings. This is where the legend of lighting cigars with hundred-dollar bills comes from — but that was at the height of the rubber boom. Housewives in Maracaibo, 2,000 miles up the Amazon, sent their laundry to England and the rubber barons built an Opera House in the jungle to attract the very best European companies, including the singer Jenny Lind. For the purposes of rubber export they built the Jungle Highway in 1905. It cost 10,000 lives and was never used.

In 1958 the president decided to build a new capital city in the jungle. In three years it was ready — in the shape of a plane. Living in the jungle brought them into contact with the world's most venomous spider. But they didn't mind. The Health Minister said, *"Fortunately, when deaths do occur, they are usually of children under seven".*

Get away from it all on Copa Cabana beach.

Nuts and colonels

The tolerant attitude to racial integration has led to a more tolerant political system than its Spanish neighbours — at least until recently. The slaves simply pretended to be Roman Catholic, while changing their god *Oxala* to Jesus Christ or *Oxossi* to St. George. Political strife usually takes an innocent form. In the northern town of Macaubas, party barbers cut party hair only. Two airports exist for the arrivals of different party members.

Perhaps this has produced the Brazilian proverb *We must be thankful for the night, because politicians sleep.* Capital punishment was not introduced until 1969 by — surprise, surprise — the military regime.

Brunei

A colony of Great Britain until 1983, Brunei last instigated a treaty between the two countries in 1979: *A Treaty of Friendship and Co-operation between her Majesty the Queen of the United Kingdom of Great Britain and Northern Ireland and the 29th Sultan H. H. Paduka Seri Bagunda Sultan and Yong di Pertuan of Brunei, Sir Muda Hassanal Bolkiah Mu'izzadin Waddaulah G.M.C.G.* So continues a relationship, even after independence, which began in the last century.

Islamic law is hard on parking offenders.

Two Japanese tourists recently decorated by the government.

Sultans

They have ruled de facto and de population since the 15th Century, when their Empire stretched from Sarawak next door to the Philippines. From the great days, a superb Islamic Mosque and several brass cannons given as dowry presents, survive. The name in Islamic for the capital is *Dar ul Salam* meaning 'City of Peace'. And because of its inaccessible position hidden amongst jungle waterways Brunei remained untouched later than surrounding countries. Now the Sultan rules supremely again after 150 years, having abolished elections in 1970 and treating the legislative assembly as a rubber stamp for palace policy. In 1962 a rebellion against his father was put down by British troops flown in from Singapore, which led to their decision to remain outside the Malay Confederation of States.

Wealth

The Sultans can afford to feel secure now. Brunei has the highest living standards in South East Asia and is one of the largest oil-producers of the Commonwealth. Oil and gas provide 99 per cent of its income. Pepper is the other major export. In addition Brunei has no personal tax at all and a very comprehensive welfare state.

Drawbacks

The population of Brunei — Malays, Chinese, Ibans, Kadazans, Indians and Europeans — have to put up with 200 inches of rain in some parts of the country while the Islamic Sultan makes sure it is a dry country in other respects. 75 per cent of the country is covered in rain forest in which pythons up to 9 metres in length flourish — longer than any snake in the world including the South American anaconda. Brunei has the world's highest death rate.

Population: A quarter of a million

Size: 2,200 sq. miles

Government: Constitutional monarchy

Main language: Malay

Religion: Islam

Capital: Bandar Seri Begawan

Currency: Brunei dollar

Tips for tourists

No one goes on the streets after about 9 o'clock in the evening. Perhaps this is because the only entertainment is Chinese Martial Arts movies and heavily censored Malay love dramas.

Tips for Japanese tourists

Between 1942 and 45 head hunting was allowed, providing the heads were Japanese. Old habits die hard.

Population: 9 million

Size: Half that of Britain, 43,000 sq. miles

Government: Communist

Language: Bulgarian

Main religion: Eastern Orthodox Church

Capital: Sofia

Currency: Lev, stotinka

Tips for tourists

A nod of the head in Bulgaria means *no*.

The National Day is September 9th. (*The Day of Freedom* — when they were forced to comply with the Soviet Union).

Eat plenty of yoghourt. Most of the milk's sour anyway, and they invented it.

The most popular pastime is *Reading Clubs*, where you go to read. Bulgaria has the oldest written Slav language and the oldest Slav literature, beginning with the works of Saint Cyril in the 9th Century.

Drugs: Bulgaria is the largest drug market place in the world.

Umbrellas: there are two kinds — with or without poisoned tips.

Bulgaria
Narodna Republika Bulgaria

An unlikely nation

Most of the countries around Bulgaria were more likely to survive as a nation. They had a greater degree of national identity before being swept away into newly created states after World War I.

Bulgaria was under Turkish domination for 500 years until 1878. Even then it had no national resistance movement until the very end. Around it, Serbia, Transylvania, Bosnia, Herzegovina, Croatia, Bessarabia, Montenegro, Banat and Bukovina disappeared, leaving Bulgaria and Romania alone.

A promising start

In the 9th Century, Bulgars from Russia colonised this land. By the 10th Century it was the most powerful kingdom in East Europe. The last Bulgar tsar died of grief when 15,000 prisoners had their eyes put out by an over-zealous commander.

After this, only ecumenical arguments raged — between the Popes of Rome and Constantinople, the bishops of Greece and vampire-believers of the mountains. Everyone was engaged in underground activity against everyone else. Plots, peasant uprisings, non-peasant uprisings and assassinations took their course.

Then three empires collapsed around them — Russia, Turkey and Austro-Hungary.

The Bulgarian police force are equipped with poison-tipped umbrellas.

Communism

The Bulgarian Communist Party was founded in 1891. King Boris banned it in 1923 but his position was too precarious to survive. The most famous communist, Georgi Dimitrov, went to Germany and won fame by standing trial accused of starting the Reichstag fire, one of Hitler's brilliant propaganda coups. He defended himself superbly, won and left for Russia where he became head of the Comintern. In 1945 he returned to become dictator of Bulgaria. Subsequently he fell out with his Soviet masters and Stalin, unable to secure his overthrow in Bulgaria, asked him to Moscow for a chat. He was taken ill there and mysteriously died.

Bad decision makers

Bulgaria chose the wrong side in both World Wars. In the first it was promised Serbia by Germany. In the second it was persuaded just in time (1944) to join the Right Side. It emerged exhausted but otherwise unscathed. Now, after promising the Allies to keep an army of no more than 55,000, it has three times that.

Modern Bulgaria

There are two political parties, the Communist Party and the Bulgarian Agricultural Union — the latter leaves the ruling of the country to the former. Since the war, industrial growth has been one of the highest in the world.

The equivalent of annual production in 1939 was achieved in three and a half days in 1978. To keep up this energetic rate of growth Bulgarians are the greatest consumers of sugar in the world. Much of their success is due to better natural resources and a harder-working attitude than the rest of the Soviet bloc, of which they are part and with whom they trade almost exclusively (i.e. lack of competition).

The Party rules through a National Assembly, called the Sobranie. Warning: Doctors say it may seriously damage your health. They maintain the closest links with Russia in the bloc. They are the world's biggest cigarette producers for the size of population and the greatest cigarette exporters (most go to Russia).

Burma

Pyidaungsu Socialist Thammada Myanma Naingngandaw

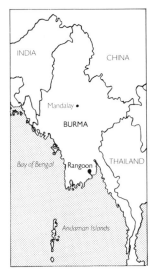

History

For a country which in ancient times was known as the Golden Land, Burma has had a tarnished history.

In the year 849 the city of Pagan was founded here. Contrary to popular belief, this was a fabulous place, full of temples, monasteries and rather nice Pagans. So nice, in fact, that they were not able to put up a decent fight when the Mongol hordes, led by Kublai Khan, over-ran them in 1287.

There were three wars between Burma and Britain in the 19th Century, the final one lasting a mere week before the Burmese collapsed. Humiliatingly, their country became a province of India until just before World War Two — when it was promptly overrun by the Japanese. It achieved independence in 1948.

Geography

Burma is shaped like a diamond with a long tail. It is a land of villages. Except for Rangoon and Mandalay there are no cities. Towns are just overgrown villages. The modern ones are easy to spot — they are rectangular; older ones are round. This is one of the wettest places on earth.

International

Of all the world's non-aligned nations, Burma is less aligned than any. Not only is it independent of the great powers of East and West, but it has even withdrawn from the organisation of non-aligned states. It refuses to be in the Commonwealth, too.

The people

The people of Burma are divided into a number of tribes with names like *Chin* and *Karen*. The Karen have the longest necks in the world (they extend them with copper coils). This does not mean that the Chin have the longest chins.

Compared with other Asian countries, Burma is under-populated. Life expectancy is 47 and a half years, which makes the official major cause of death lack credibility: it is old age. It also has the world's highest infant mortality rate.

More than 100 languages are spoken in Burma and 85 per cent of the population are Buddhists.

Politics

A socialist government was elected shortly after independence but was overthrown in 1962 in a coup led by the inappropriately named General U Win.

Burmese tribesmen value Janet Reger underwear more than anything else and will go to great lengths to protect it.

His government has followed what they call 'the Burmese way to socialism'. This consists of: banning all political parties (except its own), banning strikes, banning unions, banning employers' organisations (not that there are many employers — almost everything has been nationalised). Personal incomes are low and there is little growth in the economy, which is characterised by inefficiency.

In 1972 the Cabinet changed from military to civilian. This did not mean that the various generals were replaced — they just gave up their military titles.

Among those currently in the government are: Head of State — *U San Yu*; Deputy Prime Minister — *U Tun Tin*; Agriculture — *U Ye Goung*; Transport — *U Saw Pru*. Just about the only military man left is the Minister for Religious Affairs. He is the terrifyingly named *Colonel Bo Ni*.

Population: 36 million

Size: Three times that of Britain, a quarter of a million sq. miles

Government: Socialist Republic

Language: Burmese

Religion: Buddhism

Capital: Rangoon

Currency: Kyat and pyas

Tips for tourists

Don't go swimming. Nine hundred Japanese soldiers were killed by crocodiles here in 1945.

If you're looking for a bed for the night, don't get fooled by the YMBA. The Young Men's Buddhist Association is not what you think. It is a revolutionary organisation formed in 1906 to kick out the British. And it is still active.

Burundi

Population: Four and a half million

Size: One-tenth that of Britain, 10,000 sq. miles

Government: Republic

Language: Kirundi and French

Religions: Traditional beliefs and Roman Catholic

Capital: Bujumbura

Currency: Burundi franc

Tips for tourists

Don't bother making jokes about *Toot Toot Tutsi*. The natives won't understand. There is no railway.

And don't think you can travel by road instead. Only 150 miles of road are made up.

Go to the movies. They need you. Burundi has the lowest movie attendances in the world.

The people

The tribes of Burundi are the closest that Africa gets to *Dynasty* and *Dallas*. There are three of them:
The Tutsi are the tallest people in Africa and traditional rulers of Burundi.
The Hutu who make up 85 per cent of the population and hence are not too keen on being dominated by the Tutsi.
The Twa are few in both quantity and quality (they are pygmies). Burundi's pygmies are not like those in neighbouring countries. They have lived for centuries at high altitudes (most pygmies hide away in low lying forests) so they have got ideas above their station. These lead them to eat better food and live more openly than other pygmies.

Most people in Burundi grub a living on the land. The exceptions are the Watusi, a native aristocracy who just laze around with their cattle (that *does* sound like *Dallas*). The cattle have horns of extraordinary length, but despite their magnificent appearance, they are otherwise useless (yes, that's *Dallas*).

Overcrowding

Religion is based on a veneration of ancestors. The people have little else to venerate. Their country is the most densely-populated in Africa, one of the poorest in the world and getting poorer.

Burundi isn't only overcrowded, but overstocked. There is a saying: *'Cattle are murdering Burundi'*, which is harsh on a country which can hardly stand on its own four hoofs.

History

The Tutsi kingdom was founded 400 years ago and went through the usual tribal upheavals until the Germans conquered it in 1890 and made it part of German East Africa.

After World War One it was given to Belgium. It later became a United Nations Trust Territory until achieving self-government in 1962.

The other Prince Charles

In 1966 the king was deposed by his son, Prince Charles Ndizeye, who made himself king and Captain Michael Micombero prime minister. Micombero proved an ungrateful wretch. A mere four months later, while Charles was out of the country at a beano, Micombero declared Burundi a republic with himself as president.

In 1972 Prince Charles took on the role of Bonny Prince Charlie and returned to reclaim his kingdom. He fared no better than his Scottish namesake — in fact, far worse. He was killed in heavy fighting and so were 120,000 others (the comparative death toll in Britain would be one and a half million).

Micombero ruled for another four years until being kicked out by the army, which established a Supreme Revolutionary Council.

Geography

Burundi is a mountainous country, most of it 5,000ft. above sea level, lying across the dividing crest of the Nile and Congo. Although it is land-locked, one-tenth of its area is water — Lake Tanganyika. This justifies it having a small navy and a fishing industry. Fishing takes place at night, except when there is a full moon.

Most houses are surrounded by banana trees. Bananas are used for brewing beer. The country's only cash crop is coffee.

The Burundi 1982 Grand Prix gets off to a flying start.

Cambodia
Democratic Kampuchea

History

The first great civilisation of the Khmer people was that of the Angkor, a God-king whose rule was based on slavery. Slaves built the famous Angkor Wat, a temple mountain 130 feet high. In its foundations were buried bodies of slaves, alive and dead. Angkor controlled a network of canals that made the country the most fertile in Indo-China. Then the Siamese overthrew the cruel Angkor Empire.

History repeats itself

A French protectorate since 1864, Cambodia again nurtured nationalism in the 1930's. Ominously, the first newspaper was called *The Angkor Wat*. The first independent ruler, Prince Sihanouk Norodom, treated himself as a God-king and, in his presence, grovelling was the norm. Grovelling and obeisance were not enough, however, for the leaders of the Khmer Republic, Pol Pot and Ieng Sary, whose revolutionary Khmer Rouge forces overthrew the government in 1975 under the banner of nationalism.

So they decided to turn the clock back 12 centuries to the Angkor Autocracy — and, at the same time, create an instant Communist State. When Chou en Lai on his death bed warned them that fast food and same-day cleaning were a different kettle of fish to instant dogma, they just smiled.

A good Pol Pot joke is now a thing of the past.

Their programme involved: The emptying of the cities, the creation of a peasant state (and no-one else), the worship of manual labour, the abolition of marriage, family, property, currency, post, telephone and medicine, death to anyone on any pretext.

The outcome was that between 1975 and 79, three million people were killed (an equivalent of 20 million in the UK). City people and peasants were herded into camps in the country to toil as slaves for the glorification of Angkor. They died of starvation mostly, but hundreds of thousands were executed. First of all, the intellectuals, artists and educated people were weeded out and slaughtered. For instance:

Pre-revolution	Post Pol Pot
23,600 teachers	3,000
11,000 students	450
54 ballet dancers	4
416 sculptors	14

Even peasants were not protected in this 'Peasant State'. They were worked to death, starved to death, buried alive, torn in half, burned, beaten to death, split open and eaten (human liver was popular in the 8th Century too).

The way Pol Pot honoured peasant values was by doing the killing with hoes, spades or axes. The ox was given a place of honour under the Khmer Rouge and was referred to as *Comrade Ox*. To be more like the good ox, the Cambodians were made to draw ploughs and carry water. They worked 17 hours a day, seven days a week, on starvation rations. Malaria affected 80 per cent of the population.

American aid

The mutual hatred between Cambodians and Vietnamese was a help to the Americans when in 1969 Nixon decided to bomb the Viet Cong out of their hideouts in Cambodia. Natural skivers on other occasions, the South Vietnamese pilots *paid* to fly sorties seven days a week over Cambodia. More bombs were dropped than in the whole of the Pacific area in World War Two. Phnom Penh had grown from a city of 50,000 to 3 million because the social fabric of the country had been utterly destroyed. Thousands of square miles were left black.

Rimbauld's country *'filled with ochrous skies and drowned forest'* was unrecognisable. Nixon was particularly pleased that *'The Russians and Chinese might think they were dealing with a madman'*.

Population: 7 million

Size: 71,000 sq. miles

Government: Socialist republic

Language: Officially Khmer, also French

Religion: Traditionally Hinayana Buddhism

Capital: Phnom Penh

Currency: Riel

Tips for tourists

Don't go yet.

There are no up-to-date guide books.

The language has the longest alphabet in the world — 72 letters, some useless.

Islamic tourists bring your own copy of the Koran. The Khmer Rouge used it as toilet paper.

Don't be in a hurry to change your money into the local currency. It is one of the weakest in the world. And spend, spend, spend — Cambodia has the world's second highest inflation rate.

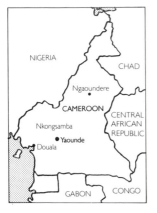

NIGERIA

CHAD

Ngaoundere

CAMEROON

CENTRAL
AFRICAN
REPUBLIC

Nkongsamba

● Yaounde

Douala

GABON

CONGO

Population: Eight and a half million

Size: Twice that of Britain 180,000 sq. miles

Government: Republic

Official languages: English and French

Main religion: Traditional beliefs

Capital: Yaounde

Currency: CFA franc

Tips for tourists

If you decide to ride on the railway, keep away from the aptly name M'Banga branch line.

To avoid malaria you must travel into the mountains. But there you are almost certain to catch dysentery.

If you hear someone say she is going home to Mum, this does not necessarily mean that a marriage is breaking up — just that someone is heading for the tiny principality in the mountains.

Cameroon

Republique Unie de Cameroun

Cameroon grew from small beginnings — its earliest inhabitants were pygmies. Their name comes from *pygmaioi*, meaning 'as tall as the distance from a man's elbow to his knuckles'. Cameroon's name comes from the Portuguese *camaroes*, meaning 'shrimps'. This is not a reference to the pygmies but to the creatures which the early European arrivals saw abounding in the waters.

History

Not much was heard of this triangular wedge in the middle of Africa until early this century. By that time it was a German colony called Kamerun. After World War One it was divided between the French and British who called their bits Cameroun (French) and Cameroon (English).

Both became independent in the early 1960's and joined together in 1972 to form the United Republic of Cameroon.

Campaigns

Cameroon's greatest achievement came during the World Cup finals of 1982. Despite being very much the underdogs they held Peru and Poland to goal-less draws and lost to Italy, the eventual winners, by a single goal. Their dashing style captured the hearts of all — except the Peruvians, Poles and, especially, the Italians.

A less successful campaign was the one run by the government in 1965 to produce hardier bananas.

Their five-year industrial plans aren't much better. This could have something to do with the names they give them — for example, *the Peasants' Plan* and *Operation 100,000 tons.*

The least successful campaign of all was the guerilla war just after independence. This was organised by the communist Dr. Felix Moumie from the safety of Switzerland. It proved not to be safe after all when in 1960 he mysteriously died. He claimed on his death bed that he had been poisoned by an organisation calling itself *the Red Hand.*

Travel

It isn't easy to get around this country, which is packed with dense forests. A railway was built in two separate short stretches. It took 50 years to join them. Nine-tenths of the country's 8,000 miles of roads are just dirt tracks.

Politics

In the 1950's there were 84 political parties in East Cameroon alone. Most of these were at tribal level. Cameroon is now a one-party state.

There are only four trade unions — one is called the Union of Denominational Workers Organisations and two of the others are for teachers.

One-fifth of the national budget goes on military expenditure.

The people

Cameroon is a racial crossroads with more than 100 different ethnic groups. One tribe, the Moundangs, live in clay *Massa* houses, which perfectly resemble the female breast, nipple uppermost.

At initiation dances, both boys and girls are completely bandaged from head to foot. This is Africa's nearest equivalent to a blind date.

Dangers of Safari. Getting your hand stuck up a wildebeest's bottom.

Canada

The deep fear of all English-speaking Canadians is that they might really be Americans. Everywhere they go they are mistaken for them, no matter how completely they cover themselves in maple leaves. Half of Canada's population lives within 200 miles of the American border — the longest undefended one in the world — and 75 per cent of their imports come from their powerful neighbour. They drive American cars, eat American food and live in American-style homes. They watch many American television programmes. In Montreal they even watch *Hawaii Cinq Zero*.

Alter ego

Canadians are not a nation of mounties and lumberjacks. There are also some housewives. One third of the population is French, living mainly in Quebec where Montreal is the largest French-speaking city, after Paris, in the world. Some of them are Indians — about 300,000 of whom 18,000 are Eskimos.

Some of the population is convinced they are British. Vancouver on the west coast is teeming with double-decker buses and bowling greens and afternoon teas. A particularly happy time for these Canadians were the years 1904-1911 when Earl Grey was Governor-General of Canada.

Geography

Everything is on an enormous scale, for Canada is the second largest country in the world. The St. Lawrence River drains a territory of 500,000 square miles which contains half the world's fresh water. Canada spans seven time zones, and the world's longest continuous road — the Trans-Canada Highway — crosses it for 5,000 miles. The climate is also extreme between north and south and between winter and summer. Montreal spent 32 million dollars just keeping the streets clear of snow during the winter of 1979.

Language

The Canadian satirist Thomas Chandler Haliburton coined some famous lines:
A nod is as good as a wink to a blind horse.
Six of one and half a dozen of the other.
I wasn't born yesterday.
Raining cats and dogs.

This Mountie appears to be unaware that his horse has ridden off without him.

History

If you thought the Pilgrim Fathers were the first to settle permanently on the North American continent you'd be wrong. The French beat them to it by 15 years — in 1605, on the east coast of Canada. They were soon joined by the British and the two colonies lived side by side until 1763 when the British beat the French in the Seven Years War and acquired the whole of Canada as part of their spoils. It became independent in 1931.

Population: 24 and a quarter million

Size: Fifteen times that of Texas, 3,800,000 sq. miles

Government: Independent Commonwealth member

Language: English and French

Religion: Christianity

Capital: Ottawa

Currency: Dollar, cent

Tips for tourists

Visit Chinatown, Vancouver, and see the world's thinnest office block — 5ft. 10ins. wide and 2 two storeys high.

Practice holding your breath for long periods — there are about 3,000 wrecked ships off the Nova Scotia coast, many of them containing treasure.

See the Copenhagen-like statue of a mermaid on a rock in Vancouver harbour — called *The girl in a Wetsuit*.

Bridegrooms beware — Niagara Falls is supposed to be a traditional haunt for honeymoon couples. But Oscar Wilde said "seeing the falls after the first night of the honeymoon must have been the bride's second great disappointment".

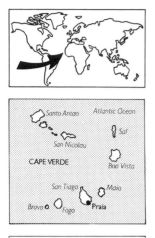

Population: 325,000

Size: 1,500 sq. miles

Government: Republic

Religion: Mainly Roman Catholic

Language: Portuguese, Creole

Capital: Praia

Currency: Escudo

Tips for tourists

Don't take a raincoat. It hasn't rained in most places for three years.

Don't expect romance. Even seagulls and terns don't breed here.

Cape Verde
Republica de Cabo Verde

Cape confusions

Perhaps from hallucination caused by insufficient water or from a low literacy rate inherited from the Portuguese, the people have some strange notions about their islands. The one they call Boa Vista — meaning Beautiful View — is a barren, arid wasteland with no trees.

A giant skunk which is extinct is protected by law; and on Brava where, so rumour has it, there are the most beautiful women in the world, there is also the greatest emigration of men. But they have always been a quaint people. In the 18th and 19th Centuries, death from disease, famine and drought led to the end of the dyeing industry.

Cape Verde is so remote that the discovery of the wheel has yet to make an effect.

Don't knows

Cape Verde *may* have been discovered in 1445 or 1456. They *may* have been discovered by Nuno Tristao or Luigi da Cadamosto both of whom were swanning around in these years in these waters. Nothing is known of the peoples already inhabiting the islands, apart from the odd rock painting on San Tiago and why anyone from Europe would want to settle there is a mystery too.

Don't cares

When the Portuguese did finally settle Cape Verde by the end of the 15th Century, they made no attempt to exploit it, calling the inhabitants 'degredados' — by which they meant Jews, beggars, slaves and convicts.

It was left to the 'degredados' themselves to do what they could with these arid, infertile and inhospitable islands. First they tried growing coffee, then cocoa and then sugar. Cape Verde was the slave warehouse on the journey from Africa to South America and in five centuries of Portuguese colonialism outdated modes of farming were meticulously preserved, leaving Cape Verde in its present, parlous state today.

Dry rot

There is chronic drought on Cape Verde and no system of agriculture yet devised could support the population. About one quarter of them left to work overseas. Famine — caused by drought — has finished off another 210,000 people this century. After independence in 1975, the government's first task — to ensure that it still had a population to govern — was to combat a ten-year drought that had all but destroyed the country's agriculture. In non-irrigated areas, all crops died and there was a 70 per cent deficit in cereal products which are the staple of the islands. On Cape Verde, if a government can control the supply of water, it controls the country and, with this in mind, the present government has decided to dam it.

Politics

The Party for African Independence for Guinea and Cape Verde was founded in 1955 by Cape Verde's most gutsy inhabitant, Amilcar Cabral. He was too gutsy for the Cape Verdeans and had to go to Guinea to raise any interest in the movement. He was murdered in 1973, probably by the Portuguese, who shortly afterwards gave the islands their independence. Today there is a one-party state governed by President Aristides Pereira who, from time to time, locks up ex-Portuguese secret servicemen agitating for a return to glorious empire.

Cayman Islands

Money and history

The state religion on the Cayman Islands is money. Its worship goes back a long way — long before the islands became a tax haven in 1966. The earliest settlers, after Columbus discovered the Caymans in the 16th Century, were an assortment of ship-wrecked sailors, buccaneers and debtors, while pirates used the place as a hang-out.

Money and the present

The special relationship with money continues today. There is no income tax, no property tax, no corporation tax, no capital gains tax. More than 14,000 companies — almost one for every islander — register here for obvious

reasons. They may do so care of any of the 400 banks which offer them mail drops and the opportunity to push cash into un-numbered bank accounts.

Facts only vaguely related to money

Planes don't only carry sackfuls of financial correspondence to these islands 500 miles south of Florida. Two hundred thousand tourists come every year attracted by the climate and keen to escape from problems that don't exist in this bankers' paradise — unemployment, unions, political parties, independence movements and racial strife.

Culture

There is none.

Population: 17,000

Size: 100 sq. miles

Government: Colony

Language: English

Religion: Anglican

Capital: George Town

Currency: Cayman Island dollar

Tips for tourists

Don't send a postcard home. Send a telex. There is one telex machine for every 100 people, the highest per capita number of telex numbers in the world.

Annual festival: Pirates' week, celebrated every autumn.

New arrivals at the Cayman Islands preparing to open a bank account.

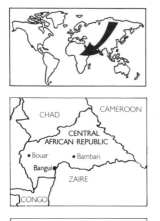

Central African Republic

Population: 2 and a half million

Size: Three times that of Britain, a quarter of a million sq. miles

Government: Republic

Main language: French, Sango

Main Religion: Traditional beliefs

Capital: Bangui

Currency: CFA franc, centime

Tips for tourists

Visit the town of Abba of happier memories.

Laugh at the *Mbum* tribe.

Be careful of the cost of living — one of the highest in West Africa.

Ruminate on the national sense of self-parody on the *Bimbo Mountains*.

Be prepared to feel isolated. Fewer tourists come here than anywhere else. But they spend more than visitors to almost any other country.

Origin and originality

The Central African Republic is indeed in Central Africa, in the heart of the Dark Continent. No name could be found more suitable for this very central place. But whereas advanced economies use the words *central* and *centralisation* to mean advancing still further along the path of administrative and economic efficiency, in the Republic being central means being undeveloped, lacking communication and being poor. It is surrounded by Cameroon, Chad, Zaire, Congo and Sudan. You couldn't be much more cut off than that.

The area was settled by people fleeing the slave trade on the coast. Since then it has had few advantages. Perhaps because all the able-bodied in the area were enslaved. Inhabited by pygmies, the country has played host to half a dozen different tribes, with the Bantu now predominating.

The National Anthem today is called *Le Renaissance* and starts *"O Central Africa, cradle of the Bantu..."* (trad.arr.)

The French

In 1899 the French defeated Sultan Rabah Zubayr who put up a stiff fight and was rewarded after the last battle by being executed. Then in 1928 Andre Gide exposed, in *Voyage au Congo*, the scandal of the 20,000 who had died in construction camps (they weren't even building a railway in their own country). The much vaunted abolition of slavery obviously took time to filter through to these backwoods French colonists. They went on enjoying it until 1945 when Barthelemy Boganda, 'father of the country', founded the *Social Evolution Movement of Black Africa.*

Independence

The country's luck fell short again when, a few days before independence in 1960, Barthelemy died in an air crash (there were no trains or roads). His nephew, David Dacko, took over. *He* was overthrown by *his* cousin, Colonel Bokassa, in 1966. The first three presidents were all members of the Mbaka tribe and clearly thought tribal methods better after 100 years of French republicanism. Bokassa ruled as Colonel, General, Field Marshal and finally Emperor until deposed in 1976 by Dacko, backed by the French. General Andre Kolingba assumed power in 1981 in a bloodless coup. Everyone else assumed more of the same.

Bokassa

Jean-Bedel Bokassa (or Papa Bok) like so many petty dictators should have been born 200 years ago or, preferably, not at all. You know the one about the bloke who thought he was Napoleon? Well Bokassa stepped right into the joke with gusto. Perhaps because his initials are the same as James Bond, Bokassa tried to out-Napoleon Napoleon.

In 1977, crowning himself Emperor, he had a 30 ft long train made (the only train in the country) encrusted with 785,000 pearls and 1,220,000 crystal beads. It cost one quarter of the country's annual income. Not content with bankrupting his very own empire, he did his best to destroy it in other ways. In 1969 he executed his minister of health. He made his government ministers work several days a month in the fields. He made friends with Amin and South Africa. And in a last desperate attempt, he started to eat his own people.

The Emmanuels model one of their rejected designs for Bokassa's coronation.

Poverty

Avoiding dying is awkward in other ways too. The average calorie intake is 2,170 (minimum recommended 2,300). There are 80,000 wage earners, 2 indigenous doctors, 60 miles of paved road, no railway, and curiously 85 per cent of the people work in subsistence farming while 41 per cent of them live in towns. They all have to migrate to eat. Industry in the capital consists of a flour mill, a vegetable-oil mill and a soap factory. Diamonds would be a greater benefit than they are (40 per cent of exports) if so many weren't smuggled out.

Chad

Republique du Tchad

Geography

Chad is a vast, bleak, poverty-stricken country. Half of it is so dry that nothing will grow. Yet most of the western frontier is Lake Chad — making Chad not just a land-locked country, but a land-and-lake-locked one.

History

Civilisation came late here and didn't stop long. The Kingdom of Kanem, which was founded in the 9th Century, couldn't really be called civilised. Neither could the Arabs who moved into the north 500 years later (they were welcome to it — there is practically nothing there but the Sahara).

It wasn't until 1897 that the first Europeans arrived. Britain, in a rare display of colonial generosity, told France she could have it. A wise move. The French ran into strong local opposition and even after conquering the country couldn't make up their minds what to do with it.

Chad became independent in 1960. Civil war has been going on almost non-stop ever since.

Politics

The first president was Francois Tombalbaye. He ran into almost immediate trouble with breakaway groups in the Moslem north and centre. As hostility to him grew, the president tried to show that he was a good African by changing his name from Francois to M'Garta. It didn't do him much good. He was assassinated in 1975.

The new rulers banned all political parties and established what they called the Transitional Government of National Unity (GUNT for short). It was doomed to failure. Civil war broke out in 1980 and troops came in from neighbouring Libya to sort things out.

The government of national unity was always far from united. For example, it had three separate armies. The president had the Forces Armees Populaires, the Vice-President the Forces Armees du Nord (severely weakened since being thrashed by the Libyans). The main result of the latest coup is that the street lights have been fixed in N'djamena and water pressure increased.

Life and death

This is one of the most sparsely populated African countries with only eight people per square mile. Life expectancy is 29 for men and 35 for women. The main causes of death are dysentery, pains in the stomach and pains in the chest.

No town life exists outside the capital, N'djamena. There are 20 ethnic groups, the largest of which is called Sara. Only one in six children attends school, one of the lowest levels in Africa.

This is one of the world's poorest countries and its people are getting poorer. 96 per cent of them work in subsistence agriculture.

Their cattle don't fare much better. The main breed is the long-horned Bos Taurus. Unfortunately, there is as little to eat for them as there is for the humans. For six months of the year, the animals are kept half-starved. This means they calve late and give little and poor milk. They are hardly ever eaten. However, they do bring prestige to their owners — which may seem better than nothing to them, but can hardly be better than food.

Travel

No railway. Just 150 miles of roads.

Population: Four and a half million

Size: Five times that of Britain, 500,000 sq. miles

Government: Republic

Religion: Islam and traditional beliefs

Language: French, Arabic and 100 local dialects

Capital: N'djamena

Currency: CFA franc

Tips for tourists

Don't get toothache. Chad has only five dentists. If the population all want six-monthly check-ups, each dentist needs to see 8,000 patients a day.

Want to get away from it all? Try the northern region of Chad. In an area the size of France, there are only 50,000 people.

Women from Chad make good ashtrays.

Population: 11 million

Size: 3 times that of Britain, 300,000 sq. miles

Government: Republic

Language: Spanish

Religion: Roman Catholic

Capital: Santiago

Currency: Peso

Tips for tourists

Take sun-tan lotion — the province of Antofagasta in Northern Chile has the highest solar intensity in the world.

Take clean hankies — and see the *cucca*, a dance where couples mime a courtship which climaxes as the woman invitingly lays her increasingly grubby handkerchief across her shoulder and her partner picks it off.

Chile

Republica de Chile

History

This 'long and friendly' land has gone through periods of deep unfriendliness. The native Indian population was conquered in the 16th Century by the Spanish, who had come looking for gold and silver (see *Peru*). In their unsuccessful search the Spanish trampled heedlessly over the vast copper deposits that are today the backbone of the Chilean economy.

They soon realised their error and began trampling over the Indians, subjecting them to forced labour in mines in appalling conditions. And they made the Indians trade with them on terms familiar to Britain in the EEC — the Indians were obliged to buy anything that the Spanish had too much of. Thus, barefoot Indians bought silk stockings and razors, and even glasses, after the Spanish discovered they had a surplus and passed a law making the wearing of them by Indians compulsory on certain occasions.

Embracing the religion of their conquerors provided the Indians with little protection. One Catholic priest was irritated by one of his Indian converts claiming to be Christ so he persuaded the other Indian converts to test him out by crucifying him.

Rescue eventually came in the early 19th Century when the Chilean people (Indians and Creoles - people of Spanish descent) rebelled against their masters. Led by the charismatic Bernardo O'Higgins they defeated the Spanish in 1818 and established Chile as an independent country.

Present-day politics

There followed 150 years of political instability culminating in 1970 in the world's first democratically elected Marxist government under Salvador Allende. He made the fatal mistake of trying to carry out his election promises. There was a military coup in which Allende was killed and a military junta under General Pinochet has been in control every since.

The regime is characterised by the firm handling so typical of military dictatorships — opponents disappear, trade union activity is 'discouraged' and political parties are (according to one ingenious guide-book) *temporarily in recess*. Hope is on the horizon, however. A new constitution introduced in 1981 provides for a return to democracy after a minimum period of eight years. There is no maximum period.

'Helping the police with their enquiries' at Valparaiso police station.

Geography

Chile may not be friendly but it *is* long — 2,650 miles, with an average width of 120 miles. The Andes, the world's second highest mountains, run the entire length of the country. There's every kind of climate and landscape, from the Atacama desert — the world's driest — in the north, to the icebergs and fjords in the far south. It was in the Chilean Andes in 1834 that Charles Darwin first noted the similarities between animals recently extinct and still living and began to ponder on the possibility of evolution.

People

Chileans love answering questions in the affirmative. So they can't say no to a drink. They have the world's highest rate of deaths from cirrhosis of the liver. They are also an emotional people who have trouble handling good news — presumably because they've had so little of it. General Miller in his 19th Century *Memoirs* describes the reaction of the citizens of Santiago to the news of a Chilean victory over the Spanish: *"People embraced each other, laughed, wept and shrieked as if deprived of their senses. Some went mad and one or two of them have never recovered their reason. One man dropped down and expired instantly."*

Bread

Chile has had the world's highest inflation rate in recent years. Once it hit 273 per cent. A loaf of bread which cost 10p in 1970 would have cost £260 by 1980.

China, People's Republic of

Zhonghua Renmin Gonghe Guo

The first 4,000

China became a unified nation in the 8th Century BC after a painful birth — 600 years of wars. In some, thousands of men battled in lines extending for hundreds of miles.

Seventh Century China was dominated by the Empress Wu, who rose from a low-ranking concubine to absolute ruler. The 9th Century was dominated by eunuchs. They ran the country disastrously. The hundred years from the middle of the last century was disastrous, too. China was in a permanent state of anarchy.

The last 40

Civil war broke out as soon as the war against Japan ended in 1945. Four years later the People's Liberation Army, led by Mao Tse-tung, controlled the mainland. It won not by force of reason but by sheer force. Sometimes it had half a million men in battle.

From 1966 to 69 the country suffered under the Cultural Revolution. Schools were closed so that millions of youths could become Red Guards who proceded to denounce 'bourgeois academic values in schools' (i.e. having to learn). Party, government and factory officials were sacked, to be replaced by teenagers. When the violence got out of hand schools were re-opened — but only so that the pupils could read Chairman Mao's little red book.

The current 1,000 million

China is the third largest country (after Russia and Canada) and has more people than anywhere else — more than 1,000 million at the last count. It takes up one-fourteenth of the world's land area and contains one-fifth of the earth's population. About one-third of it is mountainous, including part of Mount Everest (known locally as *Chu-mu-lang-m a Feng*) on the border with Nepal.

Population control

China's proudest boast at the moment is that 100 million couples of child-bearing age now use contraceptives. The government discourages men under 28 and women under 25 from marrying. Couples with only one child get a monthly cash handout. Those with more are accused of 'anarchy in parenthood'.

Other Chinese methods of keeping the population down are even less pleasant. It holds the record for having more major disasters than the rest of the world

together. Like: the worst civil war (30 million dead in the 19th Century 'Great Peace' rebellion), the worst famine (20 million dead, 1969-71), worst flood (3 and a half million dead, 1931), worst earthquake (830,000 dead, 1556). They also hold the records for worst landslide, panic, fire and mining accident, with a mere few thousand killed in each.

Name names

Most common name: *Chang* — there are 75 million of them, all resisting the temptation to add an *e* for a change.

Most appropriate name: The president of the Bank of China is *Mr. Bu Ming*.

A major contribution of the Cultural Revolution. The raffia tea cosy hat.

Culture

During the Great Leap Forward (the second five-year plan of 1958 to 63) peasants and workers were encouraged to write poetry, songs and plays. This bore fruit during the Cultural Revolution with such catchy numbers as *Embroidering for Chairman Mao, Chairman Hua and the Chairman of the Standing Committee of the National People's Congress* and *The herdsmen of the prairie love you, Chairman Hua.*

The national anthem, *March on, brave people of our nation*, was composed collectively in 1978.

Top TV show: the public execution of a Communist Party official for graft.

Health

About a quarter of the more-than one million doctors practise 'Chinese medicine'. Another one and a half million are 'barefoot doctors' who, after three months' training, treat simple ailments in communes. They get their name from going barefoot in rice paddies during the wet season.

Population: 1,008 million

Size: 42 times that of Britain, 3,700,000 sq. miles

Government: Communist

Main Language: Mandarin

Religion: None

Capital: Peking (now called Beijing)

Currency: Yuan, jiao and fen

Tips for tourists

Eat. After the French, the highest expression of gastronomic art is reckoned to be that of the Chinese.

Take a cat. Rat-plagued Chinese villages offer 5 yuan (£1.50) for cats, with a 2 yuan bonus for each litter of kittens. Don't take rat poison instead. It is banned for killing too many cats.

If you appear in court — repent. That is a precondition for getting your sentence reduced.

45

Colombia

Republica de Colombia

Population: 28 million

Size: Five times that of Britain, 450,000 sq. miles

Government: Republic

Language: Spanish

Religion: Roman Catholic

Capital: Bogota

Currency: Pesos, centavos

Tips for tourists

Look at (but don't touch) the coins minted for use in leper colonies in the museum in Bogota.

Don't invite a native to dance too close. It may be the *cumbia*, a dance where the girl holds a lighted candle.

Take your binoculars. Look for the mirla, a tropical bird that has the power of looking glum and talking.

Old gold

Centuries before the discovery of America, Chibcha Indians in Colombia were creating the legend of El Dorado. Literally sitting on a gold mine, the Indians found various ingenious ways to get rid of the stuff. One of these was to roll their chief in gold dust every year and then get him to wash it off in a lake. Hence El Dorado, which means 'the gilded one'.

New world

Rumours of this golden country began to spread and hordes of adventurers headed for Colombia. It took the first Europeans several centuries to arrive only to discover that the practice had long since been discontinued. Travel is now faster and Colombia today has the second best civil aviation service in South America.

Even though they couldn't find 'El Dorado', the Spanish did of course find gold (see *Peru*) and so they decided to stay until the early 19th Century. They ruled with their usual popularity. By 1810 the Colombians had had enough and in Bogota the ubiquitous revolutionary Simon Bolivar declared independence. Unfortunately he realised too late that he had forgotten to raise an army first so he departed to Jamaica to find troops, leaving Bogota to be crushed by the Spanish.

A bridge too far

Bolivar returned after five years to defeat the Spanish and he became the first president of the new republic. However, he was not well-liked, and was eventually forced to flee from his palace and go into hiding under a bridge. Dampness and understandable depression aggravated a touch of the TB and he died shortly afterwards in 1830.

Politics

Subsequent events in Colombia showed that Bolivar was lucky to live under a bridge. A continuous and bloody struggle for power followed between the Liberal and Conservative parties. There were bloodless palace revolutions. It was mass violence all over the country in which the whole population was involved. Finally in 1948 a civil uprising broke out which triggered off a new wave of nationwide violence lasting 10 years without a break. In Bogota, during this period, the police fought the army while farmers regularly streamed into the city and burned it to the ground.

Finally, in 1957, the few Colombians left alive decided that democracy was far too dangerous. They devised a brilliant system in which the office of president would be rotated every four years between Liberals and Conservatives while the members of the Cabinet would be drawn equally from the two parties. This government was called the National Front and it lasted for 16 years. Elections were then resumed and today Colombia is back to normal, i.e. plagued by civil unrest and guerilla activity. With centuries of such training it is hardly surprising that Colombia was the only Latin American country to participate in the Korean War.

Economy

Perhaps Colombians are just over-stimulated from drinking coffee. Colombia is the second largest coffee producer in the world and her economy is overly dependent on it. But her mineral wealth is also staggering. There is more coal than in the rest of South America put together and they supply 90 per cent of the world's emeralds. Not to mention the gold and silver.

A Choco indian shows a tourist how to get from Bogota to Barranquilla.

Comoros
Republique federale islamique des Comores

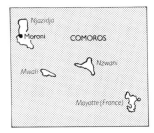

Hell and high water

The Comoros are mountainous and have a tropical climate, but no drinking water. The lush vegetation is only sustained by an extremely high humidity. Water of a salty kind is in abundance, however. In the summer, water spouts and cyclones, torrential downpours and tidal waves are common. In winter, monsoons keep you thoroughly drenched.

There are four main islands in the Comoro group and they each have two names. One is the former French name the other the post-independence Arabic or Swahili one — Grande Comoro (Njazidja), Anjouan (Nzwani) Moheli (Mwali) and Mayotte (Mahore).

The French had a trick up their sleeve. Against all historical, ethnic and economic sense, the island of Mayotte, at French instigation, voted to stay with France. When the main group got independence, the president, Ahmed Abdallah, said: *"I am telling the foreigners that they can still feel at home here"*. The French quickly transferred all their troops and equipment to Mayotte.

Poor benighted people

There are only three towns of any size in the Comoros. The capital, Moroni, has a population of just 16,000. There are 150 miles of road on which they drive 4,000 cars. There is no television although two cinemas can seat a three-hundred-and-seventy-sixth of the whole population. They have a navy — a landing craft donated by France — and an airplane.

Scent from Heaven

For long the Comoros have been called the *Islands of Scents*. The main skilled occupation on the islands is the production of essential oils for the French perfume industry. The Comoros produce more Ylang -Ylang essence than anywhere else in the world and are second to Madagascar in production of vanilla. They also make citronella and lemon grass.

Population: 400,000	
Size: 800 sq. miles	
Government: Republic	
Religion: Islam	
Language: Swahili	
Capital: Moroni (on Njazidja)	
Currency: CFA franc	

Tips for tourists

If political upheaval isn't enough for you, visit the active volcano on Njazidja, visible for 100 miles.

Don't be fooled by the French name *Iles Glorieuses*. The islands are made of bird shit.

Emigration from the Comoros is extensive.

The winner of the Moroni Annual Garden Fete — Pineapple category.

Devil in disguise

The French connection began in 1841 when Admiral de Hell took on the ruling Sultan of Johanna. In the unequal contest between Johanna and Hell, Hell uncharacteristically came out on top.

France ruled absolutely until 1961. After that, they let the locals take control of public sanitation and primary education. Nationalist Comorans, however, were unsatisfied to be merely glorified lavatory attendants and in 1974 a referendum resulted in 95 per cent of the population demanding complete independence.

Congo
Republique Populaire du Congo

Population: One and a half million

Size: One and a half times that of Britain, 130,000 sq. miles

Government: Communist

Language: French, Lingala and Kikongo

Religion: Traditional beliefs and Roman Catholic

Capital: Brazzaville

Currency: CFA franc

Tips for tourists

Good news: there are few lions.

Bad news: there are plenty of cobras, pythons, green mambas, puff adders, eagles, wild dogs, vultures, crocodiles, hawks, tsetse flies and mosquitoes.

Don't have twins. In some villages, a mother is put to death if she has twins — they are supposed to be proof that she has been unfaithful.

Doing the splits

This country is dominated by splits — geographic, social and political.

The Equator splits the Congo in half. This means that in the north, the dry season is November to March and the rainy season April to October — while in the South, it is the other way round.

Doing their sums

Half the population lives in towns. There are 12,000 pygmies and the same number of (considerably taller) Europeans, mainly French. The pygmies were there first — in fact, they were the earliest inhabitants.

The pygmies have struck up a good working relationship with other tribes. The pygmies give them meat and warn them of the approach of elephants. In exchange, they are given pottery and bananas. This has had a disturbing side effect. Through eating bananas, pygmies have contracted the disease *kwashiorkor*, a protein-deficiency which turns the hair red. However, pygmy mothers continue to wean their babies on bananas.

The population is extremely young. More than half are under 19 and only 5 per cent over 60.

Ten years ago, the Congo had one of Africa's lowest literacy rates. Now the government claims it is 95 per cent. Perhaps its numeracy has not kept pace with its literacy.

Doing their best

Farming is still the main industry and its methods have not changed much over the centuries. Men clear the land by burning, leaving their women to work the fields with hand tools. The only thriving industry there has ever been here was slavery.

Being done

The French adventurer Savorgnan de Brazza imposed what he called 'peaceful colonisation' on the natives. This meant exterminating any tribes which resisted. Those who survived were forced to become native bearers since there were no pack animals in the country (and supermarket trolleys had not been invented).

The Congo became independent in 1960 and ten years later was the first African state to declare itself communist. Since then, its leaders have subjected each other to a comradely stream of coups and counter-coups.

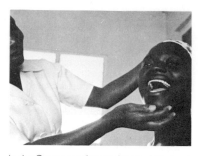

In the Congo, you have to be *taught* to laugh.

A new constitution in 1979 declared that *'The people are the source of all state power'*. However, this does not stop the president being picked by his mates on the Central Committee of the sole political party, the Parti Congolais du Travail (the Congolese Workers' Party). Neither are the party's ranks open to all 'the people'. Only *'true, sound and militant revolutionaries'* are admitted.

The truth is, the dominant political force in the Congo is not Communism but tribalism, as it always has been. That is why its history is one of underdevelopment, and deep social and political divisions.

Doing nothing

The local radio station is called the Voice of the Congolese Revolution.

Costa Rica
Republica de Costa Rica

Costa Rica has no army and a shabby police force. Recently, when an employee stole jewellery from the shop where he worked, the shopkeeper had to pay cab fares for police to track down the thief because they had no cars. *"The cab fares got so expensive I finally dropped it"* said the shopkeeper after three days of fruitless — and expensive — pursuit.

Costa Rican police preparing themselves for a march by primary school children.

Police

Costa Ricans would prefer to spend money on education rather than on security. This means that they have the highest literacy rate in Central America, at 90 per cent, but that guards at the presidential palace wear civilian clothes and street shoes because there is no money for uniforms and boots.

Government officials also complain that some civil guards are carrying guns so ancient that ammunition for them is almost impossible to obtain.

Insecurity

This is one of Latin America's few genuine democracies, and political stability has brought many benefits, including the highest life expectancy in Central America — 67 years. But reality is creeping over the borders from

neighbouring El Salvador and Nicaragua, whose terrorists find Costa Rica a useful base for operations. With no army, Costa Rica is hardly in a position to resist. Instead of 'military aid' therefore, she has been asking for 'police aid' from friendly countries.

People

Costa Rica is the most Spanish of all the countries in the region. The population is very largely white. There is one priest for every 4,200 Catholics — again the highest ratio in the region.

Place

Costa Rica means 'Rich Coast', so named by the Spanish following rumours of vast gold treasures to be found here. These never materialised. The country is known as the Switzerland of Central America but several active volcanoes explode this myth. Two volcanoes have paved roads running to the rims of their craters. The Atlantic coast has 300 days of rain a year. Unsurprisingly, swamps are everywhere.

Bananas

This was the first country in Central America to go bananas, and by 1913 was exporting 11 million bunches. Nearly all the railways were built as plantation lines by a man called Minor Keith, a feat that was achieved with major loss of life. In the first 20 miles of tracks laid, more than 4,000 men died from malaria, yellow fever, dysentery, snake bites, floods, landslides and beriberi.

Today children go to school on these trains as there are no roads through the old plantations. Costa Rica recently began operating a programme to develop fuel alcohol from sugar cane and bananas.

Prison

San Lucas Island is a place to avoid. It has a penal colony where the 'inmates' are allowed to live in comparative freedom, earning a modest income from work, receiving visits from wives and friends, and with a key to their own place. Two German tourists were murdered here in 1981, and one tourist was raped in 1980. If tourists insist on going, they will have their bags searched on arrival by security guards — and probably again later by the inmates. Capital punishment has been abolished in Costa Rica.

Population: Three and a quarter million

Size: A fifth that of Britain, 20,000 sq. miles

Government: Republic

Language: Spanish

Religion: Roman Catholic

Capital: San Jose

Currency: Colone

Tips for tourists

If you are planning to bring in your car, you should know that tyres without rims are confiscated and burnt by Customs.

If you can sing and play the guitar the locals will never let you go.

Try drinking *chan* — it looks like mouldy frogspawn and tastes like penicillin.

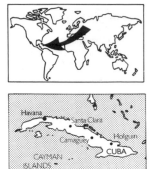

Tips for tourists

Avoid newspapers — typical headlines read: *We have accepted the challenge of nature and victory will depend on our organisational capacity in this struggle!* and *Let us reinforce work discipline during the revolutionary offensive!*

Smoke some of the 15,800,000,000 cigars and cigarettes produced annually.

Men: Avoid wearing shorts and sandals — you will be mistaken for a homosexual. NB. Cubans do not like homosexuals.

Avoid political rallies — Castro is fond of eight-hour speeches.

News travels fast here. Cubans send more telegrams than anyone except the people of Monaco.

Cuba
Republica de Cuba

The history of the Cuban people is symbolised by the Cuban heel — a small race trying to appear taller. Although their president, Fidel Castro, appears to be 6ft 7ins, informed sources have noted that he is never photographed below the ankles.

The Castro regime

Castro came to power in a revolution in 1959, proclaiming *"I am not a Communist"*. He had promised to introduce a 'social democracy' and guarantee freedom of the press, free speech and free elections. Shortly after gaining power he said that democracy was a 'betrayal of the people' and opened the Karl Marx cement factory. There are some hopeful signs, however. The new Constitution, adopted in 1962, committed the state to the 'protection of the family'. And Castro and his brother Raul, who is Cuba's First Vice-President, have shown tremendous zeal in upholding it. They are helped by the world's largest armed forces for size of population.

Pre-Castro

Cubans are used to broken promises. There have been quite a few in their history. Not from the Spanish, however, who colonised Cuba in the 16th Century. The native Indian population knew exactly where they were with the Spanish — dead, as it turned out. They were exterminated by the colonists. The Spanish had to replace their workforce with new slaves from Africa, and today one third of Cubans are black. Although there was no gold in Cuba the Spanish turned to 'crunchy white gold' — sugar, which became the main wealth of the island and its ruling landowners. But it was not only 'Spanish Eyes' that coveted

In remote parts of Cuba news of the discovery of Kit Williams' *Golden Hare* has not yet filtered through.

Cuba. In 1840 the United States had offered Spain 130 million dollars for Cuba, but had been turned down, which was just as well since in 1898 it came free as part of the spoils of the Spanish-American war. In 1902 Cuba was granted 'independence' by the US, who had the right to intervene in Cuban affairs. Immense amounts of American capital were pumped into Cuba. Havana became one of the world's great emporia of vice and prostitution. Seventy per cent of Cuba's exports went to the US and 65 per cent of her imports came from the same source.

The new government

Most Cuban governments were corrupt or worse. In the first 25 years of independence there were five attempted revolutions by groups trying to gain independence, protect individual liberty, life and so on. Each one was thwarted by the intervention or threatened intervention of US Marines determined to protect independence, individual liberty, life and so on. US troops landed in Cuba in 1906, 1912, and 1920. But American intervention was unable to prevent the eventual revolution in which Fidel became President of the republic, and Che Guevara, his famous Argentinian sidekick, president of the Cuban National Bank. These days, America and Cuba have learned to live with each other in festering hatred.

Hello education

The slogan of Cuban school children is Study: Work: Rifle, and surprisingly in the first ten years of the revolution the number of pupils and teachers was multiplied by five. The answer was total literacy. All teachers and children are obliged to spend 45 days a year in the fields doing agricultural work which is called *The School in the Countryside*. The fields make Cuba the second largest sugar producer in the world.

Cyprus
Kypriaki Dimokratia/Kibris Cumhuriyeti

Cosmopolitan

Cyprus is like a rampant sexual disease. Everyone seems to have had it at one time or another. Egypt conquered it in 1500 BC. It later became:
Mycenaean
Phoenician
Assyrian (under King Sargon)
and *Egyptian* again.
Then followed 100 years of independence (out of a total of 109).

It was then Persian, Greek, Egyptian *again*, Roman, Byzantine — followed by Syrian, Arabic, Byzantine Empire and English — for the first time (under Richard the Lionheart). Then it tried Jerusalem (to whom Richard the Lionheart gave it because the Knights Templar couldn't afford it), French (because the king of Jerusalem was French), Venetian and Egyptian *again*.

By this time it was 1426. It was ruled by Egypt through James the Bastard who was an Archbishop. Then it was Venice's turn again and the Turks at last brought some consistency, from 1570-1878. It was finally Great Britain's turn again until it was left for Greece and Turkey to fight it out.

The last battle

The Greeks wanted it to be unified with Greece but the Turks were against it. The British solution was to *share* Cyprus — a very British and very un-Turkish/Greek sentiment. In 1960 they tried. So, in 1963 there was a civil war. Luckily Cyprus had joined the UN just in time to get a peace-keeping force. In 1974, the Greeks and Turks separated completely after a civil war and remain that way.

The spoils

Cyprus's name comes from the Latin *cuprum*, meaning 'copper'. When the Romans controlled the area, their fleets were made from Cypriot trees and most of the island until quite recently was forested. Now, though copper is still important, trees are dropping off. The Turks, with only 15 per cent of the population, control 36 per cent of the island's total area and 60 per cent of its agricultural and industrial potential.

Tourism is chiefly exploited in the Greek, southern, part. But the future of the island as a whole seems to lie in acting as a service station for the Middle East.

Dangers

Zeus's father, Chronos, had his penis cut off in an argument in a part of heaven just above Paleo Paphos in western Cyprus. The penis fell, ejaculating into the sea giving birth to Aphrodite, the goddess of love, in a sea shell. Nothing so unnerving is likely to happen to the modern visitor.

The biggest danger today must be the food and wine. Hiromeri is a dish of pork marinated for 40 days in red wine and sea salt, crushed to a sixth of its normal size by mill stones and smoked for a whole winter. To wash it down, don't risk Commandaria — a truly mediaeval wine. Most of the wines of Cyprus are 'equal to the wines of Spain', which are disgusting.

The locals keep large cats to reduce the viper population. Stray dogs, though, are shot on sight ever since the first British Governor left his camel tied to the front gate of his house and returned to find it had been eaten by them. Many of the houses have very low doorways to prevent Turks stabling their horses in people's homes.

Population: 620,000

Size: 3,500 sq. miles

Government: Republic

Religion: Greek Orthodox, some Islam

Language: Greek and Turkish

Capital: Nicosia

Currency: Greek Cypriot pound, Turkish Cypriot pound

Tips for tourists

The name to associate with Cyprus and independence is Makarios — an archbishop (the Turks have a mufti).

There is still 99 sq. miles of British sovereign territory. If you're British don't go to the Turkish bit — Britain doesn't recognise it and it might work both ways.

The white wine of Cyprus is called The Beautiful White Wine of Cyprus.

When entering a Cypriot house you may be offered preserves. These should be taken sparingly but never refused.

Celebrate Okhi Day — or No Day — when the Cypriots said 'No' to the Italians in 1940.

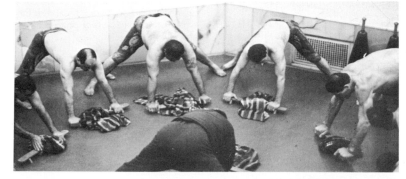

Turkish Cypriots are taught what to do in the event of a traditional Greek attack.

Population: 15 and a quarter million

Size: Half that of Britain, 50,000 sq. miles

Government: Communist

Languages: Czech and Slovak

Main religion: Roman Catholic

Capital: Prague

Currency: Koruna and haler

Tips for tourists

You won't have much trouble getting into the Strahov stadium in Prague. It takes a quarter of a million spectators — but get there early or you won't see much.

Try going to the pictures. The Czechs love a movie and have 3,180 cinemas.

Don't buy the paper Rude Pravo thinking it is a dirty mag. It is the Communist Party daily and doesn't even have pin-ups.

In restaurants, avoid *jaternice* (intestines) and *povidla* (prune goo).

Czechoslovakia
Ceskoslovenska Socialisticka Republika

Geography

Czechoslovakia is, according to its national anthem, 'a paradise to look at'. Travel guides describe it as being both in the heart and on the roof of Europe, which shows that travel writers know little about anatomy. What they mean is that it is in the centre of the continent and is rather mountainous.

It lies on the boundary between the Communist and capitalist countries — and the join shows. Mind you, it was messed about a lot even before the cold war began.

History

The Czechoslovak state was formed after World War One when the Austria-Hungarian empire was dissolved. It was two separate countries briefly. Then the Slovaks said they wanted to unite with the Czechs. That brought together the lands of Bohemia, Moravia, Silesia, Slovakia and Subcarpathian Ruthenia.

In 1938, as part of a shameful concession to Hitler, the UK, France, Germany and Italy carved the country up. On liberation Czechoslovakia was put back together again, but without Subcarpathian Ruthenia, which was given to the Russians, probably because it sounds like a disease.

Whoever looks away first is an idiot (and is then shot).

Politics

The Communist Party won little more than a third of the votes in the 1946 elections but it headed a coalition government. Two years later all the non-Communist ministers resigned when they found Reds being infiltrated into positions of power. Elections were called and Communists swept the country. They haven't looked back — except over their shoulders.

By 1968 there was growing pressure for liberalisation. The new leaders, under Alexander Dubcek, introduced many reforms in the so-called *Prague spring*. But winter was not far off. Four months later, on August 21st the tanks and troops of Warsaw Pact countries invaded. The government was forced into a policy of 'normalisation' (i.e.normal by Soviet standards).

Czechoslovakia now consists of two parts, the Czech Socialist Republic and the Slovak Socialist Republic. Constitutionally they have equal rights. But the real power lies elsewhere (not a million steppes from the Kremlin). Results at the last election were:
Number entitled to vote: 10,789,574
Number voting: 10,736,312
Number voting Communist: 10,732,017
It is not known what happened to the 4,000-odd who didn't support the Party.

The people

Czechoslovakia's population is growing slowly and ageing fast. The life span is 68 for men and 74 for women. A quarter of a million gipsies live here.

Czechs like dressing up in folk costume, making cheese and processing fruit. Half the families in Prague have a second home in the country.

Discrimination

Czechoslovakia has one of the highest rates of female employment in the world — almost half the workforce is women. However, male workers earn two and a half times more than women.

Industry

This is the second most prosperous country in the Communist bloc (after East Germany). It is Eastern Europe's largest foreign trader for the size of population and its biggest supplier of cars and trains. Even its agriculture is advanced (by Soviet standards). It is the world's third biggest beer producer for size of population.

Religion

There are 18 different faiths, including *Hussites, Czech Brethren, Slovak Lutherans, Silesian Lutherans* and *Reformed Christians*. Clergymen are paid by the state, which controls the churches.

Denmark

Kongeriget Danmark

Denmark is a low sort of place. The highest point is only 568 feet above sea-level — less than half the height of the Empire State Building. And no-one lives more than 33 miles from the sea. It is the smallest of the Scandinavian countries — about half the size of Scotland.

The Vikings

The Vikings are famous, like Millwall supporters, for rape, pillage and generally laying waste. But only when playing away from home. At their own ground it was a different story. Rape was a capital offence — as long as the woman screamed immediately she was touched. And grounds for a Viking wife being able to divorce her husband were if he wore women's clothing or did not fulfil his conjugal duties. And a Viking adage shows that a Viking was even concerned with what he should talk about afterwards:
A man should know how to make conversation with women whether they are young or getting on in years.
Judging by their primitive sailing technique, it's surprising that the Vikings had the energy for anything. They hadn't discovered the art of tacking — so if there was a favourable wind they sailed dead ahead. If not, the men rowed. From such practices, presumably, came one of their sailing adages:
Never stay at sea far into autumn, if the decision lies with you.

Some early Danish kings

Gorm the Old, Harald Bluetooth, Sweyn Forkbead, Canute the Great, Hardicanute, Magnus the Good, Harold III Hen, Canute II the Holy, Olaf Hunger (The Hungry), Eric Ejegod (Evergood) and Eric the Lamb.

Danish names

Denmark is full of Hansens, Petersens, Hensens etc. There are so many that Danish surnames are listed in the phone book by occupation. Originally, as in Iceland, a son or daughter took the father's name, adding 'sen' or 'datter' as appropriate. Thus the son of Peter Hansen was Lars Petersen, and his daughter Inge Peterdatter. But this was so complicated that in 1828 a law was passed requiring every family to choose a surname and keep it. The problem is that the range of available surnames was in effect limited to those Christian names in use when the law was passed.

Low living — at a high cost

Since the relaxation of Denmark's pornography laws in 1969, Copenhagen has become over-run with porn shows and sex shops. One of the results has been that sex crimes in Denmark have lessened, and the novelty has worn off for everyone except tourists. Instead the Danes commit suicide at an unusually high rate. This may be connected with the price of their beer, which is also very high.

Police crack down in Denmark's notorious red-light district.

The history of Denmark

At different times Denmark has ruled the whole of Norway and Sweden, most of the territory bordering the Baltic Sea, and much of England.

For years the Danes quarrelled with the Germans over the ownership of Schleswig-Holstein. Lord Palmerston remarked, many years later, that only three persons understood the political issues involved in this quarrel:
"One is Albert the Prince Consort and he is dead, the other is a German professor and he is in an asylum, and the third is myself and I have forgotten it."

Lego

Invented by another Danish carpenter's son — now a millionaire, Lego is today manufactured under licence in over 60 countries. In Billund 2 million plastic bricks have been used to build a model village — it contains a copy of an English provincial town, the Mount Rushmore presidents, and a Wild West saloon.

National anthem

The first line is *'King Christian stood by the lofty mast'*, which refers to a great naval battle between the Danes and the Swedes, at Koge Bay in 1677. Some sources claim that the King in fact observed the engagement from the tower of a nearby church.

Population: 5 and a quarter million

Size: A sixth that of Britain, 16,500 sq. miles

Government: Constitutional monarchy

Language: Danish

Main religion: Lutheran

Capital: Copenhagen

Currency: Krone, ore

Tips for tourists

Don't go at Christmas — Danes begin their Xmas dinner with rice pudding.

Celebrate the birthday of the old lime tree in Regensen College in May — by shaking hands with a pair of gloves hung up in its branches.

VAT is called MOMS in Denmark

Watch out for the former barracks behind 'Our Saviour's Church' in Copenhagen. This is the site of the capital's 'alternative' (i.e. criminal) society.

Don't say 'please' — in Danish only 'thank you' is used — tak.

You are likely to be mown down by platoons of cyclists in Copenhagen. A quarter of Denmark's population lives here, and they all have bikes.

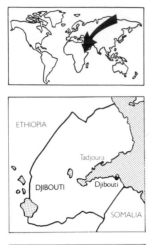

Djibouti

Jumhouriyya Djibouti

Population: About 300,000

Size: A tenth that of Britain, 8,500 sq. miles

Government: Republic

Languages: French, Arabic, Somali, Afar

Religion: Islam

Capital: Djibouti

Currency: CFA franc

Tips for tourists

Don't hire a car: *"In Djibouti chauffeurs are paid the equivalent to a general in Somalia"* — Ali Aref. Also there are only 50 miles of road.

No holiday jobs. 70 per cent unemployment and 100,000 refugees.

Water water everywhere

This tiny, wedge-shaped country squeezed between the giants of Ethiopia and Somalia looks out on to both the Red Sea and the Indian Ocean. It is at the very corner of the Horn of Africa, where it is at its horniest. (Population growth is more than twice as great as Ethiopia and Somalia). But although it overlooks a sea and an ocean, Djibouti has no comparable source of fresh water. It is an arid, volcanic, rock-strewn desert waste dotted with salt lakes. Between 1968 and 71 there was no rain in the town of Oboke.

Visits to Djibouti port by the odd liner or military vessel put an enormous strain on the capital's water supply. In three years drought killed off 15 per cent of the livestock. The nomadic Bedouins solve the problem by being great palm-wine drinkers — but punishments are severe for using the trees as wild liquor stills.

Women's emancipation has been held up by their inability to communicate with each other.

Passing water

With so little encouragement inland it was natural for Djibouti to look to the sea for its survival and the opening of the Suez Canal with the ensuing flow of traffic gave it the chance. France saw the opportunity first and in 1862 the French settled the town and port of Djibouti to balance their interests against the British in Aden.

Today the entire economy is based on the port. With half the inhabitants living here and most of the working population on the docks, Djibouti is easily affected by trouble beyond its borders. When in 1967 the Suez Canal was closed, the economy was crippled. Later the oil boom and huge tanker requirements forced Saudi Arabia to use Djibouti and the country's fortunes rallied.

In 1977, however, the war between Ethiopia and Somalia closed the railway from Ethiopia to Djibouti. Again the economy crumbled. Ethiopia imports 60 per cent and exports 40 per cent of its economy through Djibouti.

Vichy water

Independence was a watery affair. The first comment by the new President Kamil was: *"We need France and we await its aid in certain domains".* The Old Prime Minister, Ali Aref, said: *"This is the price of independence".* The French said: *"France isn't leaving because no one is throwing her out".* So the French occupation still goes on, although Djibouti gained its independence in 1977.

The French first called the country French Somaliland — then the French Overseas Territory of the Afars and Issas. Both names cause problems still. The Afars are a wandering tribe who have no regard for the national borders of the colonial powers and continually wander into and from Ethiopia. The Issas are Somalis and quote the original name of the French Territory as evidence that they should run it.

Before independence the French called a referendum, putting a barbed wire fence around Djibouti first so that a proper census could be taken. Three censuses produced three different results. Eventually, in 1967, it was decided that a vote had been taken to stay with France.

Watered down

The 1967 president was an Afar. He invited two Issas into the Cabinet but replaced Issas by Afars in the docks. In 1975, 16 died because an Issa married an Afar, but undeterred the first independent Prime Minister, an Afar, married an Issa.

Dominica
Commonwealth of Dominica

Not-so-rough

The Dominican flag contains a Sisserou parrot. If it could talk, it would say *"Who's a pretty country?"*. Dominica *is* a pretty country — ruggedly beautiful, in fact. The locals (at least, those in the expanding tourist industry) call it the Switzerland of the Caribbean, although a more suitable title would be the Tropics of Wales.

It is an island full of wonderful waterfalls, magical pools, and lush mysterious areas. The whole place is criss-crossed by rivers. In the centre are mountains covered with trees and solfataras (volcanic vents) and hot springs. The most famous of these is the Boiling Lake, 2,300 feet high, throwing 3ft high spouts of water into the air. It is the world's highest and biggest jacuzzi.

Rough passage

Dominica, the largest of the Windward Islands, was discovered on a Sunday by Christopher Columbus and named by him after the Latin for 'the Lord's Day' — *dies dominica*. The island takes its name too literally: it is closed *every* day.

It is almost impossible to travel round the outskirts of Dominica and totally impossible to get through its centre, which is packed with impenetrable greenery. Although the island boasts more than 400 miles of roads, these have more in common with the surface of the moon than a motorway.

There are few buses and almost the only way to get round the island is on the 'banana transports' — rickety old lorries which will gladly give lifts to anyone who cares to cling on to them.

Rough justice

The busiest people on the island are the 250 police officers and four magistrates, who handle some 3,500 cases a year (comparative figure for Britain would be 3 million cases). No statistics for offences are available, but they are presumably such things as handling stolen bananas, being under the influence of lime juice and breaking and entering a coconut.

Those are the only things which are produced in any quantity in Dominica. Bananas are the main product with coconuts next in importance. Limes have been important to the island for centuries. Ships used to pull in here for them to treat the sailors' scurvy. Now the lime groves are run by Rose's Lime Juice.

Rough luck

Dominica was first colonised in the 17th Century by the French. For the next 100 years the British and French squabbled over it until in 1805 it became a British colony. After a brief period in the Federation of West Indies it became an independent republic in 1978.

Rough house

Being a member of the House of Assembly is no cushy number. There are so few of them (21 elected and nine nominated) that members of the government have to double, treble and even quadruple up on jobs.

Thus the Prime Minister (currently Mary Eugenia Charles) is also Minister of Finance *and* Minister of Development. The Minister of Home Affairs is also responsible for Industrial Relations (presumably in the banana industry) as well as Housing. Another Minister has to deal with Communications, Works, Tourism and Industry.

Population: 74,000

Size: 290 sq. miles

Government: Republic

Language: English and French patois

Religion: Roman Catholic

Capital: Roseau

Currency: French franc, £ sterling, East Caribbean dollar

Tips for tourists

Do not be tempted into eating the local speciality of *mountain chicken*. It is really giant frogs' legs.

Unless you have taken aspirin with you, do not get a headache. There is only one chemist.

Remember — Dominica is pronounced *Dom-in-ee-ca*. The Dominican Republic is pronounced *Dom-in-ic-an*.

If you need to know the way in Dominica, don't ask a policeman.

Dominican Republic
Republica Dominicana

Population: Five and three quarter million

Size: A fifth that of Britain, 19,000 sq. miles

Government: Republic

Language: Spanish

Religion: Roman Catholic

Capital: Santo Domingo

Currency: Dominican dollars

Tips for tourists

Don't be tempted by the presidency.

Stand well clear of the president.

Don't eat merengues. They are dances.

Don't eat anything cooked for the president.

As in any other country in the Caribbean, don't believe anyone who says Columbus' bones are buried here.

Don't expect much snap, crackle and pop. The Republic is bottom in cereal consumption per capita (but second in fruit consumption).

Men on horseback

The history of the Dominican Republic is one of mysterious interventions by 'men on horseback' — as they were called — bandits who descended on the machinery of government from time to time and sorted it out to their own satisfaction. These 'men on horseback' are the Caribbean equivalent of roaming gangs in Spaghetti Westerns.

The modern equivalents of these powerful forces are dictators and the CIA (neither of whom are seen riding in the streets of Santo Domingo). The population still lives in fear, however, as most houses can only be reached by foot or on horseback.

The Minister for Mental Health

The good

When Columbus discovered the island, which he called Hispaniola, he was impressed: *"Once you see Hispaniola you won't want to leave".* That is exactly what happened to the thousands of Amerindians shipped in and worked to death. The cathedral Columbus built is 'the Lourdes of the Caribbean' and America's first church in America's first western habitation.

The oldest house in the western hemisphere is also on the island. When neighbouring Haiti took advantage of the French Revolution to shake loose from the French, Dominica took the hint and staged the hemisphere's first revolution — a horrific insight into its future history. So in 1821 the Dominican Republic was born. Subsequently the population referred to Spain endearingly as Espana Bobo or 'Silly Spain'.

The Minister of Defence

The bad and the ugly

The reformed French Haitians invaded in 1822 and stayed until 1844 when 'men on horseback' took over until 1899. One of them, Santana, gave the country back to Spain in return for the governorship. In 1899 Ulysses Heureux was assassinated by more 'men on horseback' who, by this time, were more like devils on horseback. Caceres was assassinated in 1911, hotly pursued by civil war.

The U.S. intervened and invited a 'man on horseback' to rule the country from 1930 to 1961. His name was Trujillo and even the Americans couldn't put up with him. They had him assassinated. His successor was overthrown and the U.S. cavalry rode in again in 1965. The president now is Blanco who continues a whitewash policy in this violent country.

Ecuador

Republica del Ecuador

Geography

Ecuador gets its name from the Equator, which crosses it. It is also crossed by the Andes mountains which run from north to south and dominate the country. They contain the world's highest active volcano, Cotopaxi *19,360 ft.*

Volcanic eruptions are only one of the disturbances the population has to contend with. Earthquakes are another (in 1949 more than 50 towns were destroyed in one). Other disturbances are man-made. For years Ecuador has been fighting Peru in a border dispute. Peru claims half of Ecuador's Amazon territories and has got them at the moment. If Ecuador could get them back it would increase its size by 75 per cent.

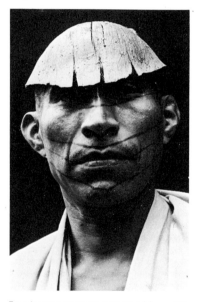

Ecuadoreans possess a toupee at blue-print stage only.

History

A Spanish colony from 1532, the country rebelled early in the 19th Century and the Spaniards were sent packing by a local army led by Marshal Sucre.

Ever since independence the country has been ideologically divided between the liberals, based in Guayaquil, and the conservatives, in Quito. The compromise has often been military rule or dictatorship. Other forms of government have included anarchy and an autocracy based on the influence of the Catholic Church.

Politics

Jose Maria Velasco Ibarra is a man who can't take a hint. Five times he has been elected president. Twice he was deposed and once he only avoided that fate by withdrawing. Other recent presidents have fared no better. One lasted for only ten days and his successor for twelve.

The national anthem is one of the most patriotic-sounding imaginable: *Salve, oh patria!*

The people

Baron Alexander von Humboldt, a German who visited Ecuador in 1802, summed up its people perfectly. He said: *They are the strangest people in the world. They live in poverty on mountains of gold; sleep tranquilly at the foot of volcanoes; and cheer themselves with sad music.*

A national minimum wage of £15 a month is laid down by law. Unfortunately, even the government fails to pay it.

Communication

There are a quarter of a million telephones, most of them in government offices. People without telephones use horses — there are more of them for the size of population than anywhere except Mongolia.

The law

Good news: the Constitution bans capital punishment and torture. *Bad news:* juries were abolished in 1928.

Tips for tourists

Don't bother hiring a car. Although there are 10,000 miles of roads most of them are narrow and liable to be blocked by landslides.

Try not to become pregnant. The main cause of death is difficult labour and birth injuries.

Keep well wrapped up. Ecuador has the world's second highest rate for death from flu.

Population: 44 million	
Size: One a half times that of Texas, 390,000 sq. miles	
Government: Republic	
Language: Arabic	
Religion: Islam	
Capital: Cairo	
Currency: Egyptian pound	

Tips for tourists

Be careful of Egyptian drivers. Their driving test involves driving 6 metres forward and 6 metres back.

Save your bacon. There are less pigs in Egypt than anywhere in the world (including Israel).

Be careful of praising your hosts' coffee (see *Love and marriage*).

Egypt
Arab Republic of Egypt

Lonely

The greatest fear of Egyptians is loneliness. Government officials invariably leave their office doors open and conduct business with several people at the same time. And there are always the secret police, waiters, taxi-drivers and shoeshine boys.

It would be nice to think that fear of loneliness drove 99 per cent of the population to huddle together in only 3 and a half per cent of the land. But the real reason is that the rest of Egypt is desert — apart from the River Nile, the world's longest.

Curses

The popular Egyptian proverb *Water will not run uphill* does not represent all that is left of 6,000 years of civilisation. There are also the three Pyramids in the desert outside Cairo, consisting of 2 and a half million square stones, each weighing 2 and a half tons.

The Tomb of Tutankhamen is thought to have cost the lives of at least 20 people in the 1920's, through accidents, assassination or suicide.

Noisy

Arabic is a very noisy and emotional language. The night before the revolution in 1952, Nasser addressed his fellow revolutionaries in English. He explained *"The Arabic language possesses no words to express the idea of calm"*. It is, however, the oldest written language.

Noisier

The Egyptian singer Umm Kalthoum was a unique phenomenon. When she died in 1975 half a million people attended her funeral. Umm could hold a single note (e.g: *Ummmmmmmmmmmm*) for more than one and a half minutes whereas ordinary singers can manage a

Passengers listen for the sound of the 3.45 from Khartoum.

maximum of only 40 seconds. Her voice vibrated 14,000 times a second, 3 times the rate of the average person. Someone did a doctoral thesis for the University of Cairo titled *An Analysis of the Voice of Umm Kalthoum*.

Modern

Modern Egypt began in 1805 with the ruler Muhammed Ali (not known as *the Cairo Lip*). The Suez Canal, built in 1869, still dominates the political scene.

In 1952, some Egyptian army officers led by Colonel Nasser staged a coup against the corrupt and weak King Farouk. Farouk abdicated with these words to his generals: *"You have done what I always intended to do myself".*

Nasser

Nasser got rid of the British and nationalised the Suez Canal in 1956. He fought for Arab unity and crushed the corrupt regime he had inherited, replacing it with a repressive police state. He was a socialist. Egypt, it was said, was Nasser, Umm Kalthoum and the Pyramids. He was passionate about Gruyere cheese sandwiches and died of a heart attack in 1970.

He was succeeded by Sadat, whose politics were less certain. The following story is told of him: Sadat was being driven through Cairo by Nasser's chauffeur when they arrived at a crossroads. *"What did Nasser do here?"* asked Sadat. *"He turned left"*, replied the chauffeur. *"Very well, signal left and turn right."* said Sadat.

Egypt now has the biggest army in Africa and spends more on defence as a percentage of national income than any other country.

Love and marriage

The television series *Dallas* has been banned as immoral. Kissing is also frowned on for Egyptians. Courting couples are forced to pretend to be tourists. They carry suitcases around with them and kiss in the airport or the central station.

Marriages are arranged. The man interviews the woman and he in turn is interviewed by her parents. After this meeting, if he says *"This is very good coffee"*, it means he wants to marry the girl.

A man only had to say *"I divorce you"* three times, whether in his wife's presence or not, to obtain a divorce. Since 1979 a husband has to inform his wife that he is divorcing her.

El Salvador

Republica de El Salvador

Death

For the past ten years, one of the major official causes of death here has been *homicide and injury purposely inflicted by other persons, and legal intervention*. Whoever wrote that classification didn't dare put in the more accurate definition: killed by the death squads. These have systematically abducted and murdered thousands.

The government's reward for turning a blind eye to this butchery has been vast — increased aid from the United States, which is now also sending in military 'advisers' (see also *Vietnam*). The Reagan administration justifies this by saying: *a)* it is stemming the tide of Communism in Central America, and *b)* it is the will of the people, as witnessed by the overwhelming victory of the extreme right-wing (i.e. death.squad) candidates in the 1982 election. (The fate of those who did not vote that way is unknown).

Politics in El Salvador are enough to drive indians to French aperitifs.

Other problems

Overpopulation. This is the smallest and most densely populated Central American state (the death squads are working on solving this problem).
Misnaming. El Salvador is the world's main source of balsam. However, the healing balsam which is grown exclusively here is known as 'Peruvian' balsam.

Miscounting. The main crop and export is coffee. This is sold in 60 kg bags, although officially they are called 69 kg bags.
Union membership. This is allowed for everyone except agricultural or seasonal workers. Virtually everyone in El Salvador is an agricultural or seasonal worker.
The roads. There are only 750 miles of them.
Volcanoes. El Salvador has the most dangerous volcanoes in America. The capital, San Salvador, has been destroyed once by one — and twice by earthquakes.

Good old days

Before the Spanish arrived in the 16th Century, this territory was peacefully occupied by five Indian tribes. They called it 'Land of the Jewel'. The Spaniards renamed it after the 'Holy Saviour'. El Salvador was one of the Central American states which tore themselves free from Spain in 1821, became independent in 1839, and has suffered ever since.

Population: 5 and a quarter million

Size: One tenth that of Britain, 8,000 sq. miles

Government: Republic

Language: Spanish

Religion: Roman Catholic

Capital: San Salvador

Currency: Colon, centavos

Tips for tourists

See the most wonderful volcano in the world, *Izalco*, 'the lighthouse'. Its red glow makes it visible to sailors at night.

Don't ask about the dam across the River Lempa. They have been building it for more than 30 years and are rather touchy about a completion date.

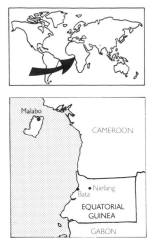

Population: 375,000

Size: A tenth that of Britain, 11,000 sq. miles

Government: Republic

Language: Spanish, Pidgin English

Religion: Roman Catholic

Capital: Malabo

Currency: Ekpwele

Tips for tourists

A PUN in Equatorial Guinea is the political party Partido Unico Nacional later changed to PUNT.

A GAG is what is put in the mouths of those who don't belong to the PUN.

There are no roads.

View the country from Mount Chocolate.

Equatorial Guinea
Republica de Guinea Ecuatorial

Bonkers

The Portuguese landed here first, naming the island they touched down on *Formosa* meaning 'beautiful'. They soon realised that if they kept naming every island they discovered 'Formosa', administration of their empire would become a real headache. So they called it Fernando Poo — Poo meaning 'dust'.

They lost it to Spain, who lost it to Britain in 1827 but got it back 50 years later. Before the Portuguese, the local dynasty of the Bonkero kings ruled — Bonkero One, Two and Three. Lunatic rule was temporarily suspended until the locals were independent again in 1968.

Mad Macias

In 1972 Macias Nguema changed his presidency into a lifelong appointment and assured the rest of the world that from now on he represented the lowest common denominator of Guineans by banning the use of the word 'intellectual'. His dictatorship, brought to an end abruptly by his nephew in 1979, went largely unnoticed in the outside world. Opponents he didn't kill, fled. No wonder this is black Africa's most sparsely populated country. Nearly half the population took this way out. Those who remained found that, although letters could be delivered to them by the postal service, they were not able to send any. Macias was a paranoid, cruel megalomaniac.

Insane Nguema

Under the electoral slogan *'Macias always keeps his promises'*, he first exceeded them by killing most of the government. His cousin looked after foreign affairs and was vice-president. His nephew, defence, finance, industry, trade, under-secretary of state etc.

He killed all the doctors, most of the educated people and some priests who wouldn't obey his order to pray only for him and acknowledge *'Macias, the sole miracle of Equatorial Guinea'*.

A colourful character (mostly red) he slaughtered, gouged out eyes, drowned, burned and even defenestrated his opponents. In 1978, the National Day was celebrated by 32 fresh executions to the strains of Mary Hopkins' *'Those were the days'*. After this even his wife fled the country, forsaking his £6 million presidential palace. The country would have had the highest 'suicide' rate in the world if Nguemas' claims were correct.

Spain's contribution

In 1904 Spain granted the status of 'legal minors' to the population and introduced forced labour, which continued until 1979. One more step towards 'independence' was taken in 1938 with the introduction of a financial qualification for freedom. 350 out of 150,000 qualified.

In 1959 the people were made Spanish citizens and until independence in 1968 had one of the highest standards of living in Africa. The legacy of Spanish rule, however, consisted of no railways, electricity, water or medicine. Malaria, fibariasis, hepatitis, dysentery and whooping cough were universal.

His people mourn the passing-on of Macias Nguema.

Ethiopia

Haile ancient

Ethiopia can claim the longest existence as a separate nation of any in the world. In Africa its historical continuity is only rivalled by Egypt. Ethiopia also had the longest succession of dynastic rulers until 1974, when the last emperor Haile Selassie was deposed. The 1955 constitution proclaimed the emperor a descendant of King Solomon and the Queen of Sheba.

The Ethiopians are obviously fairly long on naivety as well. He was also the King of Kings, the Conquering Lion of Juda, the Elect of God and Minister of Education. More successful at subduing Juda than educating the population, the emperor left a legacy of 90 per cent illiteracy. His death caused problems too, bringing into doubt his immortality.

Haile Selassie

At the time he matched his country's tradition for antiquity by being the longest reigning ruler in the world — taking control in 1928. While ensuring the 14th Century epic *The Glory of Kings* was in the shops, Selassie did try to modernise the country, doing more in 50 years than had been achieved in the previous 3,000. He created: the first standing army, the fiscal system and the Ministry of the Interior. Thus the old feudal methods were crushed.

In the arid lands of Ethiopia women stand around for up to four years waiting for it to rain.

Haile religious

In a balmy sea of Islam, Ethiopia has maintained a strong Christian majority since 325 AD. The scale of religious architecture is huge and began in the Middle Ages with 12 massive churches carved out of solid rock. The crusaders recognised this Christian haven among the infidels, basing their legend of Prester John on an Ethiopian emperor. Today religious Christian names are common, 'daughter of Zion', and 'servant of Jesus' being the most common. The people believe that the Ark of the Covenant was brought from Jerusalem to Ethiopia. Rastafarianism is derived from Selassie's real name, Ras Tafari, and he is still god in Jamaica.

Haile unfortunate

The past 20 years have brought constant wars and drought. In 1964, the war against Somalia over possession of Ogaden started. The Somalis took it, but the USSR changed sides and flooded Ethiopia with arms which drove out the Russian-armed Somalis. 2,000 million dollars of military aid was given by Russia. The repayment is in crops — this in a country where 5 million people are affected by famine. About one million dollars aid is available for this. The 1973 drought killed 200,000 and 1983 promises to be a similar disaster. Ethiopia has 20 per cent of Africa's cattle.

The internal war with Eritrea, which wants its independence, has raged for 10 years — but the opposition cannot unite and confuses the population by splitting into ELF, EPLF and ELF-PLF.

Haile amusing

Appropriately perhaps Ethiopia's national dish is *injera* — bread — and a dish called *wat* (as in wat is the national dish of Ethiopia?) In fact even their proverbs are obsessed with simple foods:
Love and porridge must be taken while hot. Once cool, those who would taste, are a lot.
This matter-of-factness extends to their views of women and mules:
Mules and women need the stick,
Mules and women will betray you.
To be betrayed by your mule in Ethiopia is a serious business as more than half the population live more than 10 miles from a road.

Population: 30 and a half million

Size: Four times that of Britain, 395,000 sq. miles

Government: Military

Language: Amharic

Religion: Coptic Christian, Islam

Capital: Addis Ababa

Currency: Ethiopian birr

Tips for tourists

The most popular newspaper is *Police and Progress* proving the lure of crime reporting.

Be careful of kissing. It is common for all but husband and wife.

The most serious insult to an Ethiopian is *evil-eyed artisan.*

See the largest monolith in the world in Aksuma (110 feet).

Drink the coffee. It grows wild and is native to the country, only being introduced to Brazil much later.

The natives clean themselves in the Awash and the Omo Rivers.

Rastafarianism encourages the smoking of marijuana in church.

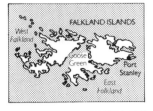

Falkland Islands
Falkland Islands and Dependencies

Tips for tourists

Men looking for holiday romance should not go to South Georgia. The population of 22 is all male.

Want some fun? The locals enjoy themselves traditionally by horse racing and steer riding. They have recently added a new entertainment — baiting British Members of Parliament who have come to investigate the Falklands problem.

The Falkland Islands used to be a huge sheep farm. Now they are a huge fortress inhabited by: 660,000 sheep, 3,500 British troops, 1,800 Falkland Islanders and 3,500,000 penguins.

Geography

There are 200 islands stretching over 1,300 miles of the South Atlantic. More than 90 per cent of the land is the East and West Falklands. There are no trees. The main vegetation is white grass and diddle-dee (which is not a reference to the conduct of the British Foreign Office).

Intent on his duty, this Ghurka fails to realise he has drifted several hundred miles to the south.

Strong man

The first recorded landing was made by the English Captain John Strong in 1690. He named the place after Viscount Falkland, then treasurer of the British Navy.

The first settlement on East Falklands was made by the French in 1764. The British settled on the west island the following year. The Spanish later bought out the French and drove out the British.

Early in the 19th Century, when the Spanish were chased out of Argentina, the Argentinians thought the Falklands would come with the victory. The British thought otherwise. They re-landed on the islands in 1833.

Strong woman

For 149 years the British occupation of what they called the Malvinas festered with the Argentines. On 2nd April 1982 their forces invaded in a desperate bid by an unpopular junta to achieve popularity. A few days later a British task force was launched to take back the Falklands in a desperate bid by Margaret Thatcher's unpopular junta.

The cost

In the war to retake the Falklands 255 British servicemen and three civilians were killed. The Argentine figure was at least four times that number. Before the war the average number of people who died on the Falklands was eight a year.

The cost of the war and its aftermath is £2 million per person (£5,450 per sheep, £1,028 per penguin) on the Falklands.

The disappeared

The population of the Falklands in 1885 was 1,800. It reached a peak of 2,400 in 1931 but it had fallen below 2,000 by the beginning of the 1970's — just about the only country in the world to have a falling population at that time.

Industry

Half the male population works with sheep. Each year nearly 5 million pounds of wool is produced, 93 per cent of exports. The only other notable product is kelp, a seaweed widely found on the island. This is how the islanders got their nickname of 'kelpers'. Postage stamps produce further income.

Communications

No railway. No roads outside Stanley. Before the war the main contact with the outside world was a charter vessel which called from Britain four times a year. There is one newspaper, called *Penguin News*. (Maximum circulation three and a half million).

Politics

There is a small Legislative Council but the islands are mainly ruled by a Governor. He is now called the Civil Commissioner and rules jointly with a Military Commissioner.

Wild life

The Falklands have provided the habitat for some of the strangest creatures on earth. The largest animal ever seen by modern man was a female whale landed at South Georgia early this century. It was 110 feet long. The seas around the islands abound with seals and sea lions and the largest seal ever known was killed off South Georgia.

There are 60 different species of birds, including the albatross (Britain's symbol for the Falklands) and of course penguins, including the king and macaroni varieties, all living happily in 18 wild life and bird sanctuaries.

Fiji

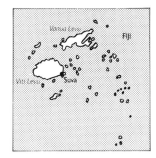

Warm welcome

Traditionally there has always been an open-armed reception for travellers and visitors. Usually the open arms have held clubs and the welcome is inspired by the natives' fondness for human flesh. Clubbing out the brain and cooking the visitor in banana leaves was a speciality.

This accounts for the islanders' current amazement that people are prepared to travel thousands of miles to visit them. They were known originally as the 'Cannibal Isles' and shipwrecked sailors, deserters, clergymen — you name it — were appreciated solely for the sweet taste of their flesh. One chief ate 999 humans — when presumably the police arrived. They even had special forks to eat human flesh.

Other native customs — until 100 years ago — included burial alive and the launching of canoes over the bodies of live girls.

Fijian women are not conventionally maternal.

Pleasures of the flesh

Today the Fijians are genuinely hospitable, echoing an earlier friendship which they offered to those they didn't want to eat. The islands are beautiful coral atolls and inland equatorial forests cover more than half.

Fiji was first visited by Abel (seaman) Tasman but the most famous visitor is undoubtedly Captain Bligh, who, cast adrift from 'The Bounty' by Marlon Brando, narrowly avoided becoming an a la carte. Bligh Water testifies to this.

But it was the abundant sandalwood which first attracted European traders who shipped it to China to be made into temples and joss sticks. These 'traders' were really brigands and buccaneers. They introduced firearms to the island, fuelling tribal wars. Soon the only articles of trade were muskets and rum.

Flesh creep

Not now having the same outlets for violence, Fijians channel it into various activities such as soldiering. They were magnificent in World War Two and the Korean War and so ingenious at jungle warfare that they were never listed as 'missing in action' but as 'not yet arrived'. In peace they amuse themselves by fire-walking — heating up stones to white hot and then walking on them. Their chief characteristic is idleness and when sugar plantations were established the British had to import Indian labour. Their main occupation, which they start at the age of three, is smoking the native weed. Not being great card players they go to fish drives instead and stand in circles until they catch them. The Fijian women sing to giant sea turtles and there is no compulsory school. Altogether pretty idyllic. They are so idle that they use the same word to mean several different things. *Kaka* = stammer, parrot and pain.

Body of state

The government is the Alliance Party but the issues are usually small. Government bodies include: the Rhinoceros Beetle Eradication Board, the Dog Control Committee and the Liquor Committee.

Population: 620,000

Size: 7,000 sq. miles

Government: Independent Commonwealth member

Language: English

Religion: Christianity, Hinduism

Capital: Suva

Currency: Fiji dollar

Tips for tourists

Don't take your children, Fijian women don't like them — the population is declining.

Don't shake hands with anyone who has more than 15 dead friends. Fijians cut off a joint of their little finger when a friend dies.

Don't be fooled by the delectable-sounding *beche de mer*. It is a sea-slug.

Finland
Suomen Tasavalta/Republiken Finland

Start

For 700 years this land was part of Sweden. Then Russia, its unfriendly neighbour, invaded a bit of it and in 1809 got the rest handed over too. So Finland became a Russian grand-duchy. After the Russian Revolution Finland declared itself independent.

In 1939 Russia invaded Finland over disputed territorial demands (Russia was demanding and Finland disputing). That led the Finns to support Germany when it invaded Russia. Consequently, at the end of World War Two, Finland was forced to sign over part of its land to Russia and pay 300 million gold dollars into the bargain.

Alcoholism is a problem in the northern wastes.

Finnish

It is always Christmas in Finland. It is a land of snow and ice in the north (the northern third of the country is above the Arctic circle), of pine trees and of reindeer (there are 245,000 of them, compared with 32,000 horses and 53,000 lorries).

Some 55,000 lakes make the country look like a green and blue jigsaw puzzle from the air.

Finland is the most remote of Scandinavian countries and none of it is more remote than Lapland in the north — the land of the midnight sun (73 days a year).

Military

Finland has been described by NATO strategists as 'a military vacuum'. It is a member of NATO with a treaty with Russia which requires it to repulse any attack from NATO. So it could end up fighting itself. This need not be a terribly bloody war as Finland is barred by the Treaty of Paris of 1947 from having more than 42,000 servicemen and 60 planes, none of which can be bombers.

Industry

Finland's economy is based almost entirely on wood. Its main products are: logs, pulp wood, newsprint, printing, writing and kraft paper, cardboard, plywood and veneers. The desperate search for ways to pay 300 million gold dollars to the Russians led to the setting up of several new industries. Wood features in some of these, too. For instance, the Finns now make the sort of pine furniture which has transformed so many trendy kitchens in the past 10 years.

Although two-thirds of Finland is covered by forests, trees are beginning to run out. This may sound potty, but so does the other big industry — Europe's largest porcelain factory, in Helsinki. The Finns have found out that money doesn't grow on trees. They are the only westerners to commute to work in Russia.

Important imports: Peace negotiators and SALT. Helsinki was the first venue of the Strategic Arms Limitation Talks.

Politics

At present eight parties are represented in parliament. This means ballot papers at elections must be long. They must also be wide as the names of some of the parties are:
Sosialidemokraatinen Puolue (Social democrats)
Kansallinen Kokoomus Puolue (Conservative)
Svenska Folkpartiet (Swedish Party)
The current president is Mauno Koivisto, a docker who became president of the Bank of Finland before getting his present job. He still cycles to work on an old bike and enjoys playing volleyball.

Language

There are two official languages: Finnish (spoken by most of the population) and Swedish (spoken by a mere 6 per cent). Both are equally incomprehensible, so it is no use trying to avoid the complexities of one by learning the other.

The local radio station captures the flavour of the language by being called *Oy Yleisradio AB*. The national anthem is reasonably pronounceable but sounds as if it should have been sung by Al Jolson. It is called *Maamme*. (That is the Finnish version. The Swedish version is called *Vart land*).

If you insist on learning Finnish, start with something simple. Try the sentence for 'Gather together the whole bonfire'. It is: *Kokoo kokoon koko kokko*.

Population: 4 and three quarter million

Size: One and a third times that of Britain, 130,000 sq. miles

Government: Republic

Main language: Finnish

Religion: Lutheran

Capital: Helsinki

Currency: Markka, pennia

Tips for tourists

Avoid Finnish culture. If you turn up at a play you are likely to be roped in to act, as they like to have huge casts. They also like huge audiences, so if you turn up to act, you may end up watching.

Even worse, avoid Finland's national epic, the Kalevala, a compilation of old ballads, lyrics and incantations.

Travel by water — there are more waterways than any country in the world, 31,000.

France
Republique Francaise

Self-delusion

'Ow can eet be zat zer French are so easily fooled? They have had the most-publicised revolution in history. Yet little changed after 1789. According to Daladier, their World War One President, 200 families have run France since the revolution.

Their other great claim to fame — as lovers — is equally self-deluded.

Lovers

A 1966 referendum among French youth voted overwhelmingly in favour of fidelity before love, beauty or intelligence. Only 22 per cent of women wanted even love from their husbands. Hardly any believed in a *Grand Amour*.

Before this century it was the same story. A Frenchman wrote *"It is doubtful whether love will be inspired by a husband."* London, with twice the population of Paris, has half as many prostitutes. One quarter of Parisian men regularly visit a prostitute.

Until recently, too much sex was believed to cause cancer. In the last century the chief preoccupation was war against masturbation. Special corsets were designed to prevent children indulging. Between the wars, one-eighth of Frenchmen died from syphilis. The saving grace, perhaps, is that old chestnut the female orgasm. The French 'discovered' it long before Marie Stopes.

Revolutionaries

The '200 families' consist of the top 200 shareholders in the Bank of France. Three-quarters of taxation was fed back to the rich via rents and contracts. Democracy was — perhaps still is — a facade.

The old still hanker for the days of Napoleon.

Although the revolution did kill aristocrats, there were subsequently several attempted coups d'etat. The Pretender to the throne, the Duke of Chambord, could recite all the dynasties of Europe by heart back to the Romans — but he couldn't tie his own shoe-laces. His tutors were told not to teach him any history after 1788.

More people were ennobled as a result of World War One than by Louis XIV, and they still kept most of the land. The revolutionary spirit won through. In 1848 Louis Philippe held the world record for most attempted royal assassinations.

Peasants

For a long time the peasants were by far the largest class in France. In 1946 37 per cent of the population was engaged in agriculture. The figure in Britain was 5 per cent. They were described as 'a sack of potatoes', and 'quadrupeds on two feet'. A priest said, *"I would love the peasant, if the peasant did not disgust me"*.

Division of land after the revolution is a myth. The bourgeois won it. The peasants were also poor and undernourished. In 1872, 325,000 men were called up. 18,000 were under 4' 10". (The average height of a Frenchman was reduced by 6 inches during the Napoleonic wars). 30,000 suffered from a feeble constitution. 16,000 were cripples. 9,000 were hunchbacks. 5,000 were 'ruined by precocious debauchery'. In all, one-third at the age of 20 were deformed.

Eaters and drinkers

The French consume more wine than anyone else. In 1953 there was one bar for every 80 inhabitants. In Britain it was 1:425. But both food and wine as a world-famous French celebration is a recent thing. Most of the population was cooking in cauldrons — some right up to World War Two.

Ironically, it was the poverty of the French that developed their cooking skills. In Britain and the U.S. there were ample supplies of good meat, making preparation unnecessary. But in France in the 1850's, when half the population was constantly ill from bad food, the aristocracy was developing the great French cuisine. Every Saturday at *Phillipes* restaurant in Paris, 18 diners ate from 6 pm — 12 pm, 12 pm — 6 am and 6 am — 12 am, each meal containing 10 courses.

Population: 54 million

Size: Twice that of Britain, 213,000

Government: Republic

Language: French

Religion: Roman Catholic

Capital: Paris

Currency: Franc

Tips for Tourists

Escoffier: *"Good cooking is the foundation of true happiness".* *"My success comes from the fact that my dishes are created for ladies".*

The French take food seriously. In 1602 a cook committed suicide because his two roasts would not be cooked in time.

They are the biggest cheese eaters.

In the last century the export of cooks was second only to the export of books.

They also invented car number plates in 1893.

Gabon
Republique Gabonaise

Population: About three-quarters of a million

Size: Slightly larger than Britain, 103,000 sq. miles

Government: Republic

Official language: French

Main religions: Roman Catholic and traditional beliefs

Capital: Libreville

Currency: CFA franc, centime

Tips for tourists

Fly. Gabon has five international airports but not much over 100 miles of good roads. The railway is still being built — and it is reserved for iron ore anyway.

If you see a woman struggling with a heavy load, don't offer to carry it for her. They are extremely proud of their strength and would be offended if a man offered to lighten their load.

Low life

Well over three quarters of Gabon is covered in forests. The only people who live there with ease are the pygmies. Whereas Europeans and Negroes find it almost impossible to walk through these dense forests, the pygmies glide through — jumping, grasping lianas and branches with their hands, and even running along low-lying branches.

The pygmies have another useful attribute for forest life. Other races claim that they exude a strong body odour. Although this is offensive to other humans, it wards off insects.

High life

Gabon is the richest nation in Black Africa for the size of its population. It needs to be. The capital, Libreville, is one of the most expensive places in the world to live. But then, all its land without trees is at such a premium that it is bound to cost a lot.

Roots

The French colonised this area in the mid-19th Century because they wanted to get at the wood. For more than a hundred years there was a lot of chopping, but not much changing. Gabon became independent in 1960.

Branching out

The French have continued to be extremely helpful. They provide the bulk of the foreign aid which Gabon's industry needs and in 1964 their troops helped to put down a military uprising.

In 1967, Albert Bernard Bongo became president at the age of 32. He announced that the country would in future be run under the slogan *Dialogue-Tolerance-Peace*. In 1977, Gabon attacked Benin. Five months later it played host to the conference of the Organisation of African Unity.

Despite its reliance on foreign aid, the government has been following a programme of 'Gabonisation'. This includes the request that all boards of directors of foreign companies hold their meetings in Gabon.

The people

This is one of the most sparsely populated countries in Africa. But there is some dispute over just how sparse the population is. The United Nations says that 550,000 people live here, but the Gabonese government claims it is 1,050,000.

There is no dispute about the largest ethnic group — it is the terrifying-sounding Fang.

Religious conversions

The president has been converted to Islam, although only one per cent of the population is Moslem. At the same time, he changed his name. Now, if you were going to change part of your name from Albert Bernard Bongo, there is little doubt which bit you'd want altered. The president was different. He changed it to Omar Bongo.

Since 1970 the Salvation Army and Jehovah's Witnesses have been banned from Gabon. This is surprising in a country which is known as 'the bastion of the cross in Africa' as half of its people are Christians.

Sex and death

Women in Gabon are customarily treated as beasts of burden. The government is now trying to change this. But it doesn't seem to have done the women much harm (or, more precisely, the men much good). The life expectancy for men is 25 and for women 45.

Land Rovers undergo every conceivable test to make them the toughest cars in the world.

The Gambia

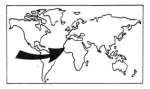

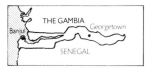

Old man river

Gambia is not only named after the Gambia River. It *is* the river. Not surprisingly the country is one of the smallest in Africa — a thin strip flowing for nearly 300 miles. It is surrounded on three sides by Senegal and on the fourth by the Atlantic Ocean. It exists solely because Britain wanted to exclude France access to the river. The river is West Africa's finest waterway and is still a mile wide 80 miles upstream. Ocean-going ships can go 150 miles inland. What isn't river is either mangrove swamps, salt flats or sandstone plateaux.

The Banjul fete. Land five discs and win a goldfish.

River of gold?

Profit, of course, was the reason Britain wanted to exclude the French. This was the common misconception from the start. After the Portuguese discovered it in 1455, they, the English and the French made explorations. Even the ruler of a Baltic State that no longer exists, Courland, bought two islands from the Kings of Kombo and Barra. In 1688 an English company called the Royal Gambia Adventurers — rather like the Famous Five — made use of the first English settlement founded in West Africa to start trading. Again there was no profit. In 1721, after continuous wars between the British and the French, only one member of the company remained faithful. These were trading wars in a land where there was no trade.

At last the British turned to the Gum Trade — but, inevitably, were soon up the proverbial tree. They couldn't even run a successful penal colony. Today the economy keeps its feet on the ground by

relying on groundnuts for over 90 per cent of its exports, and attempts at making money consistently fail. In 1948 a brilliant Gambian Egg Scheme, under the auspiciously-named Doctor Fowler, left them with egg on their face.

Sold down the river

The only thing sold here were the British garrison who, subjected to years of boredom and futility, shaved their heads to ward off disease. It was a terrible place. In one section of the capital, Bathurst, one quarter of the population died from cholera. Un-mathematically it was called Half Die. The passivity of the British and activity of the French resulted in the unreal borders of the country. The garrison's view of Bathurst (now Banjul) was that the government was 'seemingly regardless if we perish in pursuit of wealth'.

River of blood

Normally a peaceable place by African standards Gambia suffered from a 50-year desultory conflict in the 19th Century. It was between the Marabouts and the Saninki. The Marabouts were Islamic, abstained from alcohol and shaved their heads. The Saninki were not Islamic, loved liquor and didn't shave their heads. The Marabout leader had the advantage of being able to convince his followers that he could turn white men's bullets into water. Any Saninki he captured who would not renounce drink, turn to Islam and shave his head was killed.

Cry me a river

In 1965 Gambia became an independent monarchy and in 1970 a republic under Sir Dawda Kairaba. Nothing much has changed unfortunately. His minister of the Interior is called M'Boob. Still everything revolves around groundnuts and they are trying to turn them into roofing, fuel and confectionery, so watch out. In 1958 the income of the country could be judged by the fact that 13 per cent of the budget went on medical services yet there were only two doctors. But at least there is no army and all the political parties stand for much the same thing. In 1981 an attempt to become solvent was made by forming a federation with Senegal called Senegambia. The average age of males is 32 so most won't see any future changes.

Population: 595,000

Size: 4,000 sq. miles

Government: Republic within the Commonwealth

Language: English, local dialects

Religion: Islam

Capital: Banjul

Currency: Dacasi, butut

Tips for tourists

Visit Juffure, reputed home of Kunta Kinte, reputed great, great grandfather of Alex Hailey of *Roots* fame.

Eat *benachin* the Gambian speciality — meat and rice.

There is no TV.

There is one newspaper — three times a week. But there is a Radio Syd.

Keep your passport handy. Gambia is one of the few countries in the world which doesn't know its own borders.

Population: 17 million

Size: Half that of Britain, 42,000 sq. miles

Government: Communist

Language: German

Religion: Protestant

Capital: East Berlin

Currency: Mark

Tips for tourists

If you want to seduce a German girl, tell her it's healthy.

East German police don't like punks. They tend to arrest them and give them hair cuts.

Visit the Museum of German History which shows the whole history of the country interpreted from a Marxist-Leninist standpoint.

When passing along a row in a cinema or theatre, face the people in the row. It is considered impolite to turn your back.

Remember — the path to marxism leads through self-criticism.

Go by train — Leipzig has the largest railway station in Europe.

East Germany
Deutsche Demokratische Republik

East Germany is not a subtle place. A recent advert for a laxative is painfully frank: *This highly valued health aid will give your bowels an education in regularity. Even chronic constipation can be cured. Linugram is an organic laxative.*

Culture

There is little subtlety in socialist culture either.

Films — Double bill a few years ago at the local cinema:
Journey to the Centre of the Earth plus *100 per cent Price Rise.*

Theatre — At the 1964 Shakespeare Festival in Weimar, the final scene of *Hamlet* was altered beyond recognition because, the programme explained, *'we now know that men like Fortinbras did not bring happiness to their subjects'.*

Television — A selection from one evening's programmes:
The Known and Unknown CSSR: a cinematic ramble through Czechoslovakia.
Musica Viva: music, folk-song and dance programme from Dresden.
Guest on German TV: the German Communist Party
William Tell: His fight for freedom and the struggle of workers in West Germany against 'monopoly capitalism'.

Music — East German performers cannot choose where and to whom they play. The Agency for Entertainment randomly assigns punk groups to steelworkers' galas and tone-poem singers to army officers' mandatory cultural evenings. The teenage group Mona Lisa may be sent to the Soviet Union to entertain East German pipeline workers.

Exit

There is only one way to leave East Germany, unless you are a pensioner. You can marry your way out — but only after a one to two year 'consideration period'. During this time westerners newly married to East Germans may visit their spouse on a limited basis: 30 days a year, each visit to start at midnight. Queues form at crossing points just before the stroke of twelve. Some people wear pyjamas and carry love offerings of vegetables and spare parts.

Arithmetic problem from a second grade text-book

'The collectives in the neighbouring districts deliver their sugar beets to the refinery in trucks. Today the Schondorf LPG sent 34 trucks to the refinery, and the Sommerfield LPG sent 30 trucks. How many trucks carried sugar beets to the refinery?'

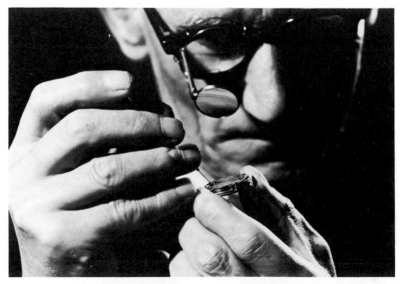

A government expert meticulously checks the 1983 Five Year Plan (for any trace of democracy).

West Germany
Bundesrepublik Deutschland

Boring

The Germans are as boring as the Belgians, but efficiently so. They are as efficient as the Japanese, but boringly so. West Germany was formed in 1949 when the zones occupied by Britain, France and the USA after World War Two became a federation of 10 states plus West Berlin (which is in East Germany).

Efficient

The Germans are so proud of their economic miracle that they have invented a word for it: *Wirtschaftswunder*. It took them only 25 years after World War Two to become the world's fourth biggest industrial power and Western Europe's greatest. It is the second largest exporter in the world (and second largest importer, too, just to balance things up).

Willi Brandt laughs at the ineffectiveness of Jomo Kenyatta's shaving brush.

Submissive

Despite their country's success, the West German people are not as well off as those of Sweden, Switzerland and Denmark. They don't seem prepared to do much to rectify this. There are few strikes and labour relations are strictly controlled by law.

Inventive but aggressive

The Germans invented motorways. Their first autobahns were built by the Nazis and they had 1,330 miles of them before the US built its first freeway. West Germany now has one of the most highly developed transport systems in the world, by road, rail, air and inland waterway. This does *not* mean that the roads are safe. There are half a million road accident casualties a year, due mainly to the arrogance of German drivers. They also have the highest rate for rape and sex crimes, after Australia.

Pride

The Germans are too proud to admit that there is anything which their forefathers didn't foresee. So when a new word is required, instead of making one up, they string together a series of old words. This makes the language very long-winded. For example, the organisation for co-operation between their broadcasting stations is called: *Arbeitsgemeinschaft der offentlich-rechtlichen Rundfunkanstalten der Bundersrepublik Deutschland.*

The Germans like to show how proud they are of their words by giving most of them — capital letters. They have 528 daily newspapers and 283 radio stations.

Language

German sayings are about as memorable as those in Icelandic or Swahili. One of the few which has stood the test of time are the words of the Prussian military theorist Karl von Clausewitz, who said in 1830: *"War is a continuation of diplomacy by other means."*

Prejudice

Foreigners think of Germans as beer-swilling loudmouths in lederhosen listening to brass band music. As it happens, that is a remarkably accurate description of the people of Upper Bavaria.

Germans only have themselves to blame for their image. They are the world's most avid travellers and have conquered more camp sites than Hitler set up concentration camps.

Sobering thoughts

Germany has the world's highest beer consumption per head and the lowest birth rate. The population actually decreased in the 1970's. One in 12 of the population is a foreign worker.

Only-sons of fathers killed in World War Two are exempt from military service. Only 0.1 per cent of the population are Jews.

Population: 61 and a half million

Size: About the same as Britain, 96,000 sq. miles

Government: Federal republic

Language: German

Religion: Christianity

Capital: Bonn

Currency: Deutsche mark

Tips for tourists

Go to an American musical. They have been popular here since 1955 when Berlin first sang-along with *Kuss mich Katchen* (Kiss me Kate).

If you want to be accepted, call yourself 'Doctor'. This title is an essential credential for advancement in German society. If you wish to be *really* admired, call yourself 'Professor'.

Don't travel by taxi. Frankfurt has the world's most expensive cabs.

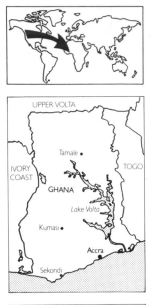

Ghana

Population: 11 and a half million

Size: Same as Britain, 92,000 sq. miles

Government: Republic

Official language: English

Religions: Christianity, traditional beliefs

Capital: Accra

Currency: Cedi, pesewas

Tips for tourists

Don't gossip. Since 1977, rumour-mongering has carried a ten-year jail sentence.

Take a stool and slippers. A stool is the symbol of office of chiefs in southern Ghana and they always wear slippers so their feet won't be polluted by the dead buried underground.

Don't drop gold in a marketplace. Special squads of police wait there to confiscate any which is allowed to fall to the ground.

Don't speak ill of the dead. Ghanaians consider their ancestors to be ever-present and capable of influencing the living.

Gold

This used to be called the Gold Coast because its economy was based on gold. On independence in 1957, it was renamed after a monarchy which may or may not have ruled this region a thousand years ago. How much more appropriate it would have been if it had been renamed the Brown Coast: Ghana's economy is now dominated by cocoa, of which it is the world's largest producer (one in five bars of chocolate originate here). But it only produces the *forastero* bean, which is reputedly of inferior taste to the South American *criollo*.

Gold is still produced and so are diamonds. They are part of the exotic economy which also includes pineapples, ginger and avocadoes. But the most important government office remains the Cocoa Affairs Ministry.

Golden boy — 1

Tetteh Kwashi's story is a real 'Jack and the Beanstalk'. Early last century, he left his native village and returned with six strange-looking beans. From them sprang the entire Ghanaian cocoa industry. What Tetteh had (which Jack didn't) was British entrepreneurial backing. Around the time that Tetteh brought his beans home, the British had taken control of Ghana and were looking for something to replace the slave trade. They chose cocoa, which made it easier for them to sleep at night.

In 1957, Ghana became the first British colony in Africa to get independence. A coup quickly followed, then years of military rule, corruption and Africa's highest inflation. Could no-one save the country?

Golden boy — 2

When the hero arose, he was an unlikely figure. Jerry Rawlings was a mere Flight Lieutenant in the airforce and was seemingly without political ambition. After leading a coup of junior officers in 1979, he *a)* restored civilian government, *b)* refused any post in the government, *c)* wouldn't even accept promotion for himself. Rawlings became idolised by the people and when the new government seemed to be as corrupt as the old, he led a second coup and became president himself. His golden image is somewhat tarnished now.

Fool's gold

In 1975 the government launched a project called *Feed yourself*. This failed as there was nothing for most of the people to eat (except cocoa).

Sixty per cent of government expenditure goes on the civil service. There are 22 times more civil servants than members of the armed forces.

Ant-hunting in Ghana.

Gibraltar

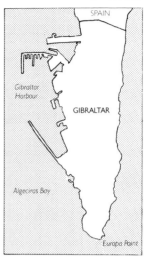

Home from home

Gibraltar is a peninisular off mainland Spain which belongs to Great Britain. The British have had this fact confirmed by three treaties. They got their hands on it in 1704 via Admiral Rooke and the Spanish were grudgingly in agreement that Britain should keep it. In return they got Florida. Gibraltar's (and Florida's) future were determined by the Treaty of Utrecht — in Holland.

Now it is firmly British after 13 sieges. Restaurants are called Paddingtons, the Oliver Twist Bar and the English Tea Room.

History

Gibraltar consists of a rock 3 miles long by three-quarters of a mile wide. The ancients thought it was the end of the world and called it one of 'the Pillars of Hercules' — the other being in Africa. Hercules was said to span the Mediterranean at its narrowest point as a bridge. For many inhabitants later it *was* the end of the world.

The Arabic name for Gibraltar is Jabal Tariq (Mount Tariq) after the Moor who captured the peninsular in 711 AD. From the first, it became an important fort for attacking Spain from Africa. 1,200 years of fortification began.

Amongst others who are commemorated on tombstones are the heroes (dead) of the Battle of Trafalgar. Nelson, however, was sent back to Britain — preserved in a barrel of brandy.

Not Viva Espana

When Spain lost its grip on Florida, they decided that treaties were made to be broken. If they couldn't keep the New World, they nevertheless wanted to retain their own borders. The British — and the Gibraltarians — were not so sure. When Franco closed the border between Gibraltar and Spain in 1969 the die was cast. Britain had hoped to appease its future NATO ally by allowing the local population to vote which way they wanted to lean. Unfortunately for Spain — and the alliance — in 1967, 12,138 Gibraltarians voted to remain a colony of Britain against 44 who wished to join with Spain.

The border has now re-opened. It is known by the locals as 'the Garlic Way'.

Rock around the clock

For three and a half centuries Gibraltar has been British. Nevertheless most of the food and buildings are Spanish. Spanish is the national language — though most people are bilingual. Education is in English, though only 77 per cent of the population is literate.

The Rock has been useful to the British on more than one occasion. In World War Two, for instance, possession ensured the freedom of the Mediterranean sea-lanes.

Apart from the Spanish and British, the only other claim to ownership of the Rock comes from the apes. They are the only wild monkeys in Europe and are said to have come to the colony through an underground tunnel from Africa. Legend has it that if the apes disappear, so does British rule. This is taken seriously and when, in World War Two, the apes were dying out Winston Churchill ordered more from Africa. The British won the war.

Gibraltar has the tallest person on record.

Population: 30,000

Size: 2.3 sq. miles

Government: Colony

Language: Spanish and English

Main religion: Roman Catholic

Capital: Gibraltar

Currency: Pound sterling

Tips for tourists

There is no fresh water. So the government has built a thirty-acre concrete sheet over the east side of the rock to catch rainwater. One millimetre of rain produces 200,000 gallons of water.

The airplane to Morocco is called *Yogi Bear*.

Pick the native 'candy-tuft' — found only on Gibraltar.

Don't take a car. There are only 10 yards per vehicle.

The airport is closer to the city centre than any other in the world — 880 yards.

Gibraltar is the world's oldest colony.

Population: 9 and three quarter million

Size: Just over half that of Britain, 50,000 sq. miles

Government: Republic

Language: Greek

Religion: Greek Orthodox Church

Capital: Athens

Currency: Drachma

Tips for tourists

Don't drive. Greece has the highest road accident rate in Europe.

Don't ask for contraceptives in a chemist's shop. Although they are sold, it is against the law to ask for them by name. You must ask for 'therapeutics'.

Don't bother watching TV or listening to the radio during Easter week. Nothing but religious programmes are on.

The Greeks will be offended if you call their coffee 'Turkish' (although it is the same).

Greece
Elliniki Dimokratia

A feast of feasts

Greek life is dominated by feasts and public holidays. These include:
January 1st: Everyone eats the Cake of St. Basil.
January 6th: The Earth is rid of *callicantzari*, the demons with red eyes, monkeys' arms and cleft hooves who run amok after Christmas, riding piggy-back on mortals and polluting food.
Clean Monday (at the end of Lent): A spring fertility rite at which the relatives arrive riding donkeys backwards.
Maundy Thursday: Housewives dye eggs red. The first egg in the dye belongs to the Virgin Mary.
June 24th: Sea bathing and the eating of water melon begin officially. Thus the proverb: *'Do not swim before you see water melon peel floating on the sea.'*
July 17th: St. Marina is worshipped as protectress against smallpox and the scourge of all insects.
August 29th: Anniversary of the beheading of St. John the Baptist.
October 28th, Ochi Day: This commemorates the date in 1940 when Greece cabled the reply 'No' to an Italian invasion ultimatum.
December 24th: Little boys ring doorbells and ask *"Shall we tell them?"* They then sing carols while beating metal triangles with miniature hammers.
December 31st: All Greeks play cards.

If this were what you were famous for, you'd have let the British take it 100 years ago.

Feast your eyes

Greece consists of a mainland and 1,425 islands. The mainland is three-quarters covered with mountains and its coastline goes in and out more often than the government of Bolivia. Only 166 of the islands are inhabited, including the holiday resorts of Crete, Rhodes and Corfu. Some islands are home for only a handful of shepherds or monks, while others shelter only a handful of millionaires.

Over-indulgence

Greece was the birthplace of democracy. So it was a shameful day when, on 21st April 1967, the country was taken over by a gang of colonels — a fate usually reserved for countries like Bolivia. The colonels — described (but not out loud) as *'smooth hard-faced men in dark suits, dark glasses and polished black Mercedes'* — banned (among other things) the smashing of wine glasses after a toast. Democracy — and glass smashing — returned in 1974.

Indulgence

Greece has a fun economy. Its main products include beer, wine and cigarettes. Unfortunately, the best-known Greek wine is *retsina*, one of the most revolting drinks invented. It is better to stick to cocktails, for which Greece produces a million tons of olives a year.

The Greeks like things that float. They are the world's biggest ship owners and produce 50 tons of sponges a year. It is difficult staying afloat in Athens. After Tokyo, it is the world's most polluted city (two-thirds of the country's motor vehicles are on its streets).

Grenada

Geography

This is the island that makes you wonder about Christopher Columbus's eyesight. He spotted it in 1498, named it Concepcion — then sailed on past. Yet it is strikingly beautiful — a wonderland of mountains and valleys, black and white beaches, and marvellous harbours.

The capital, St. George's, is the most picturesque port in the Caribbean. Had Columbus stopped, he would surely have sung: *"Grenada, you've got me under your spell."*

The country consists of three islands, Grenada (the most southerly of the Windward Islands, measuring 21 miles by 12), Carriacou and Petit Martinique. The last two are the southernmost islands of the Grenadines, the best cruising area in the world for yachts.

History

By the time Columbus sailed past, the island was inhabited by the Caribs, who had driven off the Arawaks. The Caribs also drove off various attempts by the British and French to establish a colony. Eventually, in 1650, the French succeeded. Soon after, fighting broke out between the French and Caribs and the Indians were forced further and further north. Finally a group of Caribs threw themselves from a high cliff into the sea rather than be taken prisoner. This spirit of the lemming still rules Grenadian politics today.

The French proceeded to repopulate the island with African slaves. Then the British wrested the island from them — but still went on introducing slaves. In 1796 a group of slaves followed the example of the Caribs by throwing themselves into the sea from the same high cliff. Slavery was abolished soon afterwards, but the cliffs remain unfenced.

Grenada became an independent state of the West Indies in 1967 and got its independence in 1974.

Politics

In 1950 the country's first union was formed: the Grenada Manual and Mental Workers' Union. This is a strange name, but then the chap who formed it, Eric Gairy, was a strange man. And ambitious. He went on to form a political party, which won the first elections, so he became the first Prime Minister.

His party was the Grenada United Labour Party, known as GULP for short. This meaningful use of initials for political parties was copied by the opposition, who set up MAP (Movement for Assemblies of the People) and JEWEL (Joint Endeavour for Welfare, Education and Liberation).

Gairy's rule was known for widespread corruption (8 per cent of the national budget went on his office, almost as much as on housing and health together), persecution, torture and murder. But the British knew how to deal with such a despot. They gave him a knighthood.

Sir Eric was kicked out in a coup in 1979 and a Marxist government took over. This shocked the Americans — after all, St. George's *was* the top yachting centre in the Eastern Caribbean.

The CIA has been accused of trying to destabilise the new revolutionary government. In response, the Prime Minister, Maurice Bishop, has called on all persons possessing bird guns or air rifles to lend them to the People's Revolutionary Army.

Industry

Grenada is known as the Isle of Spice. Nutmeg, pepper, cloves, cinnamon, ginger and vanilla are grown here, but the main crops are banana, cocoa and coconuts. Almost half the population is unemployed, so there's not much spice in their life.

Sport

Most popular is cricket — hardly surprising on an island which is oval shaped.

A German war criminal wittily gives the Nazi salute.

Population: 110,000

Size: 135 sq. miles

Government: Independent Commonwealth member

Main language: English

Main religion: Roman Catholic

Capital: St. George's

Currency: East Caribbean dollar

Tips for tourists

If you want to cure yourself of eating chocolate pay a visit to a cocoa plantation and watch men polishing the cocoa by treading on it with their sweaty feet.

If you want to give yourself piles take a ride on one of the island's brightly coloured wooden buses. They have quaint names, but plank seats.

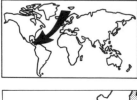

Population: 7,375,000

Size: Half that of Britain, 42,000 sq. miles

Government: Republic

Language: Spanish

Religion: Roman Catholic

Capital: Guatemala City

Currency: Quetzal

Tips for tourists

In some parts of the country 'it rains 13 months of the year'.

In 1913 Guatemala was being called 'Land of the Future'. Nothing has changed.

Visit Progreso — the most ironically-named town.

Guatemala
Republica de Guatemala

Population control

The Spanish came in 1522. They had an idea of 'altars of gold and palaces lined with silver'. The author Las Casas writing on woodcut (English translation 1699) tells us they killed 40 million Indians looking for them. Volcanoes *(mountains vomiting water)* destroyed the old capital Antigua leading to the building of Guatemala City.

Even after the worst excesses of the Spanish and the volcanoes, however, Guatemala was still the most populous country in the West Indies. Then in 1917, earthquakes destroyed the capital. They struck again in 1976 killing 25,000. And where the Spanish left off, the modern military took over. 20,000 people disappeared between 1966-1976 and criminals were defined as 'people who have been killed by the authorities' to aid the process. Death squads, or 'a programme for pacification', are the instrument of the government in this affair. In 1960 Guatemala had one of the highest death rates in the world.

Family planning

War is the other great helper in the tricky matter of keeping the population with its toes turned up. Guatemala was originally the Spanish name for the whole of Central America apart from Panama and part of Mexico. After the Spanish left, their old provinces took on national status. First there were the nationalist wars between provinces. Next came the internal wars. At the turn of the century all males between the ages of 18 and 30 were regular soldiers. It is no accident that Guatemala comes next to 'Guerrilla

The deep sea diving industry has had disappointing results in Guatemala.

warfare' in the *Encyclopaedia Britannica.* Today, General Rios Montt, who 'assumed' the presidency after the 1982 elections were annulled, is fighting:
the National Revolutionary Unit
the Guerilla Army of the Poor
the Rebel Armed Forces
the Revolutionary Organisation of the People in Arms
the Guatemala Labour Party
the Communist Party.

It's almost enough to make a dictator give up his vocation. Particularly as Guatemala has the oldest revolutionary guerrilla movement in Central America.

Wars were political (Conservatives v Liberals) or religious (Clerics v Anti-clerics) but they were never economic. The hero Carrera's battle-cry was *"Viva la religion y muerte a los extranjeros".*

Religious fanaticism

It all started with the Spanish of course. The Indians did their best but they didn't get it quite right. Indian magic blends with Christian beliefs. For instance, they believe that St. John and the Virgin Mary had an affair the night of the crucifixion. Therefore, the night before Easter, their images are removed from churches and locked up in the local gaol, apart. Next morning, they are bailed out for around 200 pesos each. The Indians do have their own gods as well — one called Mundo (the World) is worshipped at Manostenango which has so many altars it is a sort of celestial Harley Street.

Basically they use Christian myths as an excuse for fiestas. In fact any excuse will do. They even celebrate the *baile de los conquistadores* — a festival of their own defeat and enslavement by the Spanish. As a rule they don't care about marriage and death but are totally sold on christening. They see it as the opening gambit in the game of life which they will otherwise lose.

In 1889 Carrera tried to get the Cult of Minerva going. It ran for a bit but worship of the Goddess of Wisdom could never last very long in Guatemala.

Most unusual sign
'No musing by Order'

Most unlikely newspaper
El Imparcial.

Most likely newspaper
La Manana.

Guinea
Republique populaire et revolutionnaire de Guinee

There is only one name you need know in Guinea: Ahmen Sekou Toure. He has been president since the country got its independence from the French in 1958 and is worshipped almost as a god by those citizens he hasn't executed, thrown into prison, tortured or terrified into fleeing.

Guided Toure

For two decades, Toure ran Guinea as a Soviet client state, with himself in the part of Stalin. Until Idi Amin came on the scene, he was favourite to get the first Nobel Atrocity Prize. Different categories of people were treated in different ways:
Opponents: These were killed, or tortured and killed.
Potential opponents: These were thrown into the world's most inhumane prisons.
Others: These were deliberately starved.

To save himself a lot of trouble sorting people out into these various categories, Toure set up a military camp at Boiro where he could do whatever he liked. And he did.

Paranoia

Toure's brutality seems to have been caused by a feeling that nobody loved him. This led to a quite unlovable over-reaction. In 1970, after an abortive invasion by a few mercenaries, Toure said it was a NATO plot, arrested hundreds of people and hanged many of them publicly. The following year he accused the Army chief-of-staff, several cabinet ministers and the archbishop of

plotting to overthrow him. In 1973 he claimed that 'imperialism' wanted to assassinate him and three years later he accused his own Minister of Justice of leading a plot.

Bottoms up

It took the women of Guinea to change him. They organised a remarkable demonstration in which they took to the streets and bared their bottoms. This was to signify displeasure but President Toure seems to have taken it as a sign of love. He changed his policies, improved people's conditions and even visited the United States to ask for investment (he had refused to leave the country for 13 years at the height of his paranoia). Most importantly, he allowed television to be introduced.

Graffiti

Guinean walls are plastered with political slogans, mainly praising the president. The most enigmatic being: *Revolutionary syndicalism needs no slogans.*

The people

Guinea contains Africa's nicest sounding ethnic group, the Kissi. The Fulani tribe takes the class system to ludicrous extremes — its upper classes live on hillsides while its lower classes are made to live in valleys.

Before independence 90 per cent of the population were illiterate and even now only a third of the children go to school. However, this saves them from having to read the only paper, *Horoaya*, which is the party daily and sells 5,000 copies.

Twenty years ago life expectancy was only 28 years. It is longer now — unless you fall out with the president.

Industry

This is a mineral-rich country, particularly in bauxite (aluminium ore) which accounts for more than half the country's exports, and iron ore, of which it has one of the world's largest deposits. There are also gold and diamonds.

Population: 5 and a quarter million

Size: The same as Britain, 95,000 sq. miles

Government: Republic

Official language: French

Main religion: Islam

Capital: Conakry

Currency: Syli, cauri

Tips for tourists

When the president's name is mentioned, applaud. Everyone else does.

Beware the Fulani. They consider themselves the country's aristocrats, but are actually its conmen — smooth, specious and with elastic standards of honesty.

Guineans have to have medical treatment before 'voting' for President Toure.

Population: About three quarters of a million

Size: One-seventh that of Britain, 14,000 sq. miles

Government: Socialist republic

Language: Creole and Portuguese

Main religions: Traditional beliefs and Islam

Capital: Bissau

Currency: Peso

Tips for tourists

If you visit the coast in summer take your wellingtons. The whole area turns into a vast swamp.

Walking is safer than swimming. There are few lions left but plenty of sharks hang about out in the estuary.

Guinea-Bissau

History

This unhappy bit of West Africa and its offshore islands were discovered in 1446 by Portugal's Nuno Tristao. They became a separate colony in 1879, called Portuguese Guinea.

Industry and religion

The Portuguese Guinea Company was granted permission by the Church in 1697 to run the area's slave trade. This monopoly was not acceptable to the capitalists of France, England and Holland, who like to see some free enterprise in the trade (except for slaves). However, the Portuguese managed to hold out until slavery ended in 1840.

Industry and war

The slave trade led to almost uninterrupted tribal warfare as rival tribes battled to get hold of each other's people so they could sell them to the Portuguese.

This man has just heard that his life expectancy is 33.

More history

Once the slave trade had ended and there was nothing more to fight over, it dawned on the natives that the Portuguese were exploiting *all* of them. An independence movement began but it didn't really take off until after World War Two. Its leader then was the young agricultural scientist Amilcar Cabral, not the sort of person who would normally soil his hands with revolution.

The insurrection followed the normal course of guerilla warfare — strikes, riots and massacres. Then in 1972 Cabral hit on the brilliant notion of holding elections. This utterly baffled the Portuguese and they granted independence the following year. But they murdered Cabral first.

Politics

A new constitution was adopted on 10th November 1980. Four days later the military threw out the president and declared a socialist republic.

Politics and culture

Amilcar Cabral had viewed the struggle for liberation as a cultural one. With this in mind, one of the first acts of the new government was to nationalise the film industry.

Politics and health

The government's favourite slogan is: *The health of the people is our greatest wealth and main strength*. Guinea-Bissau is a very poor country — its main produce and export is peanuts. Life expectancy is 33.

Geography and health

The interior of the country is a vast plateau covered with almost impenetrable thick forests. The coast is flat, swampy and very unhealthy.

More religion

Until the Portuguese left, the official religion was Roman Catholicism, although less than 5 per cent of the population was Catholic. The Portuguese encouraged the spread of Islam because they believed this would counteract the growing influence of Marxism. This shows they were better capitalists than they were Christians (for confirmation of this, see *Industry and religion* above).

Architecture

Villages are almost non-existent. Families live in groups of huts with fortified walls to keep out cattle thieves.

Anthropology

Each tribe is easily distinguishable: *The Balante* grow rice, are keen nationalists and worship their ancestors. *The Fulani* grow manioc and peanuts, are Muslims, fight non-believers they can't convert, and are polygamous if they can afford it. *The Malinke* are farmers but used to be warriors. Their hobbies are trading and trying to convert other tribes to Islam. *The Manyako* enjoy growing palm trees. *The Bram, Biafada, Felup, Bayot, Nalu, Susu* and *Bijogo* live near the sea and mind their own business.

Guyana

Flat broke

Guyana is variously called *Mudland*, *the land of many waters* and *the land of six peoples*. The first two are more appropriate. The first piece of land above sea level is the airport — 40 feet up. Perhaps this is why they call it Ogle Airport.

From the sea, the only evidence of the existence of the capital, Georgetown, is a mass of wireless masts. The whole town is below sea-level. This is why, when the Dutch settled here in 1616, they were immediately at home, building dykes and putting the houses on stilts. Their first settlement was called *Kyk over al* — which they proceeded to do, along with the French, Spanish and British in their search for El Dorado. For his part in failing to locate the golden city, Raleigh was imprisoned (in the Tower of London) and executed. Gold was not discovered for centuries. Today 95 per cent of the population still live on the coastal plain, below sea-level. The rest is mountain and savannah.

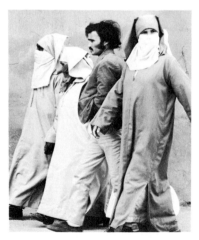

Secret police escort a dissident to gaol

The co-op

Guyana is officially called the Co-operative Republic of Guyana. But where is this co-operation? At the beginning of the century a quarter of a million Indian labourers were drafted in as forced labour. There were riots.

In the 1920's there was a sugar recession. There were riots.

In the 1930's the British Crown hung on to the country with unrepresentative government. There were riots.

After the 1953 elections the People's Progressive Party came to power under a Marxist banner. Britain suspended the constitution. There were riots.

In 1961 proportional representation at the elections was a farce. There were riots and British troops were called.

In 1963 riots killed 176.

In the early 1970's a referendum was held to see whether a referendum was needed to change the constitution. Apparently, the people said over-whelmingly that Forbes Burnham could do what he liked with the constitution. There were riots.

Real co-operation

In 1919 Hubert Critchlow set up the first trade union in the British Empire in Guyana. In 1978 the People's Temple cult got together and committed the largest mass suicide in history at Jonestown — 913 with cyanide.

Population: 925,000

Size: About that of Britain, 83,000 sq. miles

Government: Republic

Languages: English, Creole and American Indian

Religions: Hindu, Protestant and Roman Catholic

Capital: Georgetown

Currency: Guyana dollar, cent

Tips for tourists

Be careful of:
The Guyanese Water Lily — the largest leafed plant in the world. So big, it is said to be able to support a five-year old child. But this is not recommended.
The Essequibo Ferry from Georgetown. It has sunk twice.
Pirhanas, visible from the Essequibo Ferry.

Pronounce Guyana — Guy...ana.

Drink Demerara rum, particularly on the Essequibo Ferry.

Haiti
Republique d'Haiti

When asked to explain his repressive, terror-wielding rule, Dr. Duvalier, former president of Haiti, said *'Some people get crazy. They are not responsible. And I am a doctor.'* Two hundred years of rulers with similar vision have turned Haiti from France's richest colony into the poorest country in the Western Hemisphere.

God

Dr. Duvalier (known as Papa Doc) was not given to humility. In his *Catechism of the Revolution* he explained his creed: *Our Doc who art in the National Palace for life, hallowed be Thy name by present and future generations. Thy will be done at Port-au-Prince and in the provinces. Give us this day our new Haiti and never forgive the trespasses of the anti-patriots who spit every day on our country; let them succumb to temptation and under the weight of their venom, deliver them not from any evil.*
Seventy-five per cent of the population is illiterate.

Other religions

Saturday night is voodoo night in Haiti, when the islanders become preoccupied with drumming. Haitian voodoo is a mixture of African and Roman Catholic influences, and some of the voodoo spirits bear a remarkable resemblance to real characters in Haitian life:
Ti Jean Quinto — an insolent spirit in policeman form. He lives under bridges.
Limba — a rough male spirit who lives among rocks and arbitrarily persecutes human beings.
Zombie errant — a spirit of people killed in accidents.
   Zombies errant are doomed to spend their days in the woods and walk the roads by night. Under Papa Doc's rule there was a good chance they'd meet themselves coming back — the President used to exhibit the corpses of his opponents along the road to the airport. Clearly they had failed to heed his warning, *"If anyone thinks he can turn his ass left or right, I will crush it into flour and pass it through a sieve."*

Son-God

When Dr. Duvalier died in 1971, he was immediately succeeded by his son, Jean-Claude, aged 20. His regime is less terrifying, although attempts to form a political opposition still meet with failure. When Sylvio Claude announced the formation of a Christian Democratic

The Prick. A monument to Papa Doc in Haiti.

Party, for example, he was detained in a mental hospital. More recently he was sentenced to six years in prison for insulting the president. At Mr. Claude's trial an American observer noted that witnesses were not able to identify the suspect, and 'almost all the jurors were asleep during the final instructions by the judge'.

People

Luxury in Haiti is a house with a corrugated-iron roof. Half the children die before the age of four, and it is estimated that there are more Haitian doctors living in New York — to which they have been driven by the Duvaliers — than live in the whole of Haiti.
   Successive rulers have blackmailed the United States, with its fear of communism, into giving Haiti financial aid, but much of this is lost through corruption. As one UN official put it, *"Haiti is a graveyard for foreign aid".*

Population: Over 5 million

Size: 10,700 sq. miles

Government: Republic

Language: French, Creole

Religion: Roman Catholic

Capital: Port-au-Prince

Currency: Gourde

Tips for tourists

Don't expect to see many trees — once 70 per cent of the island was covered in forest, but the need for charcoal (the only fuel) has cut this to 7 per cent.

Practice speaking Creole — most Haitians can't speak French although only French is taught in schools.

Haiti is the world's main source of baseballs.

After paying contributions for 20 years, Haitians are eligible for a pension at 65. The average life expectancy is 40.

Honduras
Republica de Honduras

The main industries are growing bananas, picking bananas, packing bananas and shipping bananas. The main export is bananas. Other things *are* produced: for instance, panama hats.

History

The banana has had a long history — much longer and more interesting than that of Honduras (the Greeks wrote of it 4,000 years ago, when their sages lay in the shade of a banana tree and ate its fruit). Shortly after the discovery of the Americas, the banana was brought over from the Canary Islands. But it wasn't until a hundred years ago that the industry made a breakthrough in Honduras. That was thanks to the efforts of Captain Lorenzo D. Baker and Minor C. Keith, who developed exports to the USA.

A new type of cotton bud invented to open the government's ears to the views of the opposition.

Banana splits

This is the classic banana republic. It has had 17 constitutions since gaining independence in 1838 and a string of coups and military takeovers.

The Hondurans have devised a number of useful words for their aspiring politicians. These include:
Imposicion — meaning 'rigged elections'.

Candidato unico — meaning 'one candidate', a device used to avoid 'imposicion' and your candidate losing.
Continuismo — meaning staying in power once the legal term of office is over. This avoids both 'imposicion' *and* 'candidato unico'.

Banana travel

Most Hondurans never travel more than a few miles from home. It isn't just the desire which is missing — so is the opportunity. There are few roads and the railway is reserved almost exclusively for bananas. Indeed, most of the rail network is owned by the United Fruit Company and the Standard Fruit and Steamship Company.

Best of a bad bunch

There are 166 trade unions. Forty seven of them don't have any members. The rest average about 550 members each. In 1955 the government set up a Ministry of Labour, Social Assistance and Middle Classes. Two years later it expunged the middle classes from it.

Non-banana life

This consists mainly of moths, beetles, wasps, bees, butterflies, spiders, ants, flies and mosquitoes. The human life in the area of Gracias a Dios is still a mystery — it is largely unexplored.

Geography

Honduras is a small state full of mountains up which the people live. They only come down in any numbers to go where the bananas (i.e. work) are.

Extraordinary facts

The national anthem does not mention bananas. It is called *'Tu bander a es un lampo cielo'*. The Honduran coffee industry is picking up fast. It may soon rival bananas.

Population: 3 and a half million

Size: Half that of Britain, 43,000 sq. miles

Government: Republic

Main language: Spanish

Religion: Roman Catholic

Capital: Tegucigalpa

Currency: Lempira, centavos

Tips for tourists

Avoid the banana skins.

Don't be fooled by the government's insistence that education is compulsory. There are almost no schools in rural areas.

Take a mosquito net.

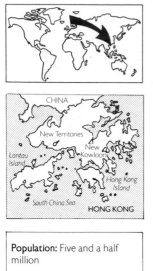

Hong Kong

Tips for tourists

Snake is a speciality for eating and drinking. Snake wine comes from live snake fermented in alcohol for anything up to 20 years. Snake restaurants bring the live snake to your table and cut out the liver for the guest. Perhaps this is why the Chinese are so hospitable.

Ma Hang prison is only a place of detention.

Apply the words of the Taoist sage (Lao Tsu, 600 BC) to Hong Kong:
The world is best ruled by letting things take their course. It cannot be ruled by interfering.

Chinese slant

The Chinese attitude to money is strange. They never entertain at home — always in restaurants. This means that some of them live in corrugated iron shacks, illegally tapping water and electricity from the mains. But they own Rolls-Royces and constantly drive to restaurants in them. Hong Kong has the greatest concentration of Rolls' in the world. They are the world's highest gamblers and greatest drinkers of brandy.

Tigers and jaguars haven't been seen in Hong Kong since the 1950's but beware of anyone who tells you there are no pythons. In 1982 the Government Snake Catcher had a job to salvage a calf from inside a 15ft. one. The method used was pouring cold water over it. The Chinese were so pleased with the success that, unnoticed, the snake slithered off.

Land of epithets

Economic nature reserve, borrowed place living on borrowed time, shop window of Asian free way of life, capitalist paradise, living fossil of early Imperial government, rumbling volcano, shoppers' paradise, commercial miracle, emporium of the east, home of laissez faire…

Bronze medal

For all its commercial expertise, Hong Kong only picks up the bronze for most things: third largest port, fleet, gold dealer and banking emporium in the world.

What it does really well is exporting more toys, textiles, radios and electronic games than anywhere. It has the largest neon sign and is the biggest Chinese laundry — laundering 40 per cent of communist China's foreign exchange. It is for this reason that Deng Xiaoping urges, *"Please tell foreign investors to put their hearts at ease."* This clarifies the old Chinese proverb, *'You can't satisfy hunger by drawing a cake'.*

Drawing a cake

You can also live in Hong Kong on the rice line. 100,000 people live on boats and the other 5 million for the most part live in more cramped conditions than anywhere. Even in 1900 there were 640,000 people per square mile. Today in Sham Shui Po there are 165,445 living in half a square mile. How they keep pace is by reclaiming land. Most of the capital of Hong Kong is reclaimed. Even so, some tower blocks contain the population of Reading, England, in an area the size of Wembley stadium. With all these cramped people, there are 6 and a quarter yards for every vehicle in the territory.

To look after its population the government is the largest landlord of rented accomodation in the world — 2 million people. In 1982 one flat was going up every 7 and a half minutes of the working day, and to cope with a population rise of 27 per cent in 10 years, 350,000 flats are planned between 1982 and 1992.

But being poor has its compensations. Eating is very cheap and the lowest denomination banknote in the world is worth one twelfth of a penny.

The government

This is controlled from Whitehall but effectively it is the governor who makes the decisions, with an un-elected executive. The population isn't interested in voting — there is only a 15 per cent turnout for urban district board elections. They have not got time to stop making money. In the worst decade for 50 years worldwide, Hong Kong's incomes doubled. In 5 years their exports to China increased 120 times. Even the social welfare situation is looking up. In 1973, they spent 81 million dollars. In 1983, 1,266 million dollars.

This experiment in traffic control has done little to help cars approaching from the right.

Hungary
Magyar Nepkoztarsasag

Early history

It was only a few short steppes from their homeland for the Magyars when they moved into the middle basin of the Danube in the 9th Century. The land they occupied became known as *On-Ogur*, which means Ten Arrows: from this name came the title Hungary. It became an independent kingdom in the year 1001.

Monarchy

Although a Communist country now, Hungary has had many interesting kings. Among these were:
Stephen I who spread Christianity throughout the land and became Saint Stephen.
Stephen II who only got the job because his father blinded all other male relatives (working on the principle *out of sight, out of line*).
Ladislav IV who undid much of Stephen I's good work by trying to reintroduce paganism.
Ladislav V known as *Posthumus* even when he was alive.
Vlaszio II called King 'Dobre' which means 'OK'. Apparently this is what he said whenever anyone spoke to him.

Wrong side

Hungary fought with the losers in World Wars One and Two. In the first it hoped to protect its empire but ended up losing two-thirds of its territory. In the second, while not supporting Nazism, it joined the Germans because it thought they would win. That makes Hungary the sort of country that should never bet on the Grand National, let alone a World War.

Right side

Hungary's greatest achievements this century were on the football field. In 1953 their side came to Wembley, where England had never lost, and won 6-3. The following year England went to Hungary and got beaten 7-1.

Another date

In 1956, fed up with Stalinist rule and Russian domination, the government introduced liberal reforms, including doing away with the secret police. A counter-government was set up which asked the Russians to help. They were only too willing. In came the troops and tanks, out went the reforms. A treaty of friendship was signed between Russia and Hungary which is still in force. With friends like that...

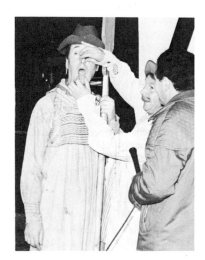

Since 1956 peasants are regularly checked to ensure their teeth are blunt.

The national anthem is *Isten alod meg a magyart*, meaning 'God bless the Hungarians'. It would be more appropriate if it were 'God help the Hungarians'.

Talking of God, there are 20 authorised religious denominations in Hungary. They survive on a state handout of around £1 million a year. This is only slightly less than the entire sum paid out in social insurance benefits.

Useless information

Land is measured in *cadastral yokes*. There are 648,900 people described as 'co-operative peasants' (presumably the unco-operative ones are shot). Radio licences were abolished in 1980 (this is the greatest measure of liberalisation since 1956).

The Hungarian People's Party, the Smallholders Party, the National Peasant Party and the Association of Working Peasants have been amalgamated into the Hungarian Socialist Workers' (i.e. Communist) Party.

Death

Hungary has the world's highest suicide rate — five times greater than Britain's. It also boasts the worst murderess of all time, the dreaded Countess Erszebet Bathory who lived 400 years ago and killed 610 young girls at her castle. The earliest recorded human remains were found in Hungary. But as they are about half a million years old, the countess is not being blamed.

Population: 11 million

Size: A third that of Britain, 36,000 sq. miles

Government: Communist

Language: Hungarian (Magyar)

Main religions: Roman Catholic and Calvinist

Capital: Budapest

Currency: Forint, filler

Tips for tourists

Don't go to lose weight — the Transylvanian Diet was not how Dracula stayed slim, but the 19th Century parliament.

Although the rest of the Communist world disdains food, Hungarians love cooking, serving and eating. Their dishes are based on lard, onions, garlic and sour cream, but the soul of their cooking is the red pepper paprika.

Hungarians are very keen on birth control — and have had a very low birth rate for most of this century. The state now offers bribes to couples who have children.

Iceland
Lyoveldio Island

Population: A quarter of a million

Size: Half that of Britain, 40,000 sq. miles

Government: Republic

Language: Icelandic

Main religion: Evangelical Lutheran

Capital: Reykjavik

Currency: Krona and Eyrir

Tips for tourists

Festivals:
Bolludagur — Children beat adults with coloured sticks to get 'Bollur' or cream buns. Monday before Shrove Tuesday.
Sprengidagur — Everyone eats salted pea and mutton soup — as a treat. Shrove Tuesday, 'Bursting Day'.
Ash Wednesday — Children tie bags of ash on unwary adults.

If you catch a cold in Iceland (which seems likely) and it turns to something worse (which seems probable), don't worry. Iceland has one of the highest standards of living in the world with the highest life expectancy — 73 years for men, 79 years for women.

A useful lullaby

*Sofur thu svind thitt
Svartus i augum
Far i fulam pitt
Fullan af Drangum*

Sleep, you black eyed pig
Fall into the deep pit full of ghosts.

History

Iceland's tourist industry has never recovered from its first visitors. Not that the Vikings who arrived in the year 874 set about raping and pillaging. There was no one to rape, nothing to pillage on this barren island in the North Atlantic.

On the contrary, the Vikings' deeds have been immortalised in sagas, the foundation of the great Icelandic culture which still survives. The popularity of these mammoth story poems took a temporary knock when the Nazis identified with most of the characters, but they now flourish again.

Industry

In the tradition of the sagas, Iceland still produces more books per head of population than any other country in the world. The only other things produced in any quantity are:
*Fish
Hot water
Hot gases.*

Geography

Just a quarter of the land is habitable and half a per cent is under cultivation. Not surprisingly. For Iceland is a wasteland of glaciers, lava fields, mountains and volcanoes. One of the 200 volcanoes, Mount Hekla, is believed to be the main gate to hell. There are frequent earthquakes, so modern houses are built from reinforced concrete. There are few trees...few foxes...and a few reindeer. But there is the largest gannet colony in the world and biggest fish catch for the size of population.

Iceland is bigger than Ireland but its population is less than a quarter of a million, more than a third living in the capital, Reykjavik. This city is famed for its great cultural life and for having the cheapest central heating in the world which uses hot springs, *solfataras*, of which Iceland has more than any other country. The largest one, Deildartunguhver, emits 55 gallons of boiling water every second.

Language

This is tricky as it is formed by joining existing words together. Thus 'The door key to the door of the Supreme Court Barrister's Secretary' is *Haestarret-tarmalaflutningsmannskkrifstofustulku-utidyralykillin.*

Travel

There is no railway and most roads are dirt tracks. But since the country is virtually impassable in winter it doesn't matter. Snow falls in the north on one hundred days a year. In the summer the temperature sometimes reaches the mid-fifties (Fahrenheit).

Politics

Iceland has the oldest parliament in the world, the *Althing* established in 930. A district council is called a *Thing*. The Althing has made many equivocal decisions, for example in the year 1,000 when it adopted Christianity as the national religion but decreed that heathen rites could still be practised if no one was watching.

The country was ruled by Denmark until 1918 when it became a sovereign state although still under the King of Denmark. In 1944 it became a republic after a referendum which gave an overwhelming 'Yes' vote for independence. Seven times more people spoiled their ballot papers than voted 'No'.

Iceland is the only NATO country without its own army or navy.

Proverbs

Iceland has many baffling proverbs. These include:
It is merely a transition, said the fox, as they flayed him alive
and
Every man likes the smell of his own farts
not forgetting
Pissing in his shoes keeps no man warm for long.

Rows and rows of cod being interrogated at the height of the Cod War with Great Britain.

India
Bharat

People

India is Earth's skid row. Forty per cent of the world's destitutes and illiterates live here. To add to this incomprehensible situation, they speak 1,652 different languages. The downtrodden are kept well under foot by the caste system. Although formally abolished in 1950, this still exists in practice. Some anthropologists claim that a person's caste may be discovered by the shape of his nose (the lower its convexity, the lower his caste). Another way to spot the lower castes is to see who people veer away from. Higher castes believe they are defiled if touched by the lower orders.

There is a worse problem than 'untouchability' — too much touching. Birth is out of control — not surprisingly, as India has the world's lowest average marriage ages: 20 for males and 14 and a half for females. But the fastest growing industry is now birth control — there are 30,000 family planning clinics.

Indians eat fewer eggs, meat and vegetables than any other peoples, although they have the largest livestock population — 344 million cattle. But more than half of the country's milk comes from buffaloes.

The Indian transport system was modelled largely, but not entirely, on the British.

Industry

There are almost 21,000 trade unions but the average wage is only £1 a week. The reason there are so many unions is that, legally, any seven persons can constitute one (so they do). The reason for the low wages is that India's economy remains dependent on tea and coffee. Poppies are also an important crop, but the opium industry has been nationalised.

Foreign companies are not too keen on investing in India since its government told them to reveal all their technological secrets. This included a demand to Coca-Cola to divulge the formula of their concentrate. Coca-Cola refused and closed its Indian factories, throwing 250,000 people out of work.

India produces more films than anywhere. They may be seen in the country's 9,017 cinemas, 2,660 of which are touring ones.

Geography

India is only the seventh biggest country in the world but it has the second largest population (after China). In the south, it is sweltering. In the north, there is more snow and ice than in any other land. That is due to the Himalayas, the world's highest mountain system.

History

For nearly a thousand years, this area was invaded by all the usual rabble — Mongols, Persians, Afghans. Sophistication came with the British, who, by the mid-19th Century had control of the whole place. Although India achieved independence in 1948 (when Pakistan was hived off for the Moslems) British rule has left as a legacy one of the most sophisticated bureaucracies in the world.

Politics

Indian politics is dominated by: *a)* corruption and *b)* Mrs. Indira Ghandi. She is the daughter of the first Prime Minister, Jawaharlal Nehru, and has triumphed despite splitting her party, forming a new one (named after herself) surviving investigations for corruption, declaring martial law and imprisoning her opponents.

Population: 700 million

Size: 14 times that of Britain, one and a quarter million sq. miles

Government: Republic

Official language: Hindi

Main religion: Hinduism

Capital: New Delhi

Currency: Rupee, paise

Tips for tourists

Take a candle. Half of India's 567,000 villages are without electricity.

Take an umbrella if you visit Cherrapunji. It is the wettest place on earth — 425 inches of rain were recorded there one year (on second thoughts, a snorkel may be more use than an umbrella).

Don't bother trying to catch a train from Khargpur unless you are very fit. Its platform is 2,733 feet long.

Indonesia
Republik Indonesia

Population: 150 million

Size: Eight times that of Britain, three quarters of a million sq. miles

Government: Republic

Main religion: Islam

Official language: Bahasa Indonesian

Capital: Jakarta

Currency: Rupiah, sen

Tips for tourists

Lazy hill climber? You'll love the one at Seria. It is only 15 feet high, the lowest recorded hill in the world, according to the Guinness Book of Records.

Frightened by thunderstorms? You'll hate it here. Some islands have more than 3,000 a night.

Geography, blast it

Indonesia consists of 13,667 islands strung out for 3,400 miles across the Pacific. Of these, 12,675 are uninhabited and 7,600 haven't even got a name — they are the orphans of world geography. But there is something worse for an island than being nameless — having a volcano. Some Indonesian islands have several (Java alone has 17).

The most famous volcanic explosion was in 1883 on Krakatoa — 163 villages were wiped out and 36,380 people killed. There was an even bigger bang 70 years earlier when the volcano on Sumbawa blew its top — the island was lowered by more than 4,000 feet.

The Suharto Memorial Hospital. This man is being vaccinated against yellow fever.

Politics

The pressures of governing Indonesia for the first 20 years of independence appear to have done something to President Sukarno. As those years wore on he scrapped the constitution, dissolved some political parties (there were 170 of them) and dissolved parliament. In 1965, after a failed revolt, some 100,000 Communists and sympathisers were murdered. The following year the military took over in the person of General Suharto. He outlawed the Communist Party (somewhat unnecessarily, as all its members were dead) and abolished Sukarno's National Front party before abolishing Sukarno himself.

Supreme power now rests with the People's Consultative Assembly. Unfortunately this meets only once every five years. This leaves power in the hands of the president, prime minister and defence minister. All three of these posts are held by President Suharto.

The largest party in the House of Representatives is the world's most boringly named political party, the Functional Group. By contrast the national anthem, *Indonesia Raya,* was written by the most interestingly named anthem writer, Wage Rudolph Supratman.

Decisions

If you want something done, there are two ways to go about it — by *mushawarah,* meaning consensus and involving extensive discussions — or bribery. This is the traditional way to do things in Indonesia and has created its own language. Thus:
pungli — these are 'wild levies' exacted by petty officials
korupsi — full-bodied corruption
catut — petty corruption
ngompreng — the use of official equipment for private purposes
ngobyek — the piece of a deal a patron gives his client.

Remember: As the Indonesian saying has it: *Being a tax collector is better than owning a clove tree.*

Industry

Indonesia has a thriving manufacturing sector and booming oil industry but agriculture is still crucial, the most important product being rubber. It is said to grow well because the soil is enriched by volcanic eruptions, which presumably makes the destruction of villages and roads worthwhile.

The salt industry has been nationalised. Weights and measures include the pikol, katti, pal and square pal.

Life

There are more than 300 ethnic groups on the islands speaking 250 different languages and belonging to virtually every religion in the world. The only thing they have in common is death, which they reach at age 45 on average, courtesy of smallpox, tuberculosis and various tropical diseases.

Animal life is much more interesting. You can find the Komodo dragon (a giant lizard), rare rhinos, walking stick insects, walking leaves and giant beetles.

Travel

To get from island to island you need a boat. To get around an island you need wings. Jakarta is worst — miles of roads choked by traffic suddenly turning, unexpectedly stopping and uncontrollably weaving. Smaller roads are blocked by pedlars. Pavements are jammed by pedestrians carrying huge bundles on shoulder sticks.

Iran

It doesn't need a historian or geographer to write about Iran. It needs a pyschiatrist. The whole country ought to be locked away in a secure institution. Even its national flag is certifiable. It contains the legend *Allah Akbar* in white Kufi script repeated 22 times, rather like an old man muttering to himself.

History

When Iran was called Persia, things were different. The first great Persian empire was founded by Cyrus the Great in the 6th Century BC and went on to dominate much of the world. But by the middle of the 19th Century, the rest of the world had come to dominate Persia. Britain was given the monopoly over its railways, trams, tobacco, minerals, road building, construction industry, phones and, eventually, the oil on which the economy came to depend.

In 1925, Reza Khan, an officer of the Cossack Brigade who had risen through the ranks, became self-proclaimed Shah after a coup. He changed the country's name to Iran and confiscated thousands of farms and businesses, which he then sold back. So by the time his son took over in 1941, the family fortune was assured. The new Shah was known as *King of Kings* and *Allah's Shadow on Earth*.

The Ayatollah

Ayatollah Ruhollah Khomeini is a most unlikely revolutionary. A religious leader, he did not object so much to the oppression of the people under the Shah as to their growing westernisation. After 15 years in exile, Khomeini returned to his homeland in triumph in 1979 after student riots persuaded the Shah that there would have to be changes. The first was that the Shah fled the country, taking about 20,000 million dollars of Iranian valuables with him.

A referendum was held by the Ayatollah to see if Iran should become an Islamic republic. The voting was: *for* — 20,288,021, *against* — 140,966. Among the changes made since then are the virtual banning of music and art, and the abolition of mixed-sex schools. But the savage penalties inflicted by Islamic justice are not much different from justice under the Shah — even then, Iran had the world's highest rate of death penalties and no proper system of courts.

Lot number 49 cost an arm and a leg.

Industry

Oil is still the main source of national income, although its production has fallen since the revolution. Opium, which used to be an important export, was banned in 1955. There are 32 million sheep (the ones with wool) providing material for Persian rugs.

Geography

A vast portion of Iran is desert, with almost no one living there. In the interior, there is an area of salt waste 200 miles long and 100 miles wide. This is supposedly where the legendary city of Sodom stood. Presumably a few grains are all that remain of Lot's wife.

Having fun

Among Iran's public holidays are: *the Birthday of the Twelfth Imam, Martyrdom of Imam Ali, Death of the Prophet, Oil Nationalisation Day* and two *Revolution Days*. If you want to do something more exciting, you could visit the extinct volcano at Damavand, where the wicked deevs are said to lurk. Their king, *Deev-i Sepid*, is a ferocious, horned, tusky white demon, with spots all over.

Population: 38 million

Size: Seven times Britain, 634,000 sq. miles

Government: Islamic republic

Official language: Farsi

Religion: Islam

Capital: Tehran

Currency: Rial, dinar

Tips for tourists

Don't commit adultery. It carries the death penalty (but only for women).

If you want to get married, take evidence of your virginity. This is required by law.

Don't get drunk. The penalty can be death. Mat weaver Hossein va'Esi Dallili was recently executed by firing squad after going on a binge despite being given 80 lashes previously for being found drunk.

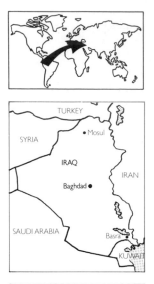

Iraq
al Jumhouriya al 'Iraqia

Mess

Iraq is the perfect example of how a well-mannered child can become a delinquent later in life. In its infancy 5,000 years ago — when, as Mesopotamia, it was one of the cradles of humanity — it was wonderfully well-ordered. It had the earliest parliament and legal code (King Ur-Hammu's). Now, army coup follows army coup, and war follows war. Is it suppressed anger from the country's adolescence?

Even the blind are taught to cut throats in Iraq.

Mesopotamia

Life in the Mesopotamian city-states of Babylon and Assyria was full of fun for the right people. The king's day would begin with his letters being read out loud to him. Then he would pay a visit to a temple to slaughter a sheep for sacrifice, or to report to the gods on state affairs. Later he would be entertained by such things as minstrels reciting fables in which the date-palm and tamarisk argued their respective merits.

Religion and sex

The gods in Mesopotamia did rather well, too. It was believed that they had to be fed four times a day — two main meals and two snacks. So these were laid out religiously for them and were always consumed (*dietary note:* priests always appeared to be extremely well fed). The gods' other basic instincts were also pandered to. 'Religious prostitutes' were kept to indulge in sexual practices to honour the goddess of love, Ishtar.

Justice and sex

Among the legal codes of the Mesopotamians were:
If a wife is caught lying with a man who is not her husband, they shall be tied up and thrown into the water. If the finger is pointed against a wife, but she has not been caught, she shall jump into the river.
If a man after the death of his father lies sexually with his mother, they shall burn both of them.
If a surgeon has saved a gentleman's life, he shall receive ten shekels of silver. If the gentleman dies, they shall cut off the surgeon's hand.

Injustice

After spending 500 years as part of Turkey's Ottoman Empire, Iraq fell under British control. It became a republic in 1958 after a coup — the first of several. The only legal political party is a coalition between the communists and the cleanest party in the world, the Ba'ath (surely election day should be known as Ba'ath night). The country is now going down the plughole as an Islamic socialist republic.

More dates

There are only two products in Iraq. One is oil, which accounts for almost 98 per cent of exports. The other is dates, which take up most of the other 2 per cent. Iraq is the largest date grower in the world, with 33 million palms producing half a million tons of dates annually.

Proverb

She's pregnant without intercourse, 'tis said;
It's by not eating she has put on weight!

More war

All male Iraqis must do two years' military service. This can be extended in an emergency. There is always an emergency in Iraq.

Population: 13 and a half million

Size: Double that of Britain, 170,000 sq. miles

Government: Socialist republic

Language: Arabic

Main religion: Islam

Capital: Baghdad

Currency: Iraqi dinar, fils, riyal, dirham

Tips for tourists

If you feel out of sorts — or out of all-sorts — take a stroll beside a river. Liquorice grows in abundance on the banks of all main rivers.

Don't bother looking for lions. The last one was killed in 1910. You'll have to make do with bats, rats, jackals and wildcats.

Tip for Mesopotamian tourists: If you've got a headache, don't visit 'the tablet house' thinking it is a pharmacist's. It is a school.

Ireland

Eire

Irish jokes

Ireland has more mental hospital beds per person than anywhere except Finland. This is no joke. There are two possible reasons. The first is simply that Great Britain had a policy of moving its lunatic poor across the sea to Ireland. The second is the Irish inheritance of poor diet, intermarriage, reliance on nervous stimulants and agricultural depression.

Blarney

Early Irish history is unrecorded legend — or blarney. Stories tell of Milesian settlers from Scythia and Egypt coming to Ierne. Of the invasion of Goidels in 500 BC and the Kingdom of Tara. They say that the Giants' Causeway is a remnant of a bridge between Ireland and Scotland. Later stories ring truer. Norwegians arrived who the inhabitants called Fingail — or White Strangers — then Danes, who they called Dubgail — or Black Strangers. Where the colour distinction comes from is a mystery.

North v South

This started earlier than is commonly thought. The south became known as *Mugs Half* and the north as *Conns Half*. Since then mugging and conning has been, with help from the English, mutual.

The English

It was the fault of the Irish — or at least Dermod McMurrough — for inviting the English to help with a local war against King Rauidrhi O'Connor. Henry II of England jumped at the chance and sent his best soldier, Strongbow. Subsequently the only English Pope gave Ireland to the English. The locals lived up to their reputation for stupidity by helping

Some Irish lifeboatmen prepare to comb the sea for survivors.

Strongbow, thinking he was Danish. By 1374 some members of the Houses of Parliament were from Ireland.

But repression followed: In the 13th Century Irish were excluded from the clergy. Richard II lost his crown there and in 1551 Henry VIII — also King of Ireland — made protestantism official. In 1560 the Church of Ireland was restored but in the ding-dong religious changes of Kings Charles, James and William, the Irish didn't know which way to turn.

Famine and emigration

In the Desmond rebellion, it took a chap like Cromwell to get control of things. His tactic of destroying crops worked and in 1739 one-third of the Irish died of famine. They got wise and planted potatoes which were not so easy to destroy and in 18 years the population doubled. By 1845 there were 9 million people, mostly living on potatoes. Then potato blight struck and only 3 million people could be fed. 300,000 died, 30,000 on 'coffin ships' to the United States. The callousness of the English response ensured a lasting bitterness. Between 1840 and 1970, when in the rest of Europe the populations doubled, Ireland's halved. Now it has the lowest population density in Europe apart from Sweden and Norway.

Writers' paradise

The Irish have always been keen on books. In 561 AD, 3,000 people died in the Battle of the Books: which must be the first recorded copyright action of any significance. The judgment of King Diarmid sparked it off: *"To every cow its calf. To every book its copy"*. Today writers are given tax exemption — perhaps because of the proliferation of great writers who have emerged from Ireland. They write books which are not allowed to be published in Ireland.

Black waters

Dubh Lina — or Dublin — means Dark Pool but today the most famous dark pool is that found in the Irish invention Guinness. It is the Guinness and potatoes which help to give Ireland the highest calorie intake in the world. But drink is doubly important to the Irish — an Irish single is equivalent to an English double. And poteen — the largest still in the world is at Midleton — is only £2 a bottle. Shannon was the world's first duty-free airport. The Irish also drink more tea than anyone else.

Population: 3 and a half million

Size: A quarter that of Britain, 26,600 sq. miles

Government: Republic

Language: English

Religion: Roman Catholic

Capital: Dublin

Currency: Irish pound

Tips for tourists

Visit North and South Slob — where half the world's Greenland geese winter.

Avoid Tipperary. It is the home of the immediate families of Buffalo Bill, Jesse James and Ned Kelly.

The only reptiles are newts.

Feel safe. Patrick Power is in charge of Defence.

Holiday romance? Ireland has a very high proportion of single people.

Israel
Medinat Israel

Genesis

This is the land of plenty, but not the one the Bible foretold. It has plenty of soldiers, plenty of trouble, plenty of financial problems and plenty of people trying to wipe it out. When it was part of Palestine, it was invaded by just about everyone. Now invaders do so at their peril.

A nice Jewish state

Israel is a country created by stealth. After World War One, the British, while acting as caretakers for the area, declared that this would be a nice Jewish homeland. But not yet, please God. God didn't listen. Jews from all over the world began sneaking in. In 1948, they got their homeland.

Holiness

One in five Jews now lives here (more live in the USA). There are two main classes of Jew, each with its own Chief Rabbi. The Sephardim were accepted as the Jewish elite because they traditionally hung around Palestine. But the Ashkenazim, although coming from Europe and America, are the biggest influence in Israel, as they led the drive for the Jewish state.

Living in a holy land is not easy for people who like a bit of fun. Haifa is just about the only place where public transport runs on the Sabbath. People who drive cars on the Sabbath have been stoned (by stones, not drugs — although that wouldn't be allowed on the Sabbath, either). And in Jerusalem there is a Committee for Guarding Modesty which has erected this sign: *'Jewish daughters, the Torah obliges you to dress with modesty. We do not tolerate people passing through our streets immodestly dressed.'*

Begin bowl

Menachim Begin threatens to do for Israel what the Titanic did for luxury cruises. He was one of the terrorists who forced the British to leave, yet in 1977 he became Prime Minister. Since then, he has managed to alienate and upset all but the most devoted Zionists. This is not a smart thing to do. Israel is still dependent on foreign aid, especially from the USA.

The country's biggest export is diamonds. The next biggest foreign-currency earner is an import — tourists.

Israel's taxes are among the highest in the world. So is its inflation — in fact, in the early 1980's, it *was* the highest.

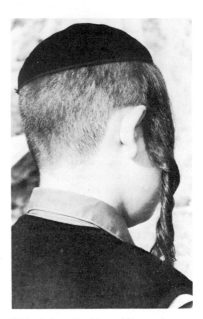

With a haircut like this, *you'd* be praying at the wailing wall.

Inflation is not to blame for the Jewish calendar being 3,760 years ahead of the usual one.

Begin and end

The average length of life is among the highest in the world, 70 for men and 73 for women. This is probably because the country is overstocked with doctors (and dentists).

The General Federation of Labour trade union is a wonderful example of entrepreneurship. 85 per cent of all wage earners are members and so are 300,000 full-time housewives. It runs the health service and has moved into banking, insurance, business and building. In fact, it is Israel's largest employer.

The national anthem is *Hatikvah*, the Hope, written by N. N. Imber. His agent is not known.

Population: 4 million

Size: Less than a tenth that of Britain, 8,000 sq. miles

Government: Republic

Official languages: Hebrew, Arabic

Main religion: Judaism

Capital: Jerusalem

Currency: Shekel

Tips for tourists

Fancy some low life? Visit Ein Bokek on the shores of the Dead Sea. It is the lowest town in the world, 1,300 feet below sea level.

Don't worry about calling people eggheads. Israel has more university professors than anywhere in the world. And, what's more, Israelis are the world's biggest egg eaters.

Join the army. One in 22 Israelis is in the forces.

For a holy evening out, go to a Bible Contest.

Italy
Repubblica Italiana

Two thousand years ago Italy had the greatest and most efficient empire that the world had ever seen. Today it is the country with the second highest number of civil disorders, and pollution problems that threaten to destroy its many hundreds of thousands of art treasures.

Other problems

Taxation — The national sport is tax evasion. About 65 per cent of the people pay no income tax at all. But their reluctance is understandable. It is estimated that if all taxes were collected fully the state would receive about 110 per cent of national income.

The Government tries to make up for this in ridiculous ways. When you buy a cup of coffee in an Italian bar you are paying 43 separate taxes on it.

Justice — The absence of justice is taken for granted. There is an old saying in Italy: *If you are right, keep away from the law courts. If you are wrong, sue, as there is a good chance of your winning.* Not only is justice absent, but it is also slow. The average length of time for a civil case to go through the courts is 6 and a half years.

Corruption — Also taken for granted.

For centuries the Italian army has been the most feared in the western world.

In 1981 the Government resigned when it became implicated in the discovery that over 1,000 of Italy's leading establishment figures belonged to a secret society with extensive criminal connections.

Recently in Sicily there were four ex-mayors, four former regional government ministers and all the members of the previous governing council facing court charges at the same time for offences connected with their terms of office.

Etiquette — Not taken for granted, unfortunately. The story is told that crossing a road in Rome a citizen stepped into the path of a bus. A passer-by wanted to shout a warning, but how to address him? He looked respectable, even distinghished; the passer-by took a chance and cried out, *Commendatore!*, instead of *Signor*. So the man paid no attention and was run over.

Bureaucracy — It is said that, in the afternoon civil servants don't come, in the mornings they don't work.

High drama

Italy is the home of grand opera. Like Italian football matches, the opera thrives on over-acting. Dying heroines rise and sing powerful arias, with perhaps an encore, before expiring. In Verdi's *Il Trovatore* the tenor wastes precious minutes singing over and over again to his companions that his mother is burning to death and there is not a moment to lose.

Nudity

In a recent judgment banning total nudity from Italian beaches, a court ruled that 'the sight of the male and female sex organs arouses a sense of uneasiness or repulsion, or perturbation or immodest curiosity or erotic excitement in the observer who possesses sensibilities, and who is not one exasperated by moral rigidity or sexual hypersensitivity'.

In 1970, the Supreme Court ruled that men who touched their genitals while fully clothed (an ancient custom supposed to ward off bad luck) were guilty of indecency because the act is 'contrary to the sense of composure held by their fellow citizens'.

But five years ago a Milan court dismissed indecency charges against a man who had been walking naked down the street. The reason was 'he was walking with complete naturalness'.

Population: 57 million

Size: Slightly larger than Britain, 116,300 sq. miles

Government: Republic

Language: Italian

Religion: Roman Catholic

Capital: Rome

Currency: Lire

Tips for tourists

Look under your bed — Italy has the 7th largest Communist Party in the world.

Hang on to your handbag — Italy has more thefts than any other country.

Get drunk — Italy is second in the world for wine production.

Wear glasses — You will then be addressed as 'Doctor' or 'Professor'.

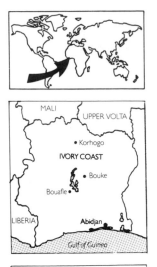

Ivory Coast
Republique de Cote d'Ivoire

Population: 8 and a half million

Size: One and a half times that of Britain, 123,000 sq. miles

Government: Republic

Main religion: Traditional beliefs

Main languages: French and Kwa

Capital: Abidjan

Currency: CFA franc, centime

Tips for tourists

Don't go out dancing. The natives like doing it on stilts.

Why not go to Cocody to try what is almost certainly Black Africa's only ice skating rink.

Stumbling

Europeans first stumbled on this square country 600 years ago. They promptly stumbled off it again. There was nothing worth staying for. For five centuries the only people who could be bothered to drop in were sailors who wanted to pick up ivory from the natives, who had picked it up from elephants' tusks (that's how the country got its name).

In 1842 the French obtained the right to colonise it. They couldn't be bothered for another 40 years. It is that sort of place. At one time, part of Upper Volta was tacked on to the Ivory Coast. It was given back a few years later. Upper Volta is that sort of place, too.

Coasting

A tribal chief and medical assistant called Felix Houphouet-Boigny started a union of small farmers in 1944. He proved adept at cultivating politics as well. He turned the union into a political party and in 1960, when the Ivory Coast became independent, he naturally became president. He still is.

The country has witnessed spectacular economic progress and extraordinary political stability (by African standards). Felix has achieved this by maintaining the closest links with France. Foreign aid has poured in. And the profits have poured out.

This does not mean that some of the natives have not benefitted from the boom. The leaders of Felix's party own a quarter of all the country's plantations and hire two thirds of the labour at half the urban rate.

This man is a fetish witchcraft priest. In his spare time he works as a cheese-grater.

A new political party has recently appeared on the scene. Is it about to disturb the tranquility? Not for Felix, it isn't. He founded it.

Thriving

The Ivory Coast thrives on coffee and cocoa. It is the world's third biggest producer of both. Unfortunately the large amount of coffee produced here is only suitable for the rotten instant kind you buy in huge tins.

These are not the only industries which have been helped by European money and know-how. White aid has also set up prostitution rackets and a crime network. Casinos have opened in Cocody, although the locals are not allowed to gamble. This is why the Ivory Coast is called the Monte Carlo of Africa.

Not all occupations are open to everyone. For example, to became a musician or griot (minstrel) you must be born into the trade.

Playing

Much of the culture here is unique to particular tribes. Thus the Senufo are known for their treatment and conservation of animal heads, the Talla for decorating doors and dancing to xylophones, the Baoule for wearing weird masks and gold jewellery.

The national sport is soccer but table tennis is becoming very popular, despite a shortage of tables.

Living

Apart from the national heroine, Queen Pokou, who is feted at every opportunity, females get a raw deal. When they grow up they will be expected to do all the work while their husbands go fishing and hunting. But they can at least feel safe. The Ivory Coast has the world's lowest incidence of rape and sex crimes.

Animals here include the bongo (a reddish-brown antelope), six kinds of dwarf antelope, giant forest hogs, pygmy hippos and the manatee, a water animal with two front flippers and a spoon-shaped tail.

Justice

There is one court.

Travel

Dominated by the rail line to Upper Volta — the world's best example of *'You ain't going nowhere'*.

Jamaica

Origin

Wans apan a taim, Breda Anansi, oed dat king av a Son. Fram di die im baan im didn waak. An Breda Anansi se iing gwain to mek dat Son waak. Nou, iz pik up iz myuuzik man, wich iz tree kakrouch, dat i tuk intu a guodi an wen ing riich about a aaf mailz, tu die king giet, im straik up di myuuzik man. Nou a gwain tu staat di myuuzik:

King oooo King oooo kimbembe King
King oooo King oooo kimbembe King
King Son a kom dong, kimbembe King
King Son a kom dong, kimbembe King

And so on: this is the language of Jamaica today. It is a Creole patois obviously closely based on English.

European origins

The Indian name, *Xaymaca* — meaning 'Land of springs' — has survived Columbus, who called the island Santiago. When the Spanish were kicked out, Jamaica became Great Britain's most important colony. Part of the reason for its capture lay in Cromwell's desire to ship the Irish as far away from England as possible.

Yo ho ho

With the British came the pirates. The most successful of all was Henry Morgan, a Welshman. Morgan rampaged through the Caribbean smashing the Spanish wherever he found them, and looting and pillaging. When Morgan went too far, however, and ransacked Panama after a treaty between the British and Spanish had been signed, he was summoned to London and put on trial. The British knew exactly what to do with a man who hung his prisoners up by the private parts and flogged them. They made him governor.

Other British entrepreneurs

The treaty with the Spanish was unpopular. A man called Jenkins was so enraged that he turned up in Parliament in London holding up what he purported to be his ear — apparently severed by the Spanish. It was probably a piece of crinkled leather (with his real ear concealed by a wig), but he persuaded the British to fight *The War of Jenkins' Ear*. Admiral 'Old Grog' Vernon was less successful.

Modern Jamaica

A rebellion in 1865 was savagely put down — The House of Assembly voting itself out of power — and hundreds of executions took place. Riots in 1938 — 100 years after emancipation — led eventually to independence in 1962. Three of the first four Presidents were related. But the motto *Out of many, one people* has been unconvincing. The 1976 and 1980 elections were both landslides — for opposing parties. The first, Manley won, the second Seaga, who set about reversing the pro-Cuba socialist policies of his predecessor. But the elections are more like battle-grounds. In the 1976 election more than 500 people died. The singer Bob Marley on two occasions got the opposing leaders on the same stage, defusing two civil wars. His song *Smile Jamaica* was his message. The country has the world's worst unemployment.

Religion

Jamaica is famous for its Ras Tafari sect, who view the late Emperor Selassie of Ethiopia as god. Selassie drew greater crowds in Jamaica than the British Queen. There is also illegal Obeah Magic. A useful dirge if you're in a hurry is: *Skarash ni-toe*. With more time you can say: *Ski bam bam chinka po*.

Proverbs

Licky-licky fly follow, coffin go a hole. (It is dangerous to follow pleasures of the palate too far)

When trouble catch bull dog, monkey breeches fit him (Loud-mouths prove blusterers)

Rocky tone a ribba bottom no feel sun hot (About people in comfortable positions not caring for others)

When cockroach gib dance, him no ax fowl (The lowly should avoid the exalted)

Jamaican hair shampoo is not yet internationally recognised for its manageability.

Population: 2 and a quarter million

Size: 4,200 sq. miles

Government: Independent Commonwealth member

Languages: English, Creole

Religions: Christianity, Pocomania

Capital: Kingston

Currency: Dollar

Tips for tourists

Look out for beautiful women rising from the sea. Jamaica is the setting for Fleming's *Doctor No.*

Look out for beautiful women. Jamaica has had three Miss Worlds.

Visit Navy Island, that modern pirate Errol Flynn's old possession.

Go for the music. Gumbay drums and the ancient 'roll-rock stone'.

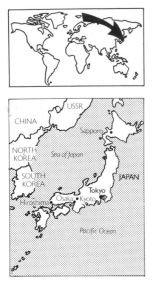

Population: 117 million

Size: One and a half that of Britain, 144,000 sq. miles

Government: Constitutional monarchy

Language: Japanese

Main religion: Shinto and Buddhism

Capital: Tokyo

Currency: Yen, sen

Tips for tourists

Don't expect to find a husband or wife here. Of all the peoples of the world, the Japanese are least inclined to marry foreigners.

Don't ask for lamb in a restaurant. There are only 12,000 sheep in the country.

Do ask for fish. The Japanese are the world's biggest fish eaters.

Don't worry about being mugged. There is very little violent crime here compared with other advanced countries.

Do travel by train. The Japanese travel more rail miles than anyone.

Japan

Nippon *or* Nihon

Japan is...

...a group of islands with most of its population living on four of them...85 per cent mountainous, so the people are forced to live in a very small area...one of the few nations never to be invaded (the Allies didn't want to after Hiroshima)...an extraordinary example of late growth: it was just a minor feudal Asian nation until late in the 19th Century.

Japan has...

...the world's longest reigning Imperial dynasty (the present Emperor Hirohito traces his family back to 200 AD)...the world's second largest shipping fleet...the world's highest circulation newspaper, *Yomiuri Shimbun* (14 million copies a day)...the largest car manufacturer and the biggest maker of zips (a quarter of the world's supply)...the world's oldest national anthem, the 1,000-year-old *Kimi ga yo wa* (but it only has four lines)...the world's largest volcanic crater (71 miles round)...twice as many TV transmitters as the USA.

Japan boasts...

...the greatest industrial growth of any nation since the end of World War Two (and it lost)...making it the third largest world economic power (after the USA and Russia)...and putting it on course for becoming the richest nation in the world by 1990.

Tokyo is...

...the world's most expensive and populous (8 and a half million people) city...*and* it has...the world's most crowded rail system — Japanese National Railways, which employs professional pushers to squeeze passengers on board...the world's fastest passenger lift — at the Sunshine 60 building...and the most expensive land in the world.

How they do it

Apart from their inscrutability, they believe in conciliation. Most police stations have a 'conciliation room'. Businesses are run like families. There are 72,693 trade unions, but they are organised on a plant basis and give little trouble. They have fewer industrial accidents than any country.

This is one of the few countries which provide a complete education for all, from kindergarten to high school. It *also* devotes a huge part of its national income to investing in industry (a third

in the 1960's, allowing productivity to double).

Little is spent on defence. The constitution does not allow them to have armed forces for aggression, so the army is called the *Ground Self-Defence Force*, the navy the *Maritime Self-Defence Force* and the air force the *Air Self-Defence Force*.

The result is that Japan now produces 14 and three quarter million TV sets a year, 15 and a half million radios, 12 and a half million cameras and 3 and a half million cars.

The Japanese are paranoid about their height.

Intolerance

Religious teaching is banned in schools and the state refuses to give a subsidy to religion. In 1945 the victorious Allies ordered the Japanese Government to stop supporting Shinto, the traditional religion which means *Way of the Gods*. This has not lessened its popularity. Shinto still has 98 million adherents.

The Japanese now appear to be intolerant of sexism. There used to be a *Girls Day* (March 3) and a *Boys Day* (March 5). These have now been amalgamated as *Childrens Day* (but the date is still March 5).

But they are tolerant of war films and make a lot of them (they are the world's second biggest movie makers).

Culture

Men like *Karate* and *Kendo* (Japanese wrestling). Women prefer *Ikebana* (flower arranging) and *Cha-no-yu* (tea ceremony), both of which they consider fits them for their future role as housewives. It is not known what the men's activities reveal about their attitudes to marriage.

Jordan
Al Mamlaka al Urduniya al Hashemiyah

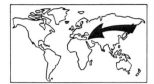

In the Biblical sense

In 7,000 BC Jericho stood here.
Abraham and the Land of Canaan
passed through, followed by the
descendants of Esau and Lot. The old
city of Jerusalem — the centre of the
Christian religion, and third centre of
Islam — was also once in Jordan's
territory. Now in Israel, Jerusalem's
importance to conflicting religions has
been a national disaster for Jordan.

The Romans, in their late empire,
Christianised the area. But Islam proved
greater than Rome. It wasn't until 1855
— for the first time since the Crusades
— that a cross was carried through the
streets of Jerusalem. Although
Bethlehem also went into Israel in 1967,
today it is only Jerusalem that is
important to the population of Jordan,
94 per cent of whom are Sunni Moslem.

The Christian minority mostly live
in Rum.

The problem

*Could we but climb where Moses stood
And view the landscape oer;
Not Jordan's stream, nor death's cold
     flood,
Should fright us from the shore.*
That's all very well. But we can't climb
where Moses stood. It might have been
better, in fact, if he'd insisted on getting
God to come down the mountain to
deliver the Ten Commandments, instead
of Moses going up. At least he wouldn't
have been able to look over the
Jordan from the West to the Promised
Land if he'd been at ground level.

The upshot is that all of Jordan west
of the River Jordan has been, since the
1967 Arab/Israeli war, part of Israel.

The effect

Losing the West Bank to Israel was a
disaster for Jordan for two reasons. In
the first place, although the West Bank
is only 6 per cent of Jordan's territory, it
supports 50 per cent of its agriculture.
Or it did. In addition the west of the
river is more sophisticated and
westernised. Which is why Jordan
annexed it in 1948, when it was
Palestine. Losing it, Jordan lost its two
main sources of income — agriculture
and tourism.

By contrast, the east bank is mostly
desert, in the east of which Bedouins
roam, and the chief product is sand.
This part was, until World War One,
under the slothful rule of the Turkish
Empire and remained undeveloped.

The inevitable casualty from the heat in the
Jordanian pilgrims' passing out parade.

Israeli annexation meant the
beginning of the end of Arab
(Palestinian) residence there.

They were driven out and went
to Jordan just across the river. There
were 700,000 refugees in 1966, an extra
350,000 in 1967 and today the total is
2 million.

Modern Jordan

King Hussein installed a constitutional
monarchy with representational
government. In other words, he
appoints the prime minister and
political parties are banned. The senate
of 30 is also appointed by him.

But his greatest diplomatic efforts
have been on behalf of the Palestinians
(and for his lost territory) and as long as
the refugees stay, Jordan will be a
'Middle-eastern trouble-spot'.
*Swing low sweet chariot —
Comin' for to carry me home;
I looked over Jordan and what did
I see?
A band of angels comin' after me —
Comin' for to carry me home.*
This negro spiritual encapsulates
exactly what Jordan doesn't need — a
load of American negroes arriving on
their doorstep having been kicked out of
the Promised Land next door.

Population: 2 and a quarter
million

Size: Just over a third that of
Britain, 35,000 sq. miles

Government: Constitutional
monarchy

Official language: Arabic

Main religion: Islam

Capital: Amman

Currency: Dinar, fils

Tips for tourists

Go in a hurry. Jordan has the
lowest crime rate in the world.

Visit Petra — a city carved out of
stone by the Nabataeans.

Greet older men 'My uncle' —
younger ones 'My son'.

It is easy to learn the words of
their songs. They love to repeat
themselves *Ahlan, ahlan, wa
Sahlan, Ahlan ahlan, wa Sahlan*.
Also after each couplet the
singer goes *Ooooooooof* for 15-75
seconds.

Eat their great gift — the
Pistachio nut.

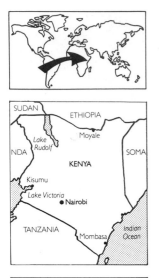

Kenya

Jamhuri ya Kenya

The population

Kenya is a huge zoo. The humans are crammed into a small part in the south. The rest of the country is occupied by lions, cheetahs, elephants, buffalo, rhinos, zebras, antelopes, gazelles, crocodiles, baboons, monkeys, snakes (including the mamba, cobra, puff adder and python) and birds (including ostrich, storks, eagles, vultures, weavers, hornbills, flamingoes, pelicans and herons).

This wild life attracts the main form of human life — tourists. More come here than to any other African country. They are wasting their time if they look for the tallest animal ever found. He was a giraffe who was sent to the Chester zoo in 1959 and christened George.

Kenya, Shmenya

The capital, Nairobi, was founded in 1900 as a railway siding. This is not as demeaning as it sounds. In those days, when Europeans were colonising East Africa, Kenya was little more to them than a railway route from the mineral riches of neighbouring Uganda to the east coast.

The territory was being fought over by other European powers, but the British shunted the French and Germans into sidings and then thought they might as well get some passengers to settle there. But no one wanted to, so the Colonial Office suggested to the infant Zionist movement that it might found a Jewish colony in Kenya. The offer was not accepted.

Kenya became independent in 1963, the new state consisting of the old East African colony of Kenya plus the mainland dominions of the Sultan of Zanzibar.

Jomo washes whiter

The outstanding political figure has been Jomo Kenyatta. Early in life he ran away to school and changed his name to Kenyatta, which is Kikuyu for 'fancy belt' (he always wore one). In 1924 he led a rebellion against the British of members of the Kikuyu tribe, Kenya's biggest. Thirty years later he was still at it and was thrown into prison by the British when the Mau-Mau rebellion broke out. This was marked by atrocities on both sides. During the eight-year state of emergency, 15,000 Africans were killed and 80,000 sent to prison camps.

On independence, Kenyatta became the country's first president under the

A government campaign to frighten big-game hunters.

slogan *Harambe* (which means 'pulling together'). When he died in 1978 his family owned vast plantations and controlled the trade in precious stones, casinos and various other industries.

Oginga Odinga

Kenyatta's first vice-president was Oginga Odinga. He resigned after a couple of years to form his own party. Kenyatta promptly had him arrested. On his release, Odinga tried to stand in the next elections, but was barred. The elections after that, he *was* allowed to stand. However, the elections were suspended.

Sex and violence

Kenya has the world's highest birth rate and the world's highest rape rate (three times higher than the United States). Neither of these is blamed on porn movies but on a certain tribal fetish: women are *supposed* to resist, so the men can't work out if they are willing or not.

Kenya has the world's lowest rates for suicide and car accident deaths. It has East Africa's largest and best-equipped police force.

Tea and a chat

Surprisingly Kenya is the biggest supplier of tea to Britain, which is the world's largest tea buyer. The other important crop is coffee. Most of Kenya's industries are controlled by foreign investment. Kenya is the world's major producer of pyrethrum, an insecticide made from chrysanthemum leaves.

Much of Kenya's trade used to be run by Asians, but in 1967 thousands were forced to leave as part of a policy of 'Africanisation'. About 75 different languages are spoken here. Although there are more than 9,000 schools, education is not compulsory and literacy among adults is 75 per cent. Kenya was the first British colony to have a regular radio service (it started in 1928).

Population: 18 million

Size: 2 and a half times that of Britain, 225,000 sq. miles

Government: Republic

Main language: Swahili

Main religion: Christianity and traditional beliefs

Capital: Nairobi

Currency: Kenya shilling, cents

Tips for tourists

Visit the Great Rift Valley, the appropriately-named place where some anthropologists believe the human race began.

Look for the oldest human footprint. It was found at Lake Turkana and is about 1 and a half million years old.

Behave yourself. Tourists have recently been accused of encouraging prostitution, homosexuality and drug trafficking, and corrupting youth. A Code of Conduct has been proposed by the Minister of Water Development.

When members of the Masai tribe die, they are laid out in the open with a clump of grass in one hand and a pair of sandals in the other. This way, they are ready for the next journey.

Don't be offended if a member of the Masai tribe offers you a handful of grass. It shows he wants to make a pact with you.

Kiribati

Position

Kiribati is the Gilbert part of the former British colony of the Gilbert and Ellice Islands. Because their verbal range is restricted by an alphabet of only 13 letters, the inhabitants' closest approximation of Gilbert is *Kiribas*. The islands consist of 30 coral atolls sitting in one million square miles of Pacific Ocean and stretch 700 miles from north to south and 2,000 miles from east to west. This causes certain central governing difficulties so the bulk of the islanders are concentrated on Bhutaritari, Abaiang, Tarawa and Abemama.

Missionary position

From the first contacts with Europeans, the islanders have had to put up with marauding missionaries. They came ostensibly to convert the population from barbaric practices such as tatooing to something more sensible and spiritually rewarding like genuflecting, crossing themselves and blowing incense all over the place. They would have been better employed converting the other Europeans who visited the islands — whalers. These people sold the natives guns and drink, and used their women for sex. Quite often they deserted to the islands, or were simply abandoned there by their ships to avoid paying them.

In 1917, the missionary position officially was, *Gilbertese women must wear drawers*. This was strange as the native women had a passion for going bare-breasted but a total horror of complete nakedness. Pre-marital sex is generally OK here and, in a dispute with the United States over Canton Island, Great Britain compounded this obsession with sexual matters by calling the island *the nudist amongst atolls*.

Stripped bare

In the late 1970s, phosphate from Banaba or Ocean Island accounted for 90 per cent of Kiribati's exports. Today it has been exhausted. In the process of mining, however, more and more of the island was eroded away, as so much of it turned out to be phosphate. The population moved into smaller and smaller enclaves until the name Ocean Island began to have some unpleasantly realistic undercurrents. As the island shrank, Chinese labour was brought in to wear it away faster.

In the 1920s the local population exploded into spectacular riots against the ubiquitous Chinese. In 1980 it was finally decided that phosphate, let alone human life, was untenable on Banaba Island and the population has been removed to another island where their roots may be able to go deeper. A vicar received handsome compensation for the loss (over £7 million) which he is to use to better their life elsewhere.

Not coconut shy

Nothing will grow properly on Kiribati apart from coconuts. The islanders have to make do with them for everything. Even the small amount of soil is made from mashed coconuts. The people drink coconut milk, make their houses out of coconut fronds, weave their mats from coconut fibre, use them to make boats and liquor, and, of course, eat them. Perhaps the most ingenious use was encountered by Europeans — as they stepped off their ships. It was coconut armour — made from coir, which is the coarse fibre from the coconut husk. It is surprisingly hardwearing — or was until the introduction of firearms.

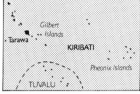

Population: 59,000	
Size: 264 sq. miles	
Government: Republic	
Language: English, Gilbertese	
Religion: Christianity	
Capital: Tarawa	
Currency: Australian Dollar	

Tips for tourists

Visit Betio, the sight of the worst Second World War Pacific fighting. There is still a huge hardware graveyard.

Stay at the Captain Cook Hotel, Christmas Island. The most un-Christmas-like food, shrimps are exported all over the world from the island.

American scientists have described a manganese find on the sea-bed as 'the best manganese nodule field in the world'.

Don't go for the breathtaking views. The islands are only 12 feet high.

Not much is left now of Banaba Island.

CHINA

NORTH KOREA

Heungnam

Wonsan

Pyongyang

Yellow Sea

SOUTH KOREA

Population: 19 million

Size: Half that of Britain, 47,000 sq. miles

Government: Communist

Language: Korean

Religion: Buddhism, Confucianism, Shamanism, Chondogyoism

Capital: Pyongyang

Currency: Won, jun

Tips for tourists

Don't bother travelling by train. The Japanese built many rail lines, but most of them don't go anywhere.

Don't bother listening to the radio. Radios are issued by the government and their dials are fixed so that they can receive little more than the speeches of Kim Il Sung.

Don't mention the Japanese. When they ruled the country (1910 to 1945) they even banned the Korean language.

North Korea

Chosun Minchu-chui Inmin Konghwa-guk

North Korea is synonymous with one man: General Kim Il Sung. He led the fight against the Japanese, led the North against the South and still leads the people of the People's Democratic Republic. Thanks to the *Seoul Shinmoon* newspaper, we have this description of the 'Sun of the Nation': *'Sunburnt brown complexion, short, modern-style hair, gentle, double-lidded eyes, dimples appearing when he smiles...though not piercingly sharp, his eyes flash sometimes when he turns his head right and left, a feeling of vitality hovering around his eyebrows.'*

Sung

The life of Kim Il Sung is chronicled in the most sycophantic biography ever written (2,000 pages, author: Baik Bong). Thus we know that the great man's father was *'Broad-minded, open-hearted, beloved by all'* and his mother *'steamed rice for many revolutionaries'*.

We also learn of the most touching moment in North Korea's history — when the General was reunited with his 'white-haired' grandmother after World War Two. She said *'Oh, you're back at last. Am I dreaming or waking?...How glad your father and mother would be in their graves.'*

According to this book, Kim Il Sung has spent most of the past 40 years giving *'on-the-spot guidance'* to workers at power stations and *'discussing draft resolutions at the Third Enlarged Meeting of the Executive Committee of the Party Central Organising Committee.'*

In fact, Kim *is* the Party, which *is* North Korea. (In the 1962 election, there was a 100 per cent turnout and 100 per cent vote for the Party). The

General's deputy is Kim Jong Il. He is the General's son and designated successor.

Sing

The national anthem is *'The Song of General Kim Il Sung.'* The chorus goes (all together now):
O dear is the name, our believed General!
O glorious is the name, General Kim Il Sung!

Allegro

Under Kim's guidance, something called *Pyongyang speed* has been established in North Korean industry. This enables, for example, a flat to be built in 14 minutes. However, this does not seem to have been translated into national prosperity. North Korea's growth rate is only a tenth that of its southern neighbour and its people's income little more than half.

Language

The Korean alphabet (Hangul) has 10 vowels and 14 consonants. This does not mean it is easy to learn. For example: *abojiga oje segumul naesiossumnida* means 'father paid his taxes today' (an important sentence in North Korea).

Religion

Even communism has not been able to wipe out the powerful hold of the various Korean religious cults. But then, Karl Marx was never a match for the great Korean philosopher Li Yi. He solved the neo-Confucianist soul-body problem like this:
One at the same time two, but not two.
Two at the same time one, but not one.

Primitive dredging methods have made it possible for ocean-going dinghies to get up-river.

South Korea
Han Kook

Smiling

South Korea is a land of smiling workaholics. They work to make their country one of the world's great economic successes. They smile because they are told to.

When it was announced that South Korea is to host the 1988 Olympics, the Home Ministry decreed 'a series of guidelines to reform the atmosphere and environment of the nation' in preparation for the great event. Citizens were advised to always wear a smile, greet everybody and to show thanks often. They were asked to clear the ground outside their houses, stand patiently in queues and to always look neat.

They were also told to stop profiteering, selling shoddy goods and dropping cigarette butts in the street. The Ministry decided to remove unseemly stores, including 'dog or snake soup shops', from main streets.

Law

Among the recent laws enacted are:
The Emigration (Amendment) Law. This encourages the deaf, dumb and blind to leave the country.
The Welfare for the Aged Law. This promotes 'respect for the elderly and honouring one's parents' by giving to the elderly half-price bus fares and reduced admission to ancient places.

Culture

The first Korean movie was *Righteous Revenge* (1919). It was designed to be combined with a stage play. The first full-length feature was *Oath under the moon* (1923). Now the most popular films are James Bond movies. The biggest home-made success of recent years was *Once again, Though hateful (or Please don't leave me) '80* (1980). Late-night movies have only just come to South Korea. A midnight 'til 4am curfew, imposed at the end of World War Two, was only lifted in 1982.

Religion

This is confusing. In a typical family, women will be Buddhists and men Confucians. But there are scores of other religious cults. These include:
Chondo-gyo — this believes that just as a child must grow in the mother's womb, so must Korea grow in the faith of Hanunim (Heavenly God). The religion's founder, Choe-Je-u was executed in 1866 for 'distorting the true ways and disturbing the right way'.

Taejong-gyo — this believes that Hwang-ung, son of Hanunim, descended on 3rd October 3457 (Heaven Opening Day) and established 2,000 communities.
Wonbul-gyo — 'Round Buddhism' — started in 1924 as a Buddhist research society, now with a million followers.

An early version of a cheap Korean space shuttle.

History

From 1392 until 1910, Korea was ruled by the Yi dynasty. We know quite a bit about life under the Yi's thanks to the autobiography of Han Joong Nok, a Crown Princess who lived in the 17th Century. Although not born a royal (her mother '*covered her window with cloth to avoid compliments about her diligence*') she was married at the age of ten to the Crown Prince. Unfortunately, he was later starved to death in a rice-chest by his father, the king. (This was an act of kindness. The prince had gone mad and taken to travelling to the palace through the sewers). A typical day in the king's life would start with him performing a sacrifice before the tablet of Confucius, after which he would '*personally administer the High Civil Service Examination to students*'.

Population: 40 million	
Size: Less than half that of Britain, 38,000 sq. miles	
Government: Republic	
Language: Korean	
Main religions: Animism, Buddhism, Confucianism	
Capital: Seoul	
Currency: Won	

Tips for tourists

Don't go looking for a husband or wife. Almost all adult Koreans are married.

See the Nakhwa-am cliff at Puyo: 3,000 palace ladies reputedly threw themselves to their deaths off it to avoid a fate worse than death from invading forces.

Don't mention communism. The school curriculum includes compulsory courses in anti-communism and communism criticism.

Get lit up. Korea has the world's largest deposits of tungsten, used for electric light-bulb filaments.

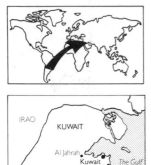

Kuwait
Dowlat al Kuwait

Population: One and a half million

Size: 7,000 sq. miles

Government: Constitutional monarchy

Language: Arabic

Religion: Islam

Capital: Kuwait

Currency: Dinar, fils

Tips for tourists

Feel safe. Kuwait has one of the lowest crime rates in the world.

Be careful of the camel spider. For its size it has the most powerful jaws of any creature.

Tourists from the third world are particularly welcome. From a population of one million people, Kuwait provides one billion dollars in third world aid.

Richer than Croesus

Kuwait is the richest country in the world. And it has no income tax. On average every Kuwaiti earns £9,000 a year. They have a £5 billion oil revenue (which is half the revenue of 1981) and their foreign assets alone earn £5 billion in interest — enough to fund all government spending. Government spending is large because there is one of the best free health services in the world and education is free. Not just tuition but books and even uniforms.

The government puts a large proportion of the country's revenue into future investment for its sons and they can produce the same amount of oil annually for the next 200 years. They are the world's third largest producer. Kuwait provides 99 per cent of its own fish. The rest is smoked salmon imported from abroad.

Government

The Arabs of Kuwait have a tradition of democracy. At the turn of the century, at *majlis* (desert courts) rulers would receive any of their subjects personally in order to air their grievances.

Today there is rule by consensus. In the words of an Arab nationalist about the country's regime, *"We are happy not to be in gaol and they are happy nobody is going to kill them."* But consensus has many different shades. For a start only 40 per cent of the population are Kuwaitis — the rest are Palestinians and Shia Moslems who have arrived in the country since 1948. These people have no vote.

But majlis are majlis and the Emirs of Kuwait ensure that there is no challenge to their supremacy. They are the al Sabah family and take the major positions of power — Prime Minister, Deputy Prime Minister, Ministers of Defence, the Interior and Oil.

With fewer than half a million people entitled to the vote, however, competition is fierce. Each vote counts. The 1975 elections were termed by cynics *'the Sheep Elections'* — because of gifts of sheep to win votes. The onward march of the 20th Century made sure that the 1981 elections were called *'the Video Elections'*.

History

The British moved in on Kuwait in the last century when the Ottoman Empire began to lose its grip. British troops fought off an Iraqi invasion earning a long-lasting friendship between the two

countries. When Sheikh Mubarak repaid British generosity by remaining neutral in World War One the British thanked him in return. They invited him to London and took him to London Zoo.

Apart from oil, Omar Sharif is the greatest gift of the Arabs to West.

Spare time

Kuwaitis are fanatical about football, ice-skating and the Muppets. They have begun a major series in Arabic of the Muppets as educational television. Some of the Muppets have been altered to look more like Arab Muppets.

Folk dancing is another popular entertainment. There are 15 troupes and the women's *freasah* dance is the most spectacular. Women dress up as men and re-enact going into battle with their husbands. As office hours end at 1pm there is a lot of time to amuse themselves. Their first all-Kuwait-made film — *The Cruel Sea* — won the Best Film Award at the Venice Film Festival.

Otherwise, there's only swimming in chilled swimming pools, water sports and camel racing.

Laos

History

The man who founded this country would not think much of it now. He was Prince Fa Ngum, the great warrior who united it 600 years ago with the help of erudite Buddhist monks and sculptors. He called it Lanxang, the Land of a Million Elephants. The elephants have disappeared now. And so has just about everything else.

By the middle of the 18th Century the country was utterly divided. French colonists moved in at the turn of this century only to be kicked out by the Japanese in 1941.

In 1953 civil war began. The French were quickly beaten leaving the battle between the rebel Pathet Lao (backed by North Vietnam, which borders on Laos), and the Royal Lao Government (backed by the U.S., which doesn't). For 20 years it raged, punctuated by a series of coups and counter-coups — like the one in 1960 which was unsuccessfully led by Colonel Kong, who fortunately did not then declare himself King.

During 1970, in an attempt to block the Ho Chi Minh trail to South Vietnam, the Americans dropped 2 and a half million tons of bombs on Laos, making it the most heavily bombed country in history. Prince Fa Ngum must have turned in his grave.

The Laos Ballet Company suffers from a chronic lack of space.

Politics

The war ended in 1973 with both sides agreeing to join in a coalition government. Within two years the Pathet Lao had taken over the whole country. King Savang Vatthana abdicated and the People's Democratic Republic of Laos was proclaimed. Prince Fa Ngum must have turned in his grave.

The Central Committee is still essentially the old Pathet Lao gang. Only the name has been changed to protect the guilty. They like name changes. They have also been called the Patriotic Front of Laos and the Front for the Reconstruction of the Motherland.

Geography

Laos is roughly the shape of an atomic explosion. There is no railway and few roads. The Chinese were building a road in the north but got thrown out in 1979. It was discovered they were really building trenches and firing posts so they could invade. The chief means of transport is by the River Mekong.

The people

There are 68 ethnic groups, the main ones being: *The Lao-Lum* (meaning Lao who live in the valley) are the biggest group and are Buddhists. *The Lao-Theung* (Lao of the mountain-sides) live in many tribes and worship spirits. *The Lao-Soung* (Lao of the mountain-tops) worship Confucius, spirits and Christ, in roughly equal proportions. *The Lao-Tai* which includes groups like Black Tai and Red Tai, so-called because of the way their women dress.

There are few towns in Laos and only 30 doctors. Almost every village has a pagoda and supports at least one Buddhist monk. Confusion surrounds the level of literacy. It has certainly improved since the 1975 Communist takeover but the government's claims seem a bit far-fetched. They boast that in 1978 alone 2 million people learned to read (out of a population of 3 and a half million).

Industry

Laos is one of the poorest countries in the world and getting even poorer faster than any other. It is so poor it can't even afford coins — it just has paper money. Not surprisingly, the currency is the world's weakest. Nine out of ten people work on the land, mainly growing rice. An attempt has been made to go into the opium business, with limited success.

There are a few puny industries producing things like rubber sandals, plastic bags, matches and ice. Plus a growing beer industry, probably inspired by the area called the Plain of Jars.

The major occupation outside agriculture is the army. Laos has one of the largest in the world for the size of its population. And there are almost as many North Vietnamese troops stationed there. Laos has four river squadrons and three quarters of a million buffalo.

Population: 3 and a half million

Size: About the same as Britain, 91,400 sq. miles

Main religion: Buddhism

Language: Lao

Government: Communist

Capital: Vientiane

Currency: Kip and att

Tips for tourists

Don't bother taking an electric razor or hair curlers. Few places here have electricity.

Take an umbrella. Parts of the south have more than 150 inches of rain a year.

Disco dancing is out. Dancing is a profession here, not a pleasure. Professional troupes travel the country performing at religious festivals and so on. All the dancers are male — boys perform the female roles.

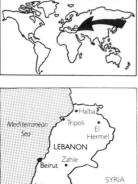

Population: 3 million

Size: 4,000 sq. miles

Government: Republic

Language: Arabic

Religion: Christian, Islam

Capital: Beirut

Currency: Lebanese pound

Tips for tourists

Out on bail? Don't worry. You'll feel at home here. The Lebanon has the world's worst crime rate.

Out of your mind? Then you'll believe the Lebanese Tourist Board's claim that their country is the Switzerland of Asia.

Lebanon

al-Jumhouriya al-Lubnaniya

For a fifth of its existence Lebanon has been ravaged by civil war. Which is eight years ravaging. Independent from the French in 1944, Lebanon's problems started in 1975, long after those of most pre-colonial states. The reasons for its early success are the same as those which in 1975 brought catastrophe. For, historically, Lebanon has been the home of ethnic minorities, different religions and dissidents from abroad. The resulting rich mixture had by 1970 made the land the biggest financial centre in the Middle East. But it also led to the falling out of several sections of the population.

French kiss

After a lingering bye-bye from the French in 1944, Lebanon became one of the world's smallest states — just 135 miles long and 30 miles wide. But its size belies the vastness of its history and experience. Some of the world's oldest human settlements dating from 3000 BC are to be found within its boundaries — Tyre, Sidon and Byblos. The history of the country involves the attentions of Phoenicians, Greeks, Byzantines, Crusaders and Arabs.

The famous cedars themselves are 956 years older than the country and have inspired poets: *exalted among all the trees in the field,* and Empresses — Queen Victoria ordered a wall to be built around the main grove to protect them. They are now the national emblem.

Healthy, wealthy and wise

By 1970 commercial prosperity had brought Lebanon the highest standard of living in the Middle East. It had the greatest number of doctors per head of population and the highest literacy rate. It was said that anything you could buy anywhere could be bought in Beirut.

Moslem women are forbidden to look upon cars.

There was 12 per cent tax: the agricultural half of the population produced only 11 per cent of the revenue. Appropriately in a country whose very name means 'white' *(labon),* the laundering of foreign money was a beautifully organised business. The country's decadence made Beirut 'the movie capital of the world'. But the most horrifying side-effect, perhaps, was the huge increase in the amount of journalists. With 40 daily papers, none of them owned by Rupert Murdoch, and six TV stations, Lebanon became a 'nation of journalists'. The population listened to more radios and watched more TV's than any other in the Near East.

Religion

Lebanon is the only Arab country not predominantly Muslim. There are *Christians:* Maronites, Greek Orthodox, Greek Catholic, Armenian Orthodox, Armenian Catholic, Syrian Catholic, Syrian Orthodox, Latin Catholic, Protestants, Chaldeans and *Jews:* 1000 approximately, as well as the *Muslims:* Sunnites (Orthodox), Shi'ite (Meterodox), Druzes (offshoot of Shi'ite).

Politics

There is sectarian apportioning in all forms of government. The president must be a Maronite. The premier must be a Sunni. The speaker must be a Shi'ite. And the seats are similarly apportioned. In this way Lebanon by 1970 became the only democracy in the Middle East. Behind the scenes, however, Muslims and Christians were not happy, Sunni and Shi'ite were tense and the Druze or Lebanese Left steered clear of all others. An unhappy calm existed until the Palestinians, mainly evicted from Jordan, started to arrive in 1970.

Catharsis

Lebanon became more complicated to understand than a plot by Frederick Forsythe is easy. Christians fought Palestinians who in turn were supported by 35,000 troops from Syria. The Israelis, encouraged by Bashir Gemayel's Christians, pulled several highly successful stunts — bombing Beirut, provoking the Palestinians, and being provoked and, finally, invading — thus ending Palestinian influence in the country. This now leaves two foreign armies in Lebanon. And the United Nations.

Lesotho

Life is hard in Lesotho, but death is easy. Its murder rate is the highest in the world — seven times greater than in the next ranking country (the Bahamas). Not surprisingly, it has proportionately more widows than anywhere else.

It is the ghetto of southern Africa — a hostage state completely surrounded by South Africa, on which it relies for access and just about everything else (except murderers). It has the highest low point on earth, nowhere being less than 4,350 feet above sea level. Despite the constant attrition of population by murder, disease, starvation and emigration, Lesotho remains desperately overcrowded. It makes life in Harlem and Watts seem relatively pleasant.

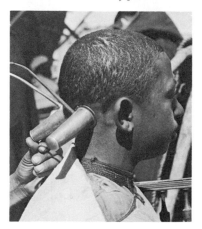

Sixth sense among some tribal peoples is due only to eyes in the back of their heads.

History

Death has always been a way of life here. The Zulus wiped out most of the inhabitants early last century, the few survivors taking refuge in the mountains. They asked for the protection of a local chieftain, King Moshoeshoe, who became paramount chief of the kingdom of Basutoland (later Paramount chiefs lived in Hollywood).

When the Boers (Dutch colonists) tried to finish what the Zulus had started, the British gave protection to Basutoland, which became independent in 1966, changing its name to Lesotho.

Politics

The political system is rather like that of Britain in the Middle Ages. Authority is firmly exercised in a system of chieftaincy extending from the paramount chief (i.e. the king) through senior chiefs (lords), subchiefs (barons), headmen (squires) and subheadmen (sheriffs). There is even an African equivalent of the House of Lords. The College of Chiefs settles disputes between chiefs, and rules on cases of inefficiency, criminality and their own absenteeism. (If this still happened in Britain the House of Lords would soon be empty).

None of this fondness for tradition has allowed Lesotho to escape the problems of a modern African state. The first election was won by Chief Leabua Jonathan who had to arrest the king to make him accept the new government. The second, in 1970, was won by the opposition party, so Chief Jonathan locked up his successful opponents, arrested the king (again), suspended the constitution and banned all newspapers (except his own). As well as staying on as Prime Minister, Chief Jonathan became Chief of State, Minister of Defence and Chief of Internal Security. This has kept him too busy to write a new constitution, although parliamentary rule has been re-introduced.

Industry

The main exports are wool (there are more sheep than people), mohair (there are almost as many goats), diamonds and people. Nearly half the workforce leaves — the highest proportion of any country. They go to South Africa in search of a better life.

For those who remain the principal occupation is still subsistence agriculture. They can't even join the army to escape — there isn't one. Life is no better for their animals. Three-quarters of the cattle die each year. Progress for the natives is replacing the thatched roofs on their huts with corrugated iron.

Discrimination

As well as income tax *and* a graded tax on wage earners, all adult males are taxed. To make matters worse (for males) there are more girls than boys in school as the latter have to work as herdsboys. Nevertheless Lesotho has the highest literacy rate in Africa. The schools are run by missionaries.

Travel

Good news: Lesotho has a railway.
Bad news: It is only one mile long (it runs from the capital, Maseru, to the South African border).

Population: 1 and a quarter million

Size: One-eighth that of Britain, 11,700 sq. miles

Government: Monarchy

Languages: Lesotho and English

Main religion: Christianity

Capital: Maseru

Currency: Loti and lisente

Tips for tourists

Be careful of dropping off at the leper colony near Maseru.

Don't get too involved in tribal initiation ceremonies. The high spot is circumcision.

Don't be fooled by the country's publicity. Lesotho is presently being promoted as *The South African Switzerland.*

Welsh visitors are especially welcome. Choir singing is very popular.

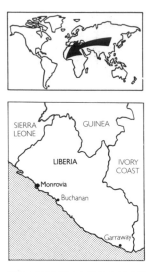

Liberia

Liberia is the most unequal country in the world. Five per cent of the population gets 60 per cent of the income. This is not what was planned when Liberia was founded in the mid 19th Century by the American Colonisation Society as a home for freed American negro slaves. It's the oldest republic on the African continent and the only black African state never to have been subjected to colonial rule. The black Africans who were already living there when the state was founded didn't notice the difference, however. By 1930 the Government (all ex-slaves) was itself being accused of slavery.

Black magic

The Americo-Liberians still number only about 50,000 but until 1980 managed to keep the one and a half million African Liberians out of power by the simple expedient of denying them the vote. The native Liberians seem to have gone to extraordinary lengths to register approval of their own repression. In the 1928 election the President, Charles B. King was returned to office with a majority of 234,000 votes. The total electorate was then less than 15,000.

Americanisation

The struggling new state was forced to seek foreign loans which compromised its independence. In 1926 the US monopoly, Firestone Tyres, took over one million acres of land for growing rubber. By 1970 all the natural resources of Liberia were controlled by foreign companies. In 1971 President Tolbert tried to negotiate a share of the profits from these companies. He was assassinated.

More Americanisation

The capital, Monrovia, is named after the American President James Monroe. Most of the money in circulation in Liberia is American notes and coinage. The University of Liberia has various schools and colleges with names like the *Mary Ann Cheeseman School of Home Economics* and the *Thomas J. R. Faulkner School of Engineering and Applied Science*. Seventy per cent of the population is illiterate.

Africanisation

President Tolbert's assassination in 1980 was part of a military coup led by Master Sergeant (later Commander-in-Chief) Samuel Doe who assumed the presidency. This marked the end of the political dominance of the Americo-Liberians. Doe suspended the constitution and banned all political parties, executing 13 former senior government officials.

Militarisation

Faced with a commitment to return to civilian rule by 1985, Doe has given all civilian ministers commissions in the army, producing total military rule. The Government is called the People's Redemption Council.

Everything these European women heard about size is confirmed.

Population

The main indigenous tribes in Liberia are the Kpelles, Bassas, Gios, Grebos, Kissis and Mandigoes. There are also the Vai tribe who, in the 19th Century, invented an alphabet which the Germans used for a code in World War II. There are two Mande tribes who are known by anthropologists as the Nuclear Mande and the Peripheral Mande. Many live in Bong County, in the Bong range of mountains.

Over half the workforce are employed on the rubber plantations, and a further 20 per cent in iron ore mines.

Shipping

Liberia has the largest merchant fleet in the world — 2,515 ships. Many countries register their ships here because Liberia maintains no control over the operation of ships flying its flag and requires only a small registration fee. Monrovia is the only free port in West Africa.

Population: 2 million

Size: 43,000 sq. miles

Government: Republic

Language: English

Religion: Christianity

Capital: Monrovia

Currency: Dollar

Tips for tourists

Watch out for monsoons.

Watch out for eight different kinds of poisonous snakes, crocodiles and scorpions.

Take confetti. Liberia has the world's highest marriage rate, more than twice as high as its closest rival, Guam.

There are no passenger railways and only 370 miles of made-up roads.

Leave your suitcase wheels behind — transport in the interior is by native porter — and go on a diet.

Libya

Al-Jamahiriyah Al-Arabiya Al-Libya Al-Shabiya Al-Ishtirakiya

Green fingers

In 1950 Libya was one of the poorest countries in the world. Its main export was grass. The average annual income was £20 and there was 95 per cent tribal rule with a king, Idris, at the head of a confederation of princes. There was no railway and the natural conditions of the place were among the most inhospitable in the world. 99 per cent of the country is the Sahara Desert with huge 'seas of sand'. On top of that there's the Surt and Libyan deserts. Just deserts. There are no rivers, only wadis, or temporary springs. In the Sabha region you will find the world's highest aridity and the seasonal 'ghibli wind' from the desert turns the sky red and reduces visibility to 20 yards. Why anyone lived here at all is a mystery: which is why Libya was the perfect place for hermits, dervishes and Tuaregs — a nomadic, hard-bitten desert tribe.

By 1969, Libya was the fourth largest oil producer in the world.

Greenbacks

At this point the ruling Senussi dynasts used the appliance of finance to bring them and their friends all the happiness they wanted. In 1969, 10 per cent of the population controlled well over half the country's income. For a while they enjoyed huge support from America. In 1959 Libya was the second largest recipient of American aid. But in 1969 Colonel Gadafy decided to re-distribute this happiness amongst the people and the king was overthrown. An attempted counter-coup in 1970 led by the Black Prince was quashed.

Green power

Since the Republic was founded, only four names have mattered — Gadafy, Gaddafy, Qadaffi and Gadaffy. He started what is called the Green Revolution. This has nothing to do with foliage. King Idris had, after all, planted 27 million trees between 1957 and 64. It was a redistribution of wealth and a political system which is indeed green on the international stage.

By 1981 Libya was generating £10 billion for its small population of three million people. A town like Augila in the desert, which was an oasis ten years ago, has now five schools, huge housing estates, four doctors and government-sponsored supermarkets. Libya now has the fastest growing population in Africa. Tribal systems have been banned, Italians, the previous colonists, deprived

Following their leader. Devotees look for hairs on the palms of their hands — the first sign of madness.

of citizenship, and a decree passed banning domestic servants — an incredible step for an Arab state. To back up his reforms Gadafy wrote a philosophy of government.

The green book

Confidently Gadafy calls his book, 'the final solution of the problem of the instrument of government'. Majority rule is unsatisfactory because some elements of society are left unrepresented. *But* 'the stronger must always rule'. 'He who produces is the one that consumes'. *Not* the Marxist 'to each according to his need'. Ties of blood and a national fanaticism are good for a nation. *But* 'they are bad for humanity'. Nevertheless Gadafy approves of them, a taste of fascism perhaps. The truth is, it is an extremely difficult book to understand — if possible at all.

Green hairs on the back of his hand

Many people think that Gadafy is mad. His old schoolfriend and colleague, Meheishi, finally described him as 'pathologically dangerous' and a despot. He makes no bones sponsoring terrorism — Carlos 'The Jackal', the IRA, Basques, Corsicans, Philippinos, Black September. Idi Amin was an old friend. The PLO are not pure or militant enough. He is crazy about gadgets — 300,000 exploding devices hidden in lamps, ash-trays and rock formations have been bought by him. It was rumoured that he wanted to be the first person to shoot down a 747. He keeps the highest soldier/civilian ratio in Africa. Is that mad? Is Meheishi right? Unfortunately, it is impossible to say as Meheishi is the one who has so far made it to a mental home.

Population: 3 and a quarter million

Size: Two and half times that of Texas, 700,000 sq. miles

Government: Communist

Language: Arabic

Religion: Islam

Capital: Tripoli

Currency: Dinar, millemes

Tips for tourists

Other inhabitants include: rodents, jackals, hyenas, skunks, wildcats, locusts and vultures.

No need to go thirsty in the desert anymore. Oceans of water numbering a quadrillion barrels have been discovered.

Best place to buy: CIA agents, weapons, an audience for your views on: assassinations, terrorism, Israel's destruction.

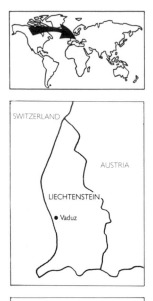

Population: 25,000

Size: 61 sq. miles

Government: Constitutional monarchy

Language: German

Religion: Roman Catholic

Capital: Vaduz

Currency: Swiss francs

Tips for tourists

If you want some false teeth, drop into the factory at Schaan. They make them there for export to 100 countries.

Look busy. There is no unemployment in Liechtenstein.

Liechtenstein

Geography

This tiny country is a big let-down for anyone who thinks that all of Europe's mini-states have the glamour of Monaco or the grace of the Vatican. Liechtenstein is little more than a 65 sq. mile factory — the world's most thoroughly industrialised nation. It nestles between Austria and Switzerland, but instead of concentrating its energy on folk singing or dancing, it beavers away producing goods for the consumer society. The industrialists haven't even been deterred by the problems of building factories up mountains (about two-thirds of the country is in the Alps).

History

On the 3rd May 1342 Count Hartmann III became ruler of the county of Vaduz. Over the next hundred years bits were added to the Hartmann domains until they reached the present boundaries.

Liechtenstein then consisted of two counties, Schellenberg and Vaduz, which were immediate fiefs of the Roman Empire. Around the start of the 18th Century the House of Liechtenstein got its hands on them and a few years later, thanks to the magnanimity of Emperor Charles VI, they became an independent principality. Since then, history has stood still.

Politics

Two of Liechtenstein's political parties are the Fatherland Union and the Progressive Citizens' Party. There are several others. This seems strange as its parliament (the Landtag) only has 15 members. These are elected by all males over 20. Women don't have the vote.

The country is ruled by a hereditary prince from the House of Liechtenstein. He can call and dismiss parliament.

Monarchy

The reigning prince is Francis Joseph II who succeeded his great uncle in 1938. He has a 400-year-old art collection which includes the world's largest private holding of Rubens paintings.

The national anthem, *Oben am jungen Rhein*, is sung to the tune of *God Save the Queen*.

Interbreeding is inevitable.

Industry

At the end of World War Two, three out of four Liechtensteiners worked in agriculture. Today less than one in 30 does. The rest are busy in the country's booming light industries.

The country's industrial success is all the more remarkable because it has no natural resources. All raw materials must be brought in. For more than 50 years it has been in a customs union with Switzerland.

Important facts

Liechtenstein has 152 goats, 101 horses and 38 policemen. There is no army.

Travel

There are 10 miles of railway and 100 of roads. The main method of public transport is by postal buses.

Luxembourg
Grand-Duche de Luxembourg

Identity

Like Wimpyburgers and Wendyburgers, Luxembourgers are almost unidentifiable. Which is why they call themselves 'Luxembourgeois': a name which doesn't inspire confidence in their individuality. Sure enough they are victims of incessant conquest and integration lasting hundreds of years. In 963 AD a man called Sigefroi built a castle in what was later to be called Luxembourg. It was the strongest castle in Europe next to Gibraltar. In 1351 Luxembourg was created the Duchy it almost is today. (Now it is a *Grand* Duchy).

The kingdom was independent until 1443 with such far-sighted rulers as John the Blind. Then it was conquered by Philip the Good of Burgundy — which was probably the last good thing that happened to this introverted little place. It passed through French and German hands (under Charles the Bold — who was so bold that he fell at the walls of Nancy). Then Spanish, French, Spanish, Austrian, French, Dutch. The Dutch gave them the Grand Dukedom and the same house (of Nassau) now rules both countries.

Genocide

The Luxembourgeois have devised a method of genocide so ingenious that it is no wonder foreign powers have now bowed out. The birthrate of the country is one of the lowest in the world. In 1976 the population actually *decreased* . The reason is that the Luxembourgeois has an exacerbated desire for prosperity — so great that he doesn't want to waste time and money on children.

Presumably a graph could be drawn to show exactly when the Luxembourgeois will die out altogether or leave, say, the richest man on the planet as the only survivor. And it wouldn't be that far away, because already 26 per cent of the total population is foreign.

Government

Since 1919 all adult citizens have been compelled to vote. They voted for a chamber of 56 people. Above this elected chamber is a Council of State which numbers 21. This Council has the power to postpone the enactment of bills by the elected chamber. Council members are chosen by the Grand Duke. You can see why it is a Grand Duchy.

Banking

Along with prosperity always comes banking in one form or other. The Luxembourgeois have jumped on the banking bandwagon. Between 1955 and 1977 the number of banks increased from 13 to 90. Savings increased by 775 per cent — almost in proportion to the decrease in the birthrate. Now Luxembourg is the host to the European Monetary Fund, the European Audit Office and the European Investment Bank. So austerity isn't a problem. In the next few years however, Luxembourg may find that the world recession starts to bite severely. Its natural mineral resources are declining, but wealth is still abundant. Luxembourg is second in the world in the number of large houses per head — the Falkland Islands are first.

Eggs are the only things to get laid in countries of declining population.

Population: 365,000

Size: 998 sq. miles

Government: Constitutional monarchy

Language: French

Religion: Roman Catholic

Capital: Luxembourg

Currency: Luxembourg franc

Tips for tourists

Don't think you can marry Marie-Astrid, Princess of Luxembourg, on the rebound from Prince Charles. She's already rebounded into the arms of another.

Keep off the road. There are more cars per head than any other EEC country and Luxembourg is third in the world for car accident deaths.

Don't turn on the radio. You're certain to hear Radio Luxembourg.

Go there at Christmas. The country gave Wenceslas to the world. He was a former king.

Drink as much as you want. Luxembourg is the top beer producer per head in the world.

Madagascar
The Democratic Republic of Madagascar

Population: 8 and three quarter million

Size: More than double that of Britain, a quarter of a million sq. miles

Government: Republic

Religion: Tribal beliefs and Christianity

Language: Malagasy

Capital: Antananarivo (Tananarive)

Currency: Malagasy franc

Tips for tourists

Avoid the *Valley of the Dead* and its surrounding mountains, the *Domain of All Past Ancestors*.

When visiting do not offend your host by entering his house against the circulation of the *vintana* (sense of fate). Thus, if coming from the north, do not walk straight down the west side of the house and come in at the door. Make a detour to come down the east side, around the end of the house, then up to the door from the south.

Superstition

Life in Madagascar is better for the dead than the living. It is a tangle of taboo, astrology, sorcery, superstition and a belief in fate. The dead are venerated. Tombs are built with more care than houses. Every few years they are opened and the bones inside are carried round town to be introduced to new members of the family. After a couple of days of feasting and merry-making the bones are re-wrapped in new silk shrouds and popped back to rest.

The people believe that days of the week have colours — Friday is red, Saturday blue and Tuesday is speckled, making it unlucky. In fact, the natives have identified 120 unlucky days in the year. Even on the un-unlucky days they take tremendous care. They almost always wear hats, never kick the walls of their homes, don't like the number eight and consult an astrologer before taking any important decision.

Other superstitious information: God is known as *The Fragrant One*, and a dozen varieties of witch are said to exist.

The Devil-Worshippers Eleven appeal for handball in a particularly cut-throat match.

Superstar

Christianity is also practised. Although much less exciting nowadays than witchcraft, it used to be a lot of fun when the missionaries first came, over 150 years ago. They and their converts were hurled to their deaths from the mountain-top palace of Queen Ranavalona, which she called *Where It Is Pleasant To Rule*.

After Roman Catholicism, the biggest Christian church is *Fianonan'i Jesosy Kristy eto Madagaskar*, which has a million followers and 5,161 churches.

Space and time

Madagascar has been described as the hyphen between Asia and Africa. It is the fourth largest island in the world and is covered with prairie grasses and bamboo trees, one of which — the travellers' tree — holds water in its trunk, like an elephant.

The first inhabitants came here not from Africa but Indonesia 3,000 miles away. The Portuguese discovered the island in 1500 AD and the French colonised it nearly 400 years later. It got its independence in 1960 since when there have been a series of coups.

The people

A mysterious bunch, quite apart from their strange beliefs. They have virtually no relations with nearby African states, still preferring to relate to Indonesia. They eat less eggs than anyone else in the world.

The people are divided into a number of tribes, one of which is named the *Inseparable Multitude*. Others are called *Those Who Do Not Cut Their Hair, People of the Thorn Bush, People of the Red Soil, People of the Sand, Those With Many Braided Hair* and *The Joyful People*.

There used to be three castes — nobles, freemen and the descendants of slaves. Now the joins only show on formal occasions like weddings and funerals.

The animals

If you think the people are strange, take a look at the animals. They are some of the weirdest in the world. There is the rarest animal anywhere, Fontoynont's hedgehog. Not to mention the tenrec, which produces litters of up to 32 young within three weeks of its own birth. Plus the world's rarest primate, the hairy-eared lemur. Lemurs like it here. It is their main home. (They are nocturnal relatives of the monkey with bright red eyes which they presumably get from staying up all night).

Four hundred of the island's butterflies are found nowhere else. Some have wings as big as a pigeon's. Chameleons grow bigger here than anywhere else.

Industry

There is almost none. Most people work on the land or rear cattle, which outnumber the people. The only thing Madagascar licks the world at is vanilla — it is its biggest producer.

Malawi

Small beginnings

Without emergent African states, it would be impossible to go from being a small-time doctor in London to leading a sovereign nation. But that's exactly what Dr. Hastings Kamuzu Banda has done. In the rich Western nations, it is enough to be a lawyer, doctor or priest. In Africa, the same people go further to become presidents for life. On July 6th 1971, seven years after 'independence' Dr. Banda was sworn in for life in this tiny African country where the chief hobby is drumming.

His mission

Taken from an interview with Doctor Banda by Douglas Brown in 1962:
Brown: Dr. Banda, what is the purpose of your visit to Great Britain?
Banda: Well, I've been asked by the Secretary of State to come.
Brown: Have you come here to ask the Secretary of State for a firm date for Nyasaland's independence?
Banda: Can't tell you that.
Brown: When do you hope to get independence?
Banda: Can't tell you that.
Brown: Dr. Banda, when you get independence are you as determined as ever to break away from the Central African Federation?
Banda: Need you ask me that question at this stage?
Brown: Well, this is as good a stage as any other stage. Why do you ask me why I shouldn't ask this question at this stage?
Banda: Haven't I said enough for any...everybody to be convinced that I mean just that?
Brown: Dr. Banda, if you break with the Central African Federation, how will you make out economically? After all your country isn't really a rich country.
Banda: Don't ask me that. Leave that to me.
Brown: Which way is your mind working?
Banda: Which way? Can't tell you that.
Brown: Where do you hope to get economic aid from?
Banda: Can't tell you that.
Brown: Are you going to tell me anything?
Banda: Nothing.
Brown: Are you going to tell me why you've been to Portugal?
Banda: That's my business.
Brown: In fact, you're going to tell me nothing at all?
Banda: Nothing at all.

Brown: So it's a singularly fruitless interview?
Banda: Well that's up to you.
Brown: Thank you very much.
Life with this man could be a very long time.

The president of Malawi tells his angry defence minister to leave his spear outside the Council Chamber.

Independence

Dr. Banda gained the country's independence through the good services of the MCP, or Malawi Congress Party. So at least he made no bones about it from the start. Nowadays he is known by government decree formally as,
Ngwazi
Saviour
Messiah
Moto
Perhaps his style is coloured by the fact that he spent 40 years in South Africa.

He subsequently fell out with other black African nations by making friends with the South Africans but he has always been confident of his own infallibility. Before independence he is quoted as saying, *"Leave all the trouble-making to me. I will do it with my tongue and brains".*

Other excesses

Malawi has a very high birth rate and hence population growth. It would be even higher but it also has a very high death rate. Between 1945 and 1966 the human population doubled and is expected to double again by 1985. In 1966 a twentieth of the population emigrated. Two-thirds of Malawi is Lake Malawi, formerly Nyasa.

Population: 6 million

Size: Half that of Britain, 45,000 sq. miles

Government: Republic

Language: English, Chichewa

Religion: Roman Catholic, Presbyterian, Islam

Capital: Lilongwe

Currency: Kwacha, tambala

Tips for tourists

Visit Blantyre, named after Livingstone's Scottish birthplace.

Do not ask the president's age. It is a capital offence. To satisfy your curiosity, he is believed to have been born in 1906.

Take plenty of pile cream. There are fewer chemists per size of population than anywhere except Zaire.

Tips for tourists

Don't call an itinerant labourer *padi*. That means 'rice'.

Don't think you can play space invaders. Video games are regarded as unhealthy. They have been banned and arcades closed.

Don't have anything to do with drugs. The Malays hang people for drug offences.

If you want to send a letter to the Lower Perak Malay Government Servants' Co-operative Thrift and Loan Society (*Syarikat Kerjasama Orang-Orang Melayu Kerajaan Hilir Perak Kerana Jimat Cermat Dan Pinjan-Meminjam Wang Berhad*, address: Teluk Anson, Perak), use their initials: S.K.O.M.K.H.P.K.J.C.D.P.W.B. — the longest of any organisation, according to the *Guinness Book of Records*.

Malaysia

Malaysia consists of two separate regions 400 miles apart. Four distinct ethnic groups live there. It has been invaded and/or ruled by the Indians, Portuguese, Dutch, Chinese, British and Japanese. Now it is governed by an elected sultan and a British-type parliament — after beating off Communist guerrillas.

Confused? You will be soon.

Geography

West Malaysia is a peninsula poking down off the end of Thailand. It is made up of 13 states, each with its own sultan, and used to be called Malaya. East Malaysia is stuck on top of Borneo and is divided into Sarawak and Sabah (formerly North Borneo).

Much of Malaysia is still covered with jungles, swamps and forests.

History

The Indians were the first to invade this area nearly 2,000 years ago. By the 15th Century the city of Malacca, founded by a displaced prince, was renowned for its splendour. When this news got through to Europe various adventurers made a dash for it. Portugal got there first and started 200 years of war, with individual states hopping from side to side.

Then the Dutch moved in and threw out the Portuguese. Then there was Chinese infiltration. Then Britain swapped the island of Sumatra for the Malay pensinsula. They got Sarawak and Sabah later in dubious deals with local sultans. The Japanese invaded during World War Two. When the war ended, the locals decided they had had enough of foreigners.

The new state of Malaysia was formed in 1963. Initially Singapore was part of it — but it left in a huff two years later.

Politics

The head of state is the *Yang di-Pertuan Agong* (meaning 'the supreme ruler'). He is elected from among the various sultans, holds office for five years and appoints the Prime Minister. The present Yang is HM Sultan Haji Ahmad Shah Al-Musta'in Billah Ibni Al-Marhum Sultan Abu Baker Ri'Ayatuddin Al-Mu'Adzam Shah, DKM, DKP, DK, SSAP, SPCM, SPMJ.

The parliamentary system is remarkably similar to Britain's. The ruling party is that of the Malacca Alliance which represents big landlords and their hangers-on — rather like the British Tory Party. The Communist Party is still outlawed.

The people

Malaysia is a melting pot of peoples, tongues and religions. There are four separate ethnic groups — the aborigines, Malays, Indians and Chinese. They have just one thing in common — they hate each other. These racial tensions are still the country's biggest problem.

The poorest people live in houses on stilts. The next step up (or down) are converted concentration camps. These were built during the war against the Communists after 1955. When hostilities ended the barbed wire was removed and the inhabitants stayed on.

To be an audio typist in Malaysia is the highest spiritual state that can be reached.

Health

It is much healthier to live in West Malaysia than East. The life expectancy is 64 compared with 55. Apart from the normal hospitals Malaysia has two institutions containing 2,688 beds for the treatment of Hensen's disease. This is so rare that it doesn't appear in any medical treatise. It must therefore be *a)* a disease confined entirely to Malaysia, or *b)* a fiction devised to rip off the health service.

Industry

Malaysia is the third richest country in Asia (after Japan and Singapore). Its success is built on rubber and tin — it is the world's biggest producer of both. The economy runs on a modified British free enterprise system — workers are exploited mercilessly. To deal with this there are 385 unions in West Malaysia alone, although their average membership is only 1,500.

Maldives
Republic of Maldives

Low life

There are 1,009 islands in the Maldives, of which 210 are inhabited. They are all coral atolls and the highest point on any of them is lower than any other nation's highest point. There are two cows, about 100 cars and the longest road is 10 miles long. One of the main sports on the islands is similar to tennis — but it is played with an eggplant instead of a tennis ball and the opposing players must have their backs to the net.

The Maldive Airline Company has one plane. It is owned by Sri Lanka.

The people

They are called Divehi, which means 'islander' and the language is also called Divehi. Tradition has it that they settled here from Sri Lanka. Maldive probably comes from *mala* — meaning 'garland' and *div* — meaning 'island'. Covered as they are with coconut trees, the islands indeed look garlanded.

One legend has it that a Sri Lankan hunter-king caught a man-beast in his net. He taught it to walk and read, upon which it married his daughter and so enraged the king that he exiled them both to the Maldives. The islands they found are still a paradise today. An indication of how unspoilt they are is that the Divehi language has no word for 'city', 'town' or even 'village'. There is nowhere the sound of the sea cannot be heard. Apart from playing with eggplants, the islanders entertain themselves by lifting large stones in competition and playing football with a ball made of leaves.

The fish

These are the staple of the people and make up 90 per cent of exports. The 'Maldive fish' is called *bonito* and provides the national dish, called *garudiya*. Instead of milk, they drink *rihakuru* — a strong fish liquid — and even wedding presents consist of fish.

Other foods are pintail birds. They catch these by wearing baskets on their heads and swimming slowly up to them. The birds think they are baskets and are caught.

Customs

The islanders, although of Muslim faith, still have fears of jinnis — or ghosts. They won't have windows in their homes for this reason.

Otherwise, they are an extremely prosaic race. Government officials who earn over 100 rupees must wear long

Accommodation in the Maldives wouldn't even get a one-star rating.

trousers, over 200 rupees a tie and over 500 rupees a coat — all in the sweltering heat.

Rarely do they marry from one island to another as it involves selling all their possessions and not being able to buy a house on their new island for 12 years. But divorce is common. In 1974, out of 100 people married, 84 were divorced — the highest rate in the world. A man can divorce his wife just by saying so. One man has divorced and re-married the same woman 81 times.

Favourite story

Stories are not common on the Maldives. The islanders are too lazy and indolent. But the favourite tells of a woman called Kamana who was extremely beautiful and refused the hands of a dozen suitors. One night she was lying on the beach when she was attacked by five men and raped. They then cut off her breasts and her vulva and threw her in the sea.

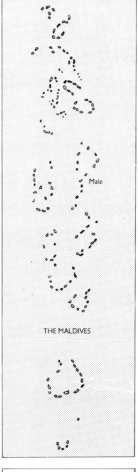

Population: 150,000

Size: 115 sq. miles

Government: Republic

Language: Divehi

Religion: Islam

Capital: Male

Currency: Rupee

Tips for tourists

Masturbation must be reported to the Attorney-General.

To get the love of another, you must bury a poem in the sand written on a young coconut, together with an iron stylus.

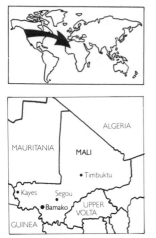

Mali
Republique du Mali

Remember the French Sudan? That's Mali. Just one of the many African countries that changed its name on independence to throw the old colonial powers off the scent. This tactic seems to have worked.

Timbuktu

No one's ever heard of the capital, Bamako, either. But we've all heard of Timbuktu, the town that symbolises the back of beyond and the middle of nowhere — a sort of African Kettering.

During the days of the Mali empire, in the Middle Ages, houses in Timbuktu were supposed to be roofed with gold. The Emperor of Mali, Mansa Musa, is said to have made a pilgrimage to Mecca in 1324 accompanied by hundreds of slaves and camels laden with gold. Timbuktu, built on a bend in the River Niger, was the terminus of the trans-Sahara caravan route. It was a thriving commercial town where Arabs from the North came to trade dates for slaves and gold from the South. For many explorers and adventurers over the next few hundred years it was also the end of the line. They perished crossing the Sahara in search of this fabled place. Those few who did make it found that the streets were paved with mud huts. Today the city is a shadow of that. Even the river has left. It suddenly altered its course and flows 13 miles further south.

Beyond Timbuktu

Half of Mali is the Sahara desert and the other half is the rich agricultural region of the Niger Valley. Over all it's a very poor country. In 1969, 250 children died for every 1,000 born. One measles outbreak had a mortality rate of 38 per cent. People here don't only work for peanuts — they even grow them, together with cotton. Other exports include live animals and fish. Mali is the cultural crossroads of West Africa but with only one railway, 400 miles long. It's land-locked so it is dependent on the good will of its neighbours for most forms of exit and entrance.

Legacy of the French

The French left in 1960. They'd only been in Mali since the turn of the century but managed to bequeath an education system in which all lessons are in French, although the majority of the population speak a variety of different tribal languages. Only 22 per cent of the children can face school.

Population: 7 million

Size: Twice that of Texas, 480,000 sq. miles

Government: Republic

Language: Maride, French

Religion: Islam, traditional beliefs

Capital: Bamako

Currency: Mali franc

Tips for tourists

If you are thirsty, visit the deepest well in the Southern Sahara, in the Azawad. It's over 300 feet deep.

Watch out for Tuareg (native tribesmen) well-diggers. They measure the depth of wells by the number of men who can stand in them upright with their arms stretched above their heads. (The Tuareg are a declining race).

Take contraceptives. The natives have the world's highest fertility rate.

If you can't stand the heat, stay out of Arovane. It's the world's hottest place, with temperatures reaching 130 degrees Fahrenheit.

Twig-gathering is a major platform for women's emancipation in Mali.

Politics

Within four years of independence the ruling party, the Union Soudanese, had stifled all opposition. Rapid inflation and hardship followed, and in 1968 there was the inevitable military coup led by Colonel Moussa Traore who until then had been passed over for promotion. As Brigadier General Traore he has not yet implemented his often declared programme of return to civilian rule.

Mali continues to suffer. A severe drought between 1972 and 74 led to accusations of misappropriation of the drought relief funds. France continues to give aid to Mali for fear that the country will fall into the hands of a power that might really help them, like Russia or Cuba.

Malta

Repubblika 'Ta' Malta

20th Century

Malta is a vast building site. Wherever you go, breeze blocks are being cemented into position in a huge building programme. They are made from the islands only mineral resource — globigerina limestone. This is a sad end to the once beautiful city Valletta, which has the best and most ingeniously defended harbour in the world, and which has served the country aesthetically and practically since the 17th Century.

From a time even before that, megalithic prehistoric temples at Mgarr and Skorba are an impressive example of architecture on a grand scale. They are the oldest free-standing structures in the world.

Life

The name Malta comes from either the Phoenician word for port, *malat*, or the Greek word for honey, *meli*. It is still a port and still has plenty of honey. Other culinary offerings are not so pleasant. It must be the greatest holiday resort in the world for people without taste buds. Even the wine — nearly as old as the temples — is disgusting.

The Maltese are manifestly unconvinced by their abilities to give tourists a good time. You can buy clothes at the *Intact Boutique*, take your car to be mended at the *Up to Date Garage* and buy sweets at the *Perfection Confectionery*. During the Nights of Malta you can go to the *Still Alive Bar*. Nevertheless twice as many tourists as the population visit every year.

Death

Because of Malta's prime position in the Mediterranean and subsequently on the route to the Suez canal, the island has always been the place for wars. When in 1530 the Knights of St. John took over the island and fortified it, the population could reasonably expect some period of calm.   But their fortifications only aroused the anger of the Ottoman sultan who besieged the city of Valetta in 1565 in one of the most cruel sieges in history. Disease, starvation and violent death could not deter the inhabitants. Even when their friends' heads were fired over the battlements by cannons, they kept *their* heads and, incredibly, won against vastly superior numbers.

This was nothing compared to World War Two however. Malta was one of the most heavily bombed places in the war because of its strategic importance. Its

only defence was three British planes, *Faith*, *Hope*, and *Charity*. The latter two were destroyed but the islanders still had Faith. Eisenhower claimed, *"Their gallant stand shortened the war by a year"* and they were awarded collectively the George Cross — the highest civilian award of the British Empire.

Our photographer has just made a Maltese cross.

Allegiance

Malta falls between Africa and Europe but is nearer Europe. It has a far higher population density than Africa (although its growth is very low). It's literacy is lower than Europe but higher than Africa. In the past ten years, oil money from Libya has poured in as aid. While Libya as a nation is far richer, income per person in Malta is higher. There are TV sets for 539 out of 1,000 people. In Libya the figure is 0.5 per 1,000.

Population: 360,000

Size: 120 sq. miles

Government: Republic

Language: Maltese, English

Religion: Roman Catholic

Capital: Valletta

Currency: Maltese pound

Tips for tourists

The principal folk festival is *Imnarja* — famous for folk singing contests and fried rabbit picnics.

The Valletta regatta is more fun than Henley.

Go to the *Mad Carnivals* in the summer.

Maltese is the only Semitic language written in Latin script.

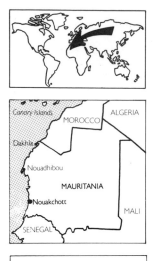

Tips for tourists

For an intimate evening out, try the movies. There are ten cinemas, each holding only 100 people.

For more excitement, try a public execution. These were revived in 1980. If you can't manage the full performance, you could watch thieves having their hands cut off (these are afterwards hung up so everyone can get a good look).

Travel: In the north, use camels. In the south, use oxen and donkeys. (Don't ask why — it's tradition). Don't plan to hire a motorbike — the Mauritanians have fewer of them than any people on earth.

Mauritania

Republique Islamique de Mauritanie

Dry information

They don't get many compliments about the scenery in Mauritania. It is amazingly flat and boring, consisting mainly of desert with a few mountains that would be called foot-hills in any self-respecting country. The man with the worst job in the place is Mohammed Ould Abby. He is director of the Green Belt Project.

This is how he got the job:
After independence in 1960, the government decided to convert a small trading post at Nouakchott into the country's capital. Being in the middle of the desert, it was convenient for hordes of people to abandon their nomadic life and settle there. Then the desert fought back. Drifting sand threatens to overrun the place. So Ould Abby has been given the task of planting a huge green belt of trees and shrubs around the capital to keep out the sand.

Nouadhibou became an important fish-drying centre in 1907. For the next 50 years, all its water had to be brought from France by tanker (it is now distilled from sea water).

The people

It must be hell being an estate agent here. Ninety per cent of the population is nomadic. They trudge around the desert with their animals (7 million sheep and goats), living in tents woven from sheep's wool.

Two-thirds of the population are Arabs and the rest negroes. The latter have become more educated than the Arabs who are suspicious of non-religious teaching. So the negroes have bagged most of the best jobs. This rankles with the Arabs.

The rankling doesn't stop there. Most of them should be moaning about their caste system, too. At the top of the Moorish society are the nobles. Then come the vassals who are protected by the nobles in exchange for tributes. Then there are the two artisan classes, blacksmiths and griots (who are a cross between musicians and genealogists). Finally, right at the bottom, come the servant classes. And below the bottom are the servants who are descended from slaves. It can't be much fun working below stairs in a tent in the desert.

Life expectancy is 36 for men and 39 for women. Only one in ten of the population can read. There are no daily papers. Slavery has been abolished three times this century. But it still exists.

History

When the French were spreading their culture through west Africa they stopped at the borders of Mauritania. It was too poor for them to exploit and too few people lived there for them to dominate with any feeling of satisfaction.

But early this century the Moors of the area made the mistake of carrying out a series of attacks. In retaliation the French went for a ramble on the Moors (they called it 'pacification').

Politics

The first president of this new republic was the ludicrously named Ould Daddah. He took his name literally and expected the people to treat him as a father figure (i.e. he abolished all political parties except his own).

As if he didn't have enough problems trying to govern a people who couldn't keep still for five minutes, he did something particularly silly in 1976. Spain withdrew from neighbouring Western Sahara and Ould Daddah claimed the southern bit of it for Mauritania. Not only did he get his wrists slapped by other African states, but he suddenly found his army of a few hundred men confronting hordes of bloodthirsty Moors from the new territory.

By 1977 military spending accounted for a third of Mauritania's budget. But increasing the size of the army didn't help. The Moors in it found they were fighting their long-lost cousins from Western Sahara and told Ould Daddah to get lost.

Recent political developments: the Military Committee for National Recovery has been abolished and replaced by the Military Committee for National Salvation.

Fouling the pavement is a capital offence.

Mauritius

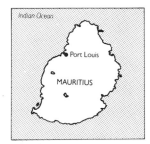

The British

The British threw French pirates off the island in 1810. Some of the British governors were more or less pirates themselves. The most famous was a man named Hook who also acted as treasurer but gave a poor performance. He dipped his hand into the national purse to the tune of £12,000. A witty man, when he was asked on his recall to England if he had left Mauritius for health reasons, he replied, *"They do say something is wrong with the chest"*. He was jailed but continued to amuse with his poetry:

*Let him hang with a curse this atrocious
    pernicious
scoundrel who emptied the till at
    Mauritius.*

Other governors were no more upright. One explained the mysterious loss of money from the treasury, saying it had been eaten by white ants.

No wonder the dodo became extinct on Mauritius.

The French

Although they were pirates for the most part, they were also good fighters in conventional warfare. Their navy at Mauritius achieved the only victory over the British in the Napoleonic Wars. They preyed mercilessly on the British trade routes to India.

The Dutch

They named the island Mauritius after Prince Maurice of Nassau in 1598.

The Portuguese

They discovered Mauritius in 1511.

The rest

Now the population consists of:
52 per cent Hindus
16 per cent Muslims
28 per cent Africans, French extraction (Creoles)
A few Chinese.

Since independence in 1968, the Labour Party has been in power. But in 1982 they didn't win *any* seats and government passed into the hands of the Mouvement Militent Mauricien. The island of Rodriguez maintains its own administration within the new regime.

The dodo

Mauritius was the home of the dodo. But like many others it decided to move on. Unfortunately it had nowhere to go.

Sugar island

Apart from piracy, sugar has been the most important money-spinner on Mauritius. In 1860, the island was the number one producer in the British Empire. Until slavery was abolished, 25,000 slaves churned the stuff out. Later it took 200,000 Indian labourers to do the same job. Fortunes were won and lost according to the fluctuations in the world price of sugar. Eventually a Mauritian, de Lesseps, built the Suez Canal and diverted all the trade routes away from Mauritius. There followed the biggest sugar slump in the world. Today 90 per cent of the economy is sugar.

Population: One million

Size: 720 sq. miles

Government: Independent Commonwealth member

Language: English

Religion: Roman Catholic, Hindu, Islam

Capital: Port Louis

Currency: Mauritius rupee

Tips for tourists

Visit the Pamplemousse Gardens built in the 18th Century by Pierre Poivre (Peter Pepper). They are one of the top three botanical gardens in the world.

But time your visit carefully. The *talipot palm* flowers once every 100 years and then dies.

Look for an 1846 Mauritius stamp. It is one of the most valuable in the world.

The three main killers are malaria, fire and cyclones which in 1865 killed one fifth of the population. Nowadays you only have to worry about the last two.

Book in advance for the movies. Mauritius has the world's second highest attendance figures per capita.

Population: 70 million

Size: Eight times that of Britain, three quarters of a million sq. miles

Government: Federal republic

Language: Spanish

Religion: Roman Catholic

Capital: Mexico City

Currency: Peso and centavos

Tips for tourists

Remember the word *mordidas*. It is the institutionalised greasing of palms without which nothing is possible here.

If you visit Mexico City's cathedral be careful where you tread. It was built over the Aztec ceremonial pyramid where living hearts were plucked from human sacrifices.

Mexico
Estados Unidos Mexicanos

Exits and entrances

Mexico has one of the world's highest murder rates and one of the highest birth rates.

The border between Mexico and the United States is the servants' entrance of the USA. It is the busiest border in the world and most of those who cross it are Mexicans travelling to a bright new future. They usually end up doing work that no U.S. citizen will do.

In the red

Mexico's revolution of 1910 did not lead to the country turning Red. It just watered down its capitalism. That has led the country into the red in a big way. It is currently the world's biggest debtor, owing some 90 billion dollars.

Mouth-watering

Mexico prides itself on introducing the world to avocados, chocolate, peanuts, vanilla and turkey — and on producing the best tomatoes.

Four-fifths of this large country is totally dry. It has no major rivers and water is scarce everywhere.

Song and dance

Mexicans have a wry attitude to entertainment. Among their most-loved songs are *El Descarrilamiento de Temem
atle* (the story of a catastrophic train wreck) and *Delgadina* (the tale of an incestuous father). One of their most popular dances is *Los Viejitos* (the Little Old Men) in which the dancers imitate people with rheumatism.

At night you may be kept awake by a swain serenading his love with Maiachi music. Worse still, he may have hired a Maiachi group to perform for him — they can be found with the meter ticking over in most large squares.

Festivals

There are more festivals in Mexico than most other places put together. Not a day goes by without one. They include:
Blessing of the Animals: cats, dogs, pigs, cows and chickens are dressed up and taken to church to be blessed. Not to be confused with:
Feast of St Anthony: kittens are dressed in gingham and pigs are painted with polka dots.
Dia de San Juan: everyone gets a bucket of water thrown over them.
The Day of the Dead: windows are painted with skeletons and shops sell things like sugar skulls.

All in the same vote

Mexico masquerades as a democracy. The ruling political party has not lost an election since it was formed in 1929. The biggest change was when it altered its name from the National Revolutionary Party to the Institutional Revolutionary Party. The word 'Revolution' does not have its usual meaning here. The ruling 'Revolutionary' party represents middle-class interests and the most right-wing party is called the 'Authentic Party of the Mexican Revolution.

Everyone over 17 has the vote as long as they 'have an honourable means of livelihood'. Thumbprints are taken of registered voters.

Oil in the same boat

Mexico has squandered its fabulous oil wealth (see *In the red*). It has failed to exploit its enormous mineral resources, with the exception of silver, in which it ranks second in world production. So it is still primarily an agricultural country. The largest money-earner is tourism.

A Mexican Villa

Mexico has had 20 centuries of turmoil, invasions, occupations and revolutions. Its best days were before the Spaniards arrived in 1519 — the time of the Aztec and Mayan Empires, some of the most brilliant civilisations the world has known.

The Spaniards ran the country until 1810 (Mexico is still the world's largest Spanish speaking country). After wriggling out from under the heel of Spain in the war of independence, Mexicans then spent 100 years under the heel of their own landed gentry. The revolution of 1910 is mainly remembered for the great folk heroes Pancho Villa and Emilio Zapata, whose imitators have given hours of fun to movie audiences.

This young child, unable to bear the stigma of further gigantic IMF loans, prepares to jump to his death.

Monaco

FRANCE

Grand Casino

MONACO

Monte Carlo

Prince's Palace

Old Town

Mediterranean Sea

Faites vos jeux

Games are the raison d'etre of Monaco. Traditionally playboys (and girls) have played them. It started with gambling, of course, in the world's most famous casino at Monte Carlo. But as Russian Grand Dukes became a dying species, the Monegasques invented new ones: car rallies and Grand Prix, the Ballet Russe de Monte Carlo presenting Diaghilev premieres in an ante room of the casino, and sailing or sitting in the world's most impressive collection of ocean-going yachts (Adnan Kashoggi leads in style at the moment with ground-to-air missiles mounted on the stern of his).

They bet on everything. This year the man third from left was again 7-1 on favourite to win the *Urinating Grand Prix de Monaco.*

Rien ne va plus

The oldest and most famous game, the casino, is a shadow of its former glory. In the last century and well into this, the casino provided most of the national income. The famous Briton who discovered an inaccuracy in the roulette wheel won so much money that it inspired the song *The Man Who Broke the Bank at Monte Carlo.* Now gambling provides only 4 per cent of the national income. Real style has left the place. There are limits on the amounts a gambler can risk and money is a more precious commodity than it used to be. Not surprisingly, Monaco has one of the highest fraud rates in the world.

Double or quits

Monaco is the second smallest independent principality in the world (after the Vatican) and has the world's shortest coastline. But, undeterred, in the past ten years it has constructed a further 500-yard beach (adding 22 acres to the existing 467) and a new town built in the sea. This is to house the latest money-making venture — conferences. Monaco has more railway track for its size than any other country.

Prince croupier

The Grimaldi family has ruled Monaco since 1297. From 1731, sovereignty passed through the female line but they kept the name. In 1793 the temporary embarrassment of the French Revolution dispossessed the family. But from 1815 to 61, Monaco was granted the protection of the King of Sardinia (after 1861 the protection of France) as crowns started to crash all around the tiny Grimaldis. But they kept theirs and it was only in 1962 that Prince Rainier renounced the principal of the divine right of kings. This was either due to an unlucky evening in the casino — or to De Gaulle surrounding the principality with French troops and threatening to cut off the water supply unless French nationals were prevented from getting tax-exemption there. Apparently God couldn't help the prince and he capitulated.

The Queen of Hearts

Rainier's jackpot was Grace Kelly, who, so locals believe, gave Monaco a new belle epoque. She took a keen interest in the arts, unthought of since the heady days of Diaghilev. Now Monaco must be the only country in the world which spends more on its orchestra than its defence. She attracted film star friends among whom Sean Connery, in an apocryphal story, won on the number 17 three times in a row. The odds are 1 in 50,653.

When the chips are down

Monegasques are not allowed to gamble by law. It is feared, if they do, they will become a burden on social security. But there are only 3,500 of them. The 25,000 foreign residents and million visitors per year amply make up for it, however. For such a small country Monaco keeps a surprisingly high profile in the world. Radio Monte Carlo broadcasts in 23 languages and plans to expand to a world service.

Population: 28,000

Size: 0.6 sq. miles

Government: Constitutional monarchy

Language: French

Religion: Roman Catholic

Capital: Monaco

Currency: Francs

Tips for tourists

Go for holiday romance. Monaco has the lowest fertility rate in the world, the second highest widowed population and, for men, the highest proportion of women to men.

Relax in safety and luxury — Monaco is top in chemists, dentists, telegrams, phones, TVs and museum attendances per capita.

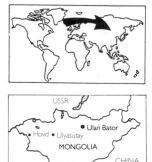

Mongolia
Bugd Nayramdakh Mongol Ard Uls

Tips for tourists

When conversing with a Mongolian, place the right palm on that of the left hand. This is a traditional sign of mutual esteem.

Don't call the natives 'mongols'. The government is trying to stop the use of this term for mentally handicapped people.

Those were the days

Although there has been a Mongolian state since 1203 it has only produced one person of note. And he wasn't someone you'd like to take home to meet your mother. Genghis Khan led his plundering hordes over much of Europe and Asia, striking such fear into other nations that it was almost 500 years before they bothered having a go at Mongolia. Or perhaps they felt it wasn't worth the bother.

In 1691 China invaded and Mongolia became one of its provinces until 1911. In the next ten years it changed hands three times, switching back and forth between Russia and China while the national hero, Damdiny Suhbaatar, fought for his country's independence. In 1921 he got his wish.

Those weren't the days

Mongolia was not the sort of place you'd like to win in a raffle. Its population of three quarters of a million was falling and expected to die out completely (the high mortality rate was not solely responsible — the country had 100,000 Buddhist monks sworn to a life of celibacy).

Most of the land and cattle were owned by feudal lords and religious leaders (lamas). Only one in 50 of the population could read — not surprisingly, as there was only one school.

How things have changed. After 60 years of communist rule the population has doubled (although Mongolia is still the most sparsely populated country in the world). The land has been handed over to huge farming collectives and almost everyone can read. No wonder the capital is called Ulaanbaatar, meaning 'Red Hero'.

Travel

Sixty years ago it was only possible to get round by camel caravans. Today there is the Trans-Mongolian railway, an airline called Mongolair and a lorry service named Mongoltrans.

Alas, not all progress is for the best. The old horse post exists no more. It had quaint features — like indicating urgent messages with a feather. There were no stamps, just a horse's-hoof symbol (meaning 'gallop' — urgent mail) or a bird ('fly, fly' — very urgent).

Industry

For centuries Mongolia has lived by its sheep, goats and horses. It still does,

The government is urging foreigners, in the strongest possible terms, to stop calling mentally handicapped people 'Mongols'.

although it now makes 2 million pairs of shoes a year as part of its growing light industry. The people of the country are outnumbered 20 to 1 by animals. One in three workers are shepherds.

Geography

Mongolia is an endless vista of hilly plains, snow-capped mountains and Gobi desert. There are 3,000 lakes with an area greater than half a square mile. On 250 days a year there is clear sunny weather.

Entertainment

In keeping with the nomadic tradition, Mongolia has 23 cinemas and 439 mobile cinemas.

The major sport, in the tradition of Genghis Khan, is killing things. The Mongolian Huntsmen's Association, which has 30,000 members, kills 3 million animals a year.

Festivals

The most famous is the annual festival of the Three Manly Sports.
Manly Sport One: Wrestling — hundreds of participants are clad in the bright colours of a special tight-fitting costume and simulate the flight of the mythical Garudi bird. Winners get titles like Titan, Lion, Elephant and Invincible Titan.
Manly Sport Two: Archery — bowmen shoot at leather targets with ancient weapons for the title of Supermarksman Exceptional winners are called Miraculous Archer or Most Scrupulous Archer.
Manly Sport Three: Horse racing — all competitors are children aged from 7 to 12. They race 20 miles across country wearing fine ornamental dresses.

Montserrat

Montserrat is the usual idyllic Caribbean island with mountains, forests, a balmy climate and a branch library. Oddly, the main political party is called the People's Liberation Movement. What can the people possibly want to be liberated from? Perhaps it's the island's black, not white, beaches — a result of the volcanic soil.

Living books

Not only does the library contain books but there are people on the island with the same names as famous authors. The prime minister is one John Osborne, while the president of the Teachers' Union is Leslie Thomas. Not to mention the name of the island itself.

Don't go to Montserrat to buy shoes.

Aggro

Perhaps the island has a dark secret that we should know about. It is ominous to note that although slavery was officially abolished here in 1834, most of the population work in what are called 'agro-based industries'. These purport to produce sea-island cotton, peppers and various kinds of livestock (mainly goats).

Natural aggro

The people may well wish to be liberated from some occasional natural bits of bother. Although there is no well-defined rainy season, the hurricane season is pretty obvious, and earthquakes are hard to miss. There are also seven active volcanoes.

Not only is there no God...

But He keeps testing your faith.
St. George's Church:
1843 — destroyed by earthquake
1899 — destroyed by hurricane
1924 — destroyed by hurricane
1928 — damaged by hurricane.

History

The history of the island is the history of sugar. The economy of the island was based on slavery and the sugar industry. After the emancipation of slaves, sugar went through a sticky time before it dissolved completely to be replaced by limes.

People

In 1805 slaves outnumbered whites by 9:1, and the islanders are still predominantly of African descent. Soon after emancipation, the Lt. Governor had to report to the Colonial Office that the persons being chosen to sit in the Assembly of his colony could 'barely read and write'.

Illiteracy is now a thing of the past, and the islanders' increasingly successful exploitation of Montserrat's tourist potential show they know how many beans make five. On the whole these are old beans — Americans, Canadians and British, many of whom come here to retire.

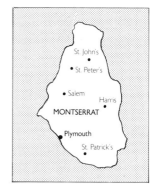

Population: 12,000

Size: 40 sq. miles

Government: UK colony

Language: English

Religion: Christianity

Capital: Plymouth

Currency: East Caribbean dollars

Tips for tourists

Careful with Irish jokes — the majority of the original settlers are Irish and most islanders still speak with an Irish brogue.

Don't bring a car, bring a jeep — the island's roads are too steep for ordinary motor vehicles.

Montserrat is sometimes called the Emerald Isle.

Morocco
al-Mamlaka al-Maghrebia

One thing above all others has brought Morocco fame: Casablanca, the town which gave its name to the film in which Bogart and Bergman loved and lost.

Of all the countries, in all the world

Morocco is a mostly mountainous country draped along the north coast of Africa. In the south it drifts into the Sahara desert. All its rivers are torrential. So even desert roads can be flooded in the spring as melting snow from the mountains overflows the rivers.

As time goes by

The 2,000 years of Moroccan history before this century read like a report of football hooliganism, with invasions by the Vandals (among others) and rule by the dynasty of Wattasid (the perfect name for a football hooligan). As France and Spain slowly occupied Morocco, they were resisted by independence forces gathered in the Rif region (Rif-raf would have been more appropriate). Morocco got its independence in 1962.

Here's looking askance, kid

In the early years of this century, Morocco was the most backward place on the Mediterranean and the most mis-governed place on earth. The only law was the sultan's whim. He appointed ministers (called *viziers*) who were selected purely for their greed. They appointed governors who in turn appointed local officials. No salaries were paid — all lived on what they could get from bribery and extortion. A share passed back along the line to the sultan.

Still the same old story

Not much has changed. The king (called the *cherif*) still holds supreme religious and political power. There are great inequalities of wealth. Two million people live in slums. They are lucky. Most of the 10 million peasants are landless and jobless. Apart from agriculture, the only main source of employment is begging, although women can get part-time jobs as *negaffas*, female wedding attendants who carry the bride around on their shoulders.

Play it, Sam

There are two public holidays: *November 18th*, Accession of the King Mohammed V, and *March 2nd*, Accession of King Hassan II — this lasts three days and is marked by displays of traditional horsemanship with much firing of ancient muskets. The Cherry Festival is in June, the Date Festival in October and the Olive Festival in December. There is a Drama Festival in June and July, but the Casablanca Fair (April-May) is not a film festival.

Biggest splash: the Orthlieb pool in Casablanca, the world's largest. It measures 1,547 feet by 246 feet.

Least successful garden party: when, in 1971, 1,400 military cadets burst into the summer palace and wiped out 90 royal guests. But they failed to kill the king (and so were unable to sing *'I shot the cherif'*).

Fundamental things

Moroccan men are allowed four wives. But only if they can afford them — and the women agree.

Population: 21 million

Size: Twice that of Britain, about 180,000 sq. miles

Government: Constitutional monarchy

Language: Arabic

Religion: Islam

Capital: Rabat

Currency: Dirham and centimes

Tips for tourists

Avoid the women. Morocco has the highest proportion of female criminals in the world.

Don't get a job. The industrial accident rate is the world's worst. (They probably cut themselves on sardine tins — Morocco has the world's largest sardine fishery).

Hashish is forbidden to tourists, but smoked openly by the locals. On the other hand, tourists can drink alcohol, but the natives can't. They must make do with mint tea.

A trip to avoid. The P39 road from Tangier to Ketaka passes through the centre of the hashish area. Aggressive sellers block the road and hurl themselves at cars.

Morocco is one of the few places in the world where you can live actually inside a fruit machine.

Mozambique
Republica Popular de Mocambique

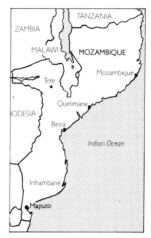

The Portuguese

Vasco de Gama discovered Mozambique in 1498 and the Portuguese held on to it until 1975. It was their second largest colony in Africa and they attempted to turn it into an extension of Portugal culturally, administratively and socially. If their ambitions hadn't been so great, they would never have got into the war for independence which finally saw them off. Between 1950 and 1970 Portuguese personnel increased from 48,000 to 150,000 as the mother country realised the increasing possibilities of exploitation.

Up until the sixties they ruled it like a 19th Century colony, apparently unaware that slavery no longer existed elsewhere. Forced labour and corporal punishment were commonplace almost until independence. But with the rise of independence movements it cost Portugal more and more. In 1969 they had 60,000 troops in the country. By 1970, wars in Angola, Guinea and Mozambique claimed 40 per cent of the Portuguese budget.

The port

One of the reasons for hanging on so long was the value of the country's main port, Lourenco Marques (now Maputo). It is one of the best natural harbours in the world and exports a high proportion of South African goods.

Before independence, South Africa featured strongly in the economy as a whole. Nearly half the southern tribesmen at some time in their lives worked in the mines there as wages in Mozambique were low even by South African standards. And taxes were high.

Effects of independence

After a long struggle the independence movement *Frelimo* won in 1975. It created a one-party Marxist state with a council of 216 appointed by Frelimo.

The national flag expresses the style of rule: a rifle crossed with a hoe on a book inside a cog-wheel. They clearly intend to be a warlike yet rustic, artistic yet scientific, new country.

The artificial influx of Portuguese before independence was reversed afterwards. In 1972 there were 500 doctors. By 1975 only 40 remained. There was a flight of capital, termination of gold payments by South Africa, sabotage of industry and an imposition of sanctions against Rhodesia to help her independence movements.

As if this weren't enough, the regime had to cope with large-scale flooding in 1977 and 1978 which affected 250,000 people.

Better effects

The new country claims the largest production of cashew nuts in the world and of tantalite. To work these heavy industries, Mozambique has the largest hydro-electric scheme in Africa, at Cabora Bassa.

What the critics say

With two of the most famous rivers in the world, the Zambezi and Limpopo, flowing through the land, it is hardly surprising they have inspired the flow of the pens of great poets. Kipling wrote:
The great grey-green greasy Limpopo
— which has a lot of g's in it. And, more prosaically, the Pirhanas pop group observed:
Zambezi Zambezi Zambezi Zam!
Not to be outdone, Bob Dylan took a shine to Mozambique:
I like to spend some time in Mozambique
The sunny sky is aqua-blue

Population: 12 and a half million

Size: Three and a half times that of Britain, 300,000 sq. miles

Government: Socialist republic

Language: Portuguese

Religion: Mainly Islam

Capital: Maputo

Currency: Escudo

Tips for tourists

Tourism ceased in 1978.

These German tourists have lost their way to the crocodile observation platform.

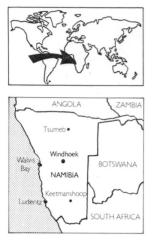

ANGOLA · ZAMBIA

Tsumeb •

Windhoek •
Walvis Bay
BOTSWANA

NAMIBIA

Keetmanshoop •

Lüderitz •

SOUTH AFRICA

Population: 1 million

Size: 3 and a half times that of Britain, 320,000 sq. miles

Government: South African colony

Main languages: English, Afrikaans

Religions: Traditional beliefs and Christianity

Capital: Windhoek

Currency: Rand, cent.

Tips for tourists

When addressing the people of Rehoboth, remember to call them *bastards*. They take great pride in this. Do not call them *coloured*, as this is a terrible insult.

Namibia
Suidwes-Afrika

Richer and poorer

There is an endangered species in Namibia. It is the whites. So to make sure they don't become extinct, the people who run the country (who are also white) have allowed them to have a special protected reservation. It is an area about 1 and a half times the size of Britain which contains most of the best grazing land and water. It supports 20,000 whites.

The rest of the population, who are mainly blacks, is allowed to occupy segregated areas of the rest of the country. This is chiefly desert, with no water or rainfall. Consequently the blacks suffer from disease, overcrowding and malnutrition. But the whites do not consider them to be endangered.

This woman is still waiting for independence in Namibia.

Better and worse

It would be wrong to think that the whites keep control of Namibia just because they like power. They do it for the money, too. Namibia is the world's leading producer of industrial diamonds and has wonderful riches of silver, copper, zinc, lead and plutonium. All mines are owned and run by South Africa, Britain and the US.

South Africa's apartheid laws have been exported to Namibia and made retrospective to 1950 (only a Boer could tell you how this is possible). Although white children make up only 20 per cent of the school population, they get 80 per cent of the education budget. Blacks are taught only in Afrikaans. Exams are held only in English and German. This leads to a low pass rate, thus proving what the whites have always believed.

Shotgun marriage

Namibia was a German state from the late 19th Century, so something had to be done with it after World War One. The League of Nations asked the South Africans, who lived next door, to look after it for a while. This was rather like lending your lawnmower to new neighbours. The South Africans refuse to give it back, still calling it South-West Africa and claiming that they administer it as 'a sacred trust of civilisation'.

In 1971 the International Court of Justice ruled that South Africa's presence in Namibia was illegal. A UN Commissioner was appointed and South Africa given until 1975 to declare its intentions. These were always obvious to anyone except UN Commissioners. The South Africans organised elections which overwhelmingly returned to power the party of whites, and bought off tribal chiefs who had just been put in position by South Africa.

Gunshots

All attempts to solve the Namibian problem have failed. The South-West Africa People's Organisation (SWAPO), which is recognised by the UN as the proper representative of Namibia, continues to fight a guerrilla war. Meanwhile, Namibia continues to be run by the white rancher Dirk F. Mudge and the equally inappropriately named Jannie deWet.

Nauru

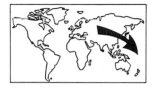

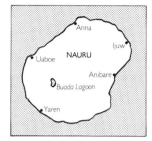

This island is built upon, exists on, and lives by and for one thing. Bird shit.

Geography

Nauru is a tiny oval-shaped island in the Pacific. It is 12 miles round and is surrounded by a reef only exposed at low tide.

Apart from a rather pretty beach on one side it consists of little more than a plateau of high-grade phosphate (i.e. ancient bird shit). But the people live very well on it. They have one of the world's highest national incomes.

Life

When last counted ('O'-level maths not required) the human population consisted of 4,174 Nauruans and 2,080 Europeans, who are mainly there to organise the shit-shovelling and educate the children.

There is little animal life, although pigs and poultry have been introduced. Surprisingly, there are few birds. No one seems to know why. Perhaps they were wiped out by an epidemic of diarrhoea.

Politics

Nauru is the world's smallest republic. Its parliament has 18 members.

Industry

There is only one industry: the mining and export of phosphate — about one million tons a year of it. This is carried to the shore by rail and then travels by a complicated system of conveyor belts and cantilevers to ships moored far out at sea. Although these offshore moorings are said to be the deepest in the world, there is no harbour on the island.

The past

The first to set foot here were the crew of a British ship (skipper, Captain Fearn) in 1798. The navigator, John Hunter, named the place Pleasant because of the friendly welcome they got from the natives. Had he set foot in something unpleasant — a chance which he surely only narrowly avoided — presumably he would have given the island a far less complimentary name.

The island was annexed by Germany (during its anal phase) in 1888. In 1914, when the Germans were conquering everywhere else, they surrendered this tiny territory to Australia. It achieved independence in 1968.

The future

Looking up has always been a problem on Nauru. Looking ahead is no better — supplies of phosphate are expected to run out in 1993.

Education

Compulsory. The school leaving age is 15 for European children and 16 for Nauruans. The island has the world's highest literacy rate.

Population: 8,000

Size: 8 and a quarter sq. miles

Government: Republic

Language: English

Religion: Christianity

Capital: None

Currency: Australian dollar

Tips for tourists

No need to queue at the movies. There are seven cinemas, the highest proportion for the population of anywhere in the world.

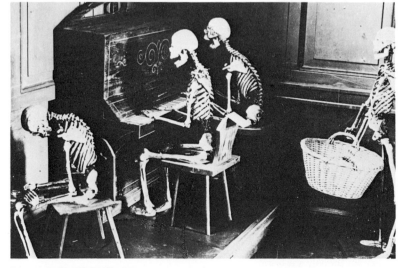

The Nauru Symphony Orchestra runs on a tight budget.

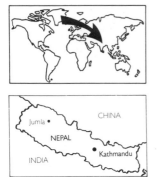

Nepal

Population: Fifteen and half million

Size: Under half that of Britain, 54,000 sq. miles

Government: Constitutional monarchy

Languages: Nepali, English

Religions: Hinduism, Buddhism

Capital: Kathmandu

Currency: Nepalese rupee

Tips for tourists

Try to see an Indian rhinoceros. It's your best chance as Nepal has 300 out of 700 in the world.

Don't fall ill. They have the fewest hospital beds in the world for size of population.

Four good reasons not to take a car:
They have the least cars per size of population.
They use the least petrol.
There are only 1,000 miles of road.
The president of the Automobile Association of Nepal is called Path.

Try eating *chang*. It is 'a species of alcoholic porridge'.

Principal occupations

The major employment in Nepal is wood collecting. This is done mainly in winter. In summer, there is grass collecting. The grass is gathered when it has grown tall enough to hide a tiger or rhinoceros. Grass-gathering is a significant cause of death in Nepal. A tiger may only be shot after it has killed three people.

Practical Nepal

A tough no-nonense race, the Nepalese are mainly of Mongolian origin with a few Indians in the south. It is the only Hindu country in the world ruled by a king. He is King Birendra Bir Bikram Shah Diva and owes his power to a revolutionary movement in the 1950's which restored the monarchy to its former supreme position — a tough, no-nonsense revolution. Before, the country had been governed feudally by families and suffered the usual family feuds.

Being one of the least developed countries in the world, with 20 per cent literacy, 420 doctors for 15 and a half million people and general lack of civilisation, it comes as no surprise that it produces some of the greatest warriors in the world. Since 1559 the Gurkhas have held a special place in the country and in both World Wars have helped Great Britain unstintingly. They are well paid by Nepalese standards — the average wage is £50 a year.

The Nepalese have a tough, no-nonsense language to match. Nepal means *'at the foot of the mountains'* and Himalaya means *'abode of snow'*. They get China to build their roads in the north and India in the south.

Spiritual Nepal

1) The Yeti
2) Buddha
Siddhartha Gotama, or Buddha, or the Enghlightened One, or the Vishnu, or Yogi or Krishna was born in Lumbini, Nepal, in 624 BC. He was an incredibly rich prince whose discovery that poverty and sickness actually existed made him go religious. He tried a group of ascetics called the Brahmins but, finding them too ascetic, sat under a tree in northern Nepal until he was enlightened. The result? The Four Noble Truths.

Basically the only way to avoid suffering is to avoid rebirth. Or birth in the first place, presumably. Avoiding rebirth is nirvana, where you simply go out like a light.

Buddhism split into two forms. In the north it produced Lamas, Zen etc. In the south, people shave their heads and wear yellow clothes. They are not allowed to carry money although they used to be permitted four old pence to make a phone-call when they came to London. Post-decimalisation Buddhism is unclear on this point.

The Nepalese are crazy about gods. Their Monkey God is revered by smearing its face with a red paste. So much paste has been applied that its features are now obscured. Kathmandu is a city of 350,000 and has over 2,000 temples. But they are not content with imaginary godheads. A Kumari Deva is chosen every so often. She is a pre-pubescent girl who is declared a goddess. She rides in cavalcades through the capital and lives in a palace. When she reaches puberty she is given a life pension and a new goddess is chosen.

Nepalese draw lots for who gets a meal in 1982.

The rest of Nepal

The country has one of the most varied climates in the world. In 100 miles there is a difference in altitude of 27,000 feet. 60 per cent of the country is covered by hills and 30 per cent by mountains. The highest, and the highest in the world, is, of course, Mount Everest. One-sixth of the country is under perpetual snow and one-third is forested. The scenery varies from tropical forest to mountain.

The Netherlands
Koninkrijk der Nederlanden

Important fact
Many people think this country is called Holland, but it's really called the Netherlands. There *is* a place called Holland and it is a part of the Netherlands — up in the top right-hand corner.

Two traditionally dressed Dutch women show their typical sense of fun by placing their Dutch caps on their heads.

History
Holland was the first bit of the Netherlands to be settled. That was a thousand years ago when all the rulers were called either Dirk or Floris. They spent their time fighting. Rather successfully, as it happens. Their country grew and grew.

It had a few setbacks. In the 14th Century, there was a civil war between the Hooks and Cods (this was *not* the first cod war). But by the Middle Ages, the Netherlands was an important nation. Its buccaneers roamed the world in the name of the Dutch East and West India Companies. Since then, it has been pretty much all downhill, although that can't be all bad for a nation of cyclists.

After various entanglements with the Spanish, French and Belgians, the Netherlands became a separate state in 1814, with its own king.

Most embarrassing moment
When the Dutch fleet was captured by the Prussian cavalry (the fleet was frozen in).

Monarchy
There are two things to remember about Holland's kings: *1.* For the past 100 years, they have been Queens, *2.* They abdicate.

The present Queen, Beatrix, took over when her mother abdicated in 1980.

Geography
The true miracle of the Dutch is that they are the people who have learned to walk — and live — on water. A fifth of their country, which is less than half the size of Scotland, has been reclaimed from the sea. Much more was once marsh land. Little of the country is more than a few feet above sea level and some of it is below. It has the most unusual government department in the world: the *Waterstaat,* meaning 'State of the Waters'.

Travelling
The Netherlands is one of the most densely populated countries in the world, but travelling is easy for the 14 million inhabitants. The country is criss-crossed by navigable rivers and canals. It has excellent roads, a vast railway system and, of course, the best cycle-track network in the world.

Industry
The blessing of the huge discoveries of oil and natural gas has not been so fortunate for those working in the traditional coal industry. All the mines have been closed. Butter and cheese, which are produced under state control, are major exports. And the Philips and Shell companies are among the richest in the world.

Politics
Dutch politics is dominated by religious divisions. For example, there are three organisations for employers and three for trade unions — one for Catholics, one for Protestants and one for 'others'. Among the political parties which have not achieved any great success are the *Unmarried Mothers' Party* and the *Party of Duped Citizens.*

Proverbs
He has been hit by a windmill vane (meaning: he is mad)
Who comes first, grinds first (meaning: obvious)

The Language
Holland has given a number of sayings to the rest of the world. These include:
Dutch by injection — a woman who lives with a Dutchman
Dutch courage — courage induced by drink
Dutch cap — form of contraceptive
Dutch oven — what the bedclothes smell like after you've farted.

Population: 14 million

Size: A seventh that of Britain, 16,000 sq. miles

Government: Constitutional monarchy

Language: Dutch

Main religions: Dutch Reformed Church and Roman Catholic

Capital: Amsterdam

Currency: Gulden, cents

Tips for tourists

The Dutch do not object to short visitors. In fact, the shortest person on record, a dwarf known as 'Princess Pauline' came from Holland.

Why not try some of Holland's cultural activities? These include:
Clog dancing (Dutch: *Klompen*).
A quiz called 'The Dutch have taken Holland'. To play this the players must say a well-known or obvious fact.
Sending messages by the set of the sails of a windmill.

New Zealand

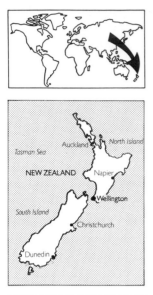

Population: 3 and a quarter million

Size: Bit bigger than Britain, 104,000 sq. miles

Government: Independent Commonwealth member

Language: English, Maori

Religion: Christianity

Capital: Wellington

Currency: NZ dollar, cents

Tips for tourists

Don't be insulted if when you say goodbye to a New Zealander he says *Hurrah*. That means 'cheerio'.

Don't worry about a New Zealander who says *I'm a box of birds*. That means 'I feel fine'.

Don't think you are off to a classical concert if you are invited to a *bach*. A bach is a weekend shack.

Language

Before embarking on a trip to New Zealand, it is important to master the Maori language, in which many place names are written. The main things to remember are that 'wh' is pronounced 'f' and all vowels must be enunciated. Thus the town of Whakatane is pronounced *Fukatarni* and when asking the way to Waiwhakamukau, you must say *Whyfukamoocow*.

The duality of language extends to the national anthems, of which there are two: *God Defend New Zealand* and *God Save the Queen*. There should be a third: *Sheep May Safely Graze*. New Zealand has 68 million of them and this is indeed a land fit for sheep. About two thirds of the two main islands (called, with startling originality, North and South Islands) are used for agriculture and grazing. No part of the country is further than 80 miles from the sea. Few parts are further than 80 feet from a sheep.

History

There was little life of any kind here before the Maoris arrived from Polynesia about a thousand years ago. The First European to drop in was Tasman in 1642 and 127 years later Captain Cook had a good look around.

From 1800 New Zealand was home for whalers, traders and convicts who had escaped from Australia. It became a British colony in 1840 when a treaty was signed with Maori chiefs. Settlers flocked in — and so did sheep. By the turn of this century, the country was virtually self-governing but it did not officially become independent until 1947.

In the rough

New Zealand has a reputation for racial harmony between whites and Maoris. The most serious racial disturbances in 100 years were in 1982, when a number of Maoris rioted and the Governor General was bruised on the chest by a golf ball.

There are a quarter of a million Maoris, three quarters of them under 30. The proportion of them in the population is growing. Since 1867 they have elected four of their own members to the House of Representatives.

Wild life

Due to New Zealand's isolation it has few wild animals (it is one of the few places in the world without snakes).

The search goes on for something of cultural interest.

Some of those it does have are weird. The tuatara is a reptile which has been extinct elsewhere for 100 million years. The gecko is a lizard born directly instead of being hatched from an egg.

New Zealanders believe in an equal society. By this they mean that everyone should behave the same. They think they should all live in a three-bedroom bungalow, wear shorts, drink plenty of beer, eat well (they are the world's top meat and protein eaters) and play and/or watch lots of sport. The whole country is sport mad. Rugby has been raised to the position of a national religion.

New Zealand has the world's third highest theft rate, and is fifth in rape and sex crimes. It has the seventh highest proportion of criminals in its population.

Easy life

New Zealand prides itself on pioneering the welfare state. It was the second country to introduce non-contributory old age pensions (Denmark was first). Industry consists of 380,000 tons of wool a year, plus more meat than from any other country.

Travel

There are 13,297 bridges. Even if you don't mind crossing them, you are still likely to get vertigo asking for *Taumata whakatangihangakoauauotamatea (turipukakapikimaungahoronuku) pokaiwhenuakitanatahu*, a hill on North Island. (It is a Maori name meaning 'The hill whereon was played the flute of Tamatoa, circumnavigator of lands, for his lady love').

Nicaragua
Republica de Nicaragua

This is the land the USA just can't leave alone. It has meddled in its affairs for 130 years, causing nothing but trouble to the people of this, the largest of the Central American republics. Will they never learn? (Answers, on a postcard, to: *President Reagan, the White House, Washington DC, USA*).

History

Columbus touched on Nicaragua at a point he called Gracias a Dios. That means 'thanks to God', which shows an astonishing lack of foresight by the great explorer. As soon as the country became independent in 1838, it was split by internal dissent. This resulted in the capital being moved from Leon to Granada and back again. And again. And again. Then there was a civil war. Then, in 1855 the US persuaded an adventurer, William Walker, to land in Nicaragua and proclaim himself president. 'President' Walker's main act was to order the reintroduction of slavery.

Here come the marines

In 1925, Washington sent in the marines. As soon as they left, the head of the National Guard, which they had established, made himself dictator. His name was Anastasio Somoza. When he was assassinated in 1956, another member of his family took over. By the time they were driven out of the country, the Somoza family controlled 95 per cent of the economy, including the transport system, best farmland and key branches of industry.

But it did not control prostitution, night clubs, gambling joints and tourist centres. These were run by officers of the National Guard. This was not easy for them, as they were also running a reign of terror and had to be ready to deal with emergencies. One of these was the earthquake of 1972 which destroyed 60 per cent of the capital, Managua, leaving 40,000 dead and 200,000 homeless. Millions of dollars poured in from international aid. This created another emergency, as it was far too much for Somoza to embezzle by himself. He had to rely on the National Guard to help out. When the Somozas were thrown out in 1978, everyone was delighted (except the National Guard, US President etc. etc. etc.)

Only known Nicaraguan

Bianca Jagger

Here come the marines — again

The United States government continues to believe that the poverty-stricken peasants of Nicaragua and their leaders threaten the most powerful nation on earth. So the CIA is sending in armed guerillas from Guatemala, Honduras and El Salvador. However, the National Guard has been disbanded, 100,000 peasants given their own land and the 70 per cent illiteracy rate (Central America's highest) is being tackled.

Population: Two and a half million

Size: Two-thirds that of Britain, 57,000 sq. miles

Government: Republic

Language: Spanish

Religion: Roman Catholic

Capital: Managua

Currency: Cordoba, centavos

Tips for tourists

Take care. The major causes of death, apart from old age, are homicide and war.

Here come the marinas: Nicaragua could be turned into the world's biggest boating park. One tenth of the country is lakes, including Lake Nicaragua, the largest freshwater lake in Central America (although it contains sea fish).

In the Managua Hilton, CIA operatives chat unobtrusively between coups.

ALGERIA
LIBYA
MALI
NIGER
• Agades
Niamey
• Zinder
CHAD
NIGERIA

Population: 5 and a half million

Size: Nearly twice that of Texas, 450,000 sq. miles

Government: Republic

Language: French, Hausa

Religion: Islam

Capital: Niamey

Currency: CFA franc

Tips for tourists

Moslems welcome. Niger is one of Africa's most Islamic countries

Don't worry about beri-beri. It is the Hausa word for the Kanuri language.

See the Wogo tribe in their matted huts.

Book early. There are only 400 hotel rooms.

Niger
Republique du Niger

Heat and Dust

More than half the Niger is desert. The other half is savannah but even in non-desert areas the average temperature can reach 106 degrees Fahrenheit. The winds that sweep up from the south clash with the northern *Harmattan* wind from the Sahara which results in frequent tornados. One-ninth of Lake Chad is in Niger — but this dries up, making it possible to walk to Chad across it. Unsatisfied with her work, Nature has inflicted regular droughts on the country — the worst this century lasting from 1968 to 1974. This was so bad that 95 per cent of the Tuareg cattle died. Peanuts, previously 85 per cent of exports, dropped to nothing. And the government fell too.

How do they cope with this heat? One tribal chief — of the Bornu — used to sit in his cage carried by his courtiers who wore 12 shirts to make them fatter.

Origins

Nature's only concession was the Niger River, after which the country is named. It is the third longest river in Africa and runs through the desert. In the Tamashek language it is called *gher n gheren* — river of rivers. Perhaps this goes too far, but when you're clutching at straws in a desert, the river is the obvious place to go. It nourishes the cram cram, a native prickly grass.

Before colonial divisions, Niger gave birth to the empires of Ghana, Mali, Songhai, Hausa, Sokoto and Bornu. In the north the Tuareg fought and beat everybody including the French.

Empire builders

Appropriately in such a hot place, the name of the chief who took Songhai from a small state to an Empire was Sunni Ali. But he was outdone in the quest for a memorable place in the history books by the Fastest Tuareg Driver in the West — Beni Hillal, who drove the Tuaregs from south to north and left them to fester in the desert. Later, in 1905, *the Blind Marabout of Koɓsi Kanda* had a crack at the French, and the history books, when he led a rebellion at Seydou.

King confusion

The French and British got involved in an unseemly attempt to colonise Niger. They both wanted to use the Niger River and control the interior. France first sent Decoeur to make a treaty with the King of Nikki. But the British said

he wasn't the king — and that the real king was the King of Bussa who had tried to allay confusion by calling himself the King of all Borgu — wherever that was. The British already had a treaty with Bussa/Borgu but France said he was not the king. When the British heard of the French expedition, they immediately sent a man called Lugard to get to Nikki first. He arrived 5 days before the French and made a treaty with the King of Nikki — just in case he was, after all, king. The French rejected this treaty.

In the end, Britain got Bussa and France got Nikki. The search for Borgu goes on. The French subsequently realised that the river at Nikki was not navigable and the affair had all been a waste of time.

An anxious tourist searches for the country's road.

Independence

Hamani Diori ruled for 18 years with a politburo containing no Hausa or Fulani — 75 per cent of the population. His ministers set African records for the length of time in office. The 1974 coup put the Hausa leader, Kountche, in charge of a military council. One reason for the coup was that relief trucks, sent to distribute grain during the drought, were used as taxis by Diori's men. There have been two attempted coups since — one led by the inauspiciously-named plotter, Mr. Boube. Since 1975 the French can no longer hold key positions which include show-promoters, hairdressers and film-producers. But feelings have always run high against the French. In 1972, in a land where these are scarce, a tomato was thrown at President Pompidou.

Nigeria

Federal Republic of Nigeria

History

Some 2,500 years ago this was where the remarkable artistic Nok culture flourished. Until the British moved in, the country followed the usual West African pattern of exploitation by the slave trade. What a relief it was to be exploited by the British instead! Throughout the 19th Century, the Brits surreptitiously took more and more land until in 1914 they could make the place a colony. Nigeria became independent in 1960.

The people

The people of Nigeria have been described by their president as 'millions of poverty-stricken, ignorant and disease-ridden peasants.' This leaves little to add, except that Nigeria is the most populous state in Africa (one in four Africans is a Nigerian) and ninth in the world. The exact number of Nigerians remains a mystery, as censuses have a habit of ending in allegations of fiddling. Three hundred African languages and dialects are spoken. To avoid confusion, the official language is none of them (it is English).

The economy

Nigeria is black Africa's wealthiest nation. This has produced one of its main imports — immigrants looking for work. In 1982 that led to a major new export — two million immigrants being thrown back to their own countries.

Oil accounts for almost half the country's income. Nigeria is Africa's largest oil producer and the seventh largest in the world. It is the second largest producer of cocoa (after Ghana) and Africa's largest rubber producer.

The war

After the military coup in 1966, the Ibos of the eastern region began to be massacred. They did not like this. They didn't like it either when the government refused to give them any oil revenues. In 1967 the eastern region declared itself an independent state under the name Biafra. A two and a half year civil war followed. The Biafrans had to cope with disease, starvation, a well-equipped Nigerian army and antagonism from the oil companies of Britain, the US, France and Italy. By the time Biafra was dragged back into Nigeria, there had been one and a half million casualties.

Most popular star

The best-known pop singer is Fela Anikulapo-Kuti. He is as well known for his lifestyle as his music. In 1978 he married 27 women in one ceremony (he describes this as 'my second marriage'). His mother, Funmilayo Anikulapo-Kuti, was a pioneer for Nigerian women's rights until soldiers threw her out of a window.

Worst party

A new capital is being built at Abuja, which used to be a cluster of huts in the bush. To celebrate (prematurely) President Shagari arranged a party for 1,000 in the new state house. This had to be covered in plastic sheeting in case it rained. The lunch was boycotted by 87 of the 90 senators because their invitations were on paper and not proper invitation cards.

Population: 90 million

Size: Four times that of Britain, 360,000 sq. miles

Government: Federal republic

Official language: English

Main religions: Islam, Christianity

Capital: Lagos

Currency: Naira, kobo

Tips for tourists

Avoid the folk opera of the south west region. This combines mime, colourful costumes and drumming. Among the best-known works are *The palmwine drunkard* and *The king did not hang*.

Don't catch cold. The main cause of death is pneumonia.

Take a candle. The national electricity board, NEPA, is known locally as *Never Expect Power Again*.

Don't hire a cab. Lagos has the world's second most expensive taxis.

Nigerian boys go around in twos and threes in case they forget where they put their trays of sweets.

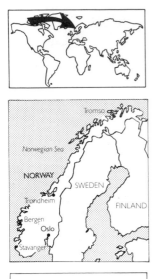

Norway
Kongeriket Norge

Norway (derived from North Way) is the northernmost country in Europe. Its North Cape is the northernmost place in Europe and Hammerfest is the northernmest city in the world. Tromso is the largest city above the Arctic Circle and has the world's northernmost brewery, university and pub. In the very north, the sun doesn't go in from May to July or come out from November to January. Perversely, the Icelanders call the people from Norway the 'East Men'.

But this doesn't mean that Norway is necessarily very cold. Its coastline is divided into fjords — some over one mile deep and 130 miles long. If the coastline were stretched out it would go half way around the world. The Gulf stream pours 150 million cubic feet of warm water per second onto this coastline and the water is stored in the fjords. In Oslo's fjord the water temperature reaches the 70's Fahrenheit, making it possible to cultivate crops which would not be possible on the same latitude elsewhere.

North men

From the fury of the North men, Good Lord deliver us was a common enough prayer around the coastlines of north Europe. They invaded Britain, Iceland, Denmark, France and Ireland. Apart from the Saracens, they had the largest fleet in Europe, and at the Siege of Paris, fielded 40,000 men. In 800 AD, they provided the Praetorian Guard (Ancient SAS) in Constantinople. They were, of course, the Vikings.

From the word *Vik* — meaning bay or creek, they put the fear of God into every bay in Britain. The suffix 'wich' in English place names is all that remains today. They were called Harald

Disguise is everything on a deer shoot.

Finehair, Eric Bloodaxe, Hallfred Crow Leg, Magnus Bare Leg etc. They drank blood from the skulls of their victims and sacrificed children. To a Viking, heaven was fighting and drinking mead forever. By the 12th Century Norway's fame was based on fish, exiled bishops and drunkenness.

North women

Norway was the first country in the world to give women the vote and admit them to the church. The *Housewives Association* is a department store in Oslo which hires out clothes for weddings.

North sea

The sea has always provided Norwegians with a livelihood, whether as violent pillagers or as a source of wealth in itself. Oil is today a major provider and Norway has the largest turn-out of oil rigs in the world.

But it is fish which Norway is really famous for. They have the 4th largest fleet in the world with more tonnage per head of population than anywhere. Bergen is the fishing capital and Stavanger the fish-canning capital (of the Western world). They know more ways of preparing fish than anyone else. To catch them, they invented the explosive harpoon.

Fresh water provides another source of income. As a result of its massive hydro-electric resources, Norway has more electrical power per head of population than anywhere in the world. They even export it to Sweden. Converting bauxite to aluminium can be done more cheaply in Norway because of water power.

North ways

Today the Norwegians are rich. They have a higher income per head than the United States. But their taxes are large. They have a king — but have abolished all titles and privileges. But they are very formal people. You must arrive at dinner on time. But you may go to up to three dinners a day. For leisure they invented skiing. A 2,000 year old ski has been found. And they publish more books than anyone. The long nights encouraged the government to give them free television and radio.

Gifts to the English language

Quisling — wartime pro-Nazi leader whose name is now synonymous with 'traitor'.

Population: 4 million

Size: One and two thirds that of Britain, 150,000 sq. miles

Government: Constitutional monarchy

Language: Norwegian (Landsmal)

Religion: Protestant

Capital: Oslo

Currency: Kroner

Tips for tourists

In Trondheim there is the smallest playable violin in the world — the size of a postage stamp.

Oslo is the fourth largest city in the world in size — with a population of less than half a million. This is a result of a decision in 1948 to simply make it 27 times larger. Most of the city is forest and park.

They are still Haralds, Svens, Thors, Lars and Rolfs, but the French are still Normans.

Oman
Sultanate of Oman

Backwards

As Swingin' Britain rocked to the Beatles and Rolling Stones in the 1960's, what was life like in oil-rich Oman? There were only three schools as the sultan, Said bin Tairmur, was totally opposed to education. He was also opposed to medicine, so there were only 12 beds in the sole hospital. Not that it mattered much, as there were no doctors.

The sultan also banned music, the cinema and 'fraternal associations'. There were no newspapers and only two roads, one of them a dirt track.

Heir today, king tomorrow

Naturally enough, the repressed people began to bemoan their lot. The British (who had controlled the country for 50 years) realised that something had to be done about the sultan. They decided to keep things in the family and arranged for the sultan's son, Qaboos bin Said, to depose his father. Qaboos was a most suitable chap. He had been educated at Sandhurst and was a fan of Gilbert and Sullivan.

A military detachment led by British officers entered the royal palace and politely asked the old sultan to leave. He was not so gentlemanly, not having been to Sandhurst and never having heard of *The Pirates of Penzance*. He grabbed a machine pistol to fight off the invaders, but unfortunately shot himself in the foot whle trying to load it. He was hopping mad. The sultan was eventually sent to spend the rest of his days in England.

Up to date — 1

There are now 257 primary schools in Oman (although 80 per cent of the population is still illiterate), a rapid road construction programme and many modern buildings. This is as good for the British as the Omanis, as their firms have landed most of the contracts.

The British also run the armed services. When the tribesmen from the Dhofar region, formerly best known for producing frankincense, rebelled, British officers spearheaded by the SAS led the sultan's troops against them. Oman continues to spend more of its national income on defence than any country other than Egypt.

The sultan still rules absolutely, although he has been helped since 1981 by a state advisory council. There are no political parties, no unions and no constitution.

Sun worship can go too far in some of the world's hottest places.

Up to date — 2

The major industry and export used to be dates. 50,000 tons a year of them are still produced, mainly for export to India. But the country's wealth now comes from something else black and rich — oil. It provides 95 per cent of the country's income, although the reserves will be used up by the year 2,000. There is almost no other industry, most of the population still working in fishing or farming.

The people

Oman is a nation of nomads, so it is no wonder that estimates of the population vary from 600,000 to one and a half million. This confusion among a people three quarters of whom live in tents extends to one of the best-known Omani proverbs: *If your neighbour dislikes you, change the gate of your house.* Equally baffling is another proverb: *By Him who made male and female at different ends truly do ye aim!*

Population: Approx. 900,000

Size: Slightly smaller than Britain, 82,000 sq. miles

Government: Absolute monarchy

Main language: Arabic

Religion: Islam

Capital: Muscat

Currency: Rial Omani, baiza

Tips for tourists

Buy a camel. The best camels in the world are bred here.

Buy a donkey. Omani donkeys are reputedly as strong as mules.

Enjoy yourself on the only national holiday, December 18th. It is the sultan's birthday.

Population: 90 million

Size: One and a half times that of Britain, 320,000 sq. miles

Government: Federal Republic

Main languages: Urdu and Punjabi

Main religion: Islam

Capital: Islamabad

Currency: Pakistan rupee, paisa

Tips for tourists

A *loo* is a hot wind

Be careful — Pakistan has the ninth highest number of civil disorders in the world.

Got a short head? Go to Baluchistan where you will be much admired. Some of the tribes even bind their daughters' heads to make them shorter.

Need a fix? Pakistan is the world's biggest source of heroin.

Don't go looking for a wife — Pakistan has the world's lowest proportion of females to males.

Pakistan
Islamic Republic of Pakistan

Guns, rifles, revolvers, sword sticks and umbrellas must be left with the attendant, reads a notice in the foyer of a museum in the North West Province in Pakistan. Strangely, in this part of the world, people with umbrellas are a lot more suspicious than people with guns — it hardly ever rains.

Hardware

Everyone is armed to the teeth — some even to the gums — in the North West. The geography is to blame. Lying on the route between the Middle East and India, the province has been on the required invading list of every major invader in history. From Alexander the Great to the cast and crew of *Carry on up the Khyber*, the local people — the Pathans — have seen two thousand years of continual action.

But instead of petitioning for a by-pass, the Pathans have decided they want independence, which they hope to achieve in the only way they know. In 1973, the Pathan leader Abdul Wali Khan told a British journalist: *"My people are not going to be bullied. They will pick up their arms and blow the hell out of everybody. We all have guns here."*
There is an old Pathan saying: war begins with peace.

This Pakistani Moslem counts to ten before she goes in search of Hindus.

Rain-making

How to make rain in one area of Pakistan: 'the villagers collect up all the dung, compost and excrement they can find and throw it into the house of the most bad-tempered person in the village. The resulting argument is supposed to attract the attention of the Almighty to the village's need for rain.'

Beginning

Pakistan came into being in order to create a separate homeland for Indian Muslims at the time of India's independence in 1947. The name was invented in 1933 by Rahmat Ali, a student at Cambridge, and is composed of letters taken from the names of the 5 provinces that go to make up the country. It's founder and first leader was Muhammad Ali Jinnah whose success as a politician was attributed to his 'capacity to take up a permanently negative attitude'.

War

In the two-week war with India in 1970, over the secession of East Pakistan (now Bangladesh), Pakistan lost half her navy, a quarter of her combat aircraft and about a third of her ground forces. Today her annual defence expenditure is one of the highest in the world.

Politics

Pakistan can't seem to handle democracy. The current ruler, General Zia Ul-Haq, has been promising elections for some time. In preparation political parties have been banned and Pakistan is being turned into a strict Islamic state. Schools have had to stop teaching in English and teach in Urdu. Textbooks have been revised. Towns and streets have been renamed. And flogging, hanging and amputation have been introduced for 'major' crimes ranging from drinking alcohol to adultery.

People

Pakistan is one of the poorest countries in the world. Industry is dominated by a group of large families and agriculture is concentrated in the hands of landlords, many of whom are absentee. Most of the people are illiterate, and the population is fast-growing. In 1968 the Family Planning Programme was the third largest employer in the country after the military and the railways.

Panama
Republica de Panama

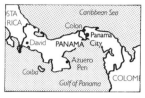

Thin excuse

Panama is the thinnest part of the Americas, a mere 37 miles wide at its most slimline point. It looks thin enough to put your hands around. So, sure enough, someone did. The USA.

Their wandering eyes first fixed on this territory a hundred years ago, when it was part of Columbia. Being so narrow, it was the perfect place to build a canal that would speed access between fast-growing California and the East coast.

However, Columbia refused to play ball. So the US fomented a separatist movement which led to the breakaway of Panama from Columbia in 1903. Fifteen days later, a Frenchman called Philippe Bunau Varilla, with no real authority, signed a treaty with the US allowing them to build a canal and operate it forever.

The canal

It is 51 miles long, up to 1,000 feet deep and in places is 500 feet wide. It is one of the two most strategic artificial waterways in the world (the other is Suez). Its most spectacular part is the 8-mile Gaillard Cut, a 200-foot deep trench. This was dug, with enormous loss of life, by thousands of black labourers from the British West Indies.

On one day every year, the public may shoot at the feet of the chief of police.

The USA still controls all land, water and installations, including the adjoining military bases. However, President Carter agreed in 1977 to let the Panamanians have their canal back. But not yet. They won't get it until 1999.

Independence

The Panama government has not been totally submissive towards the US. For example, it insists that all films shown in the country's 52 cinemas must have Spanish sub-titles. And only one of the five TV stations is run by the US army. And although the Government relies on US dollars for its banknotes, it *does* produce its own coins.

The USA's tight grip of Panama is more than merely economic and militaristic. At times it seems to be an anal fixation. It built the sewerage system of the capital, Panama City, and then refused to let the Panamanians run it for 30 years.

Off guard

The most important body in Panama is the National Guard. It acts as police, army, a para-military force and coastguard and is responsible for state security. But it was unable to prevent the coup of 1968. In fact, it organised it.

The president was deposed, the National Assembly suspended and a military junta established. Civilian rule was later restored, with the previous 42-member assembly being replaced by one with 505 members. That is inflation.

Industry

Panama means 'many fish'. Fishing is still important although ships are even more so. 11,000 are registered here, mainly because fees are low and labour laws non-existent.

The chief exports are oil, bananas, sugar and shrimps. The main items produced for home consumption are beer, whisky, rum, seco, anise and gin. Panama has the largest undeveloped copper deposits in the world. They remain undeveloped while 80 per cent of the farmers continue to earn a living growing rice.

Youth

There is a very young population due to the exceptionally high rate of population growth. The average age is 19. The education standards are high compared with other Latin American countries.

Population: 2 million

Size: One third that of Britain, 30,000 sq. miles

Government: Republic

Language: Spanish

Religion: Roman Catholic

Capital: Panama City

Currency: Balboa, US dollar

Tips for tourists

Don't be scared of catching Panama disease, even though it is commonly and frighteningly known as *banana wilt*. Although a devastating complaint, it only affects bananas.

Don't panic if your marriage breaks up. Panama has a higher proportion of divorcees than anywhere. It also has a very high proportion of illegitimate births.

Don't buy a Panama hat. The best ones come from Ecuador, where there is a plentiful supply of the screw-pine leaves needed to make them.

Papua New Guinea

Population: 3 million

Size: Twice that of Britain, 180,000 sq. miles

Government: Independent Commonwealth member

Language: Pidgin English

Religion: Christianity

Capital: Port Moresby

Currency: Kina

Tips for tourists

The national airline is called *Niugini* — which means 'stand for coconuts'. The great thing about coconuts is they fall out of the sky and kill people.

The Governor general is called Sir Lokoloko.

There are over 3,000 species of orchid: more than anywhere else.

The mountain of copper covered with gold is called Ok Tedi.

Talking disaster

The Papuans don't have a language — they have 700. It is potentially the biggest communications disaster area in the world and the Papuans solve it by speaking Pidgin English — as a recognised national language.

To make matters worse, some of the languages are extremely complex. In Kiwai, for instance, one verb performs several grammatical functions: *ai ni mi bi du mo iauri ama ri go* means 'those three will certainly see us two'. The Argoram language is still more complex. To change one word in a sentence necessitates changing the whole sentence. For instance *ame akwum kuvambakwum sumupar amenakwum salikamba* means 'I saw my two big women'. If you change 'women' to 'arrows', the sentence becomes *ame pwanggli kapanggli klupar amenakanggli salikanggliya*. The trick is never to change women to arrows.

Grey area

Only 85 per cent of Papua is mapped. Until the 1930's and 1940's the only area even vaguely known to Europeans was a 50-mile strip around the coast. It was one of the last places in the world to be explored. The Dutch kept a bit to protect Indonesia. The British kept a bit to protect Australia, which is only 100 miles away. And the Germans kept a bit to keep an eye on the British and the Dutch. The Portuguese discovered it, calling it Islas dos Papuas — or Islands of the Fuzzy Heads.

The only non-grey area is the Buka people. They are said to have the darkest skins on earth.

Modern 'politics'

Papuan politics have a distinctive flavour. In the mountains tribal warfare — clubs and spears and so forth — make centralized liberal democratic politics a nightmare. In the 1973 elections, the first anyone had heard of central government was when they were asked to vote for their parliamentary representative.

The proximity of Indonesia, which feels that Papua, and even Australia, are part of their Empire, also creates problems. New Guinea is divided between Papua and Indonesia. Suharto of Indonesia offered the islanders this choice: *"There will be an act of self-determination, of free choice, but if they vote against Indonesia, this would be treason".*

Suspicion

Most Papuans cannot understand why whites have more money than they do. The popular misconceptions are *a)* they acquired it from the spirit world, *b)* they intercepted it from the spirit world when it was intended for the Papuans, *c)* they tore out a page of the Bible which says God is a Papuan.

This obsession with where whites get their money has led to something called the 'Cargo Cult'. Papuans expect to receive money and cargo anytime from the spirit world. They have built wharves and airstrips in imitation of the white man to be ready for this heavenly hand-out. They even build offices in which they pass around pieces of paper, with nothing written on them. Another term for this strange phenomenon is *Vailala Madness*. Government-sponsored schemes have taken people to Australia to show them where the cargo comes from. But the suspicion persists. In an attempt to become more like the white man financially, the people of New Hanover even tried to buy President Lyndon Johnson so he could show them the way.

A proud father holds up the winner of the under-14's school head-shrinking competition.

Paraguay

Republica del Paraguay

Land of perpetual rain

Paraguay may be the Indian for 'place with great rivers' and rivers certainly play a major role. They are the main form of transport. The Paraguay River divides the country into east and west, while the Parana river forms the eastern and southern borders. The wettest spot on Earth is believed to be where the Parana divides into 21 arms. The floods of these great rivers ensure that one quarter of the country is marsh. This area is called *Endless Marsh*. In the past the floods were so great that *"jaguars appeared floating in the streets of Montivideo"* 1,000 miles away.

Almost everyone in Paraguay thinks he is Napoleon.

River of silver

This is the Spanish name for the River Paraguay.

Tribes were not eager to help the Spaniards. Prisoners of the Cario were fattened up and given an easy life — to be eaten. The Cario quite often married and ate their wife on the same day. One custom involved doctors. After the death of more than three of his patients, a doctor was killed. The Indians valiantly defended their territory but eventually dug so many pits, booby trapped with sharp stakes, that they fell in themselves.

Those who survived were subdued by the Jesuits — in 1537 they were thought to have made enough progress under Jesuit teaching for Pope Paul III to recognise them as humans. But the Indian threat: *"The witch will change you into a white man"* shows their side of things.

The China of America

There were 66 Spanish governors between 1536 and 1804. Between 1811 and 1948 their were 48 presidents/dictators. The first, the dictator Francia, cut off Paraguay totally from the rest of the world for 40 years. No-one could leave or enter. He ran the country with a government bureaucracy of 4 clerks and a military guard. Not surprisingly he called himself, 'El Supremo Dictator' and his policy was *'neither peace nor war'*. Less equivocally, his pseudonym after death was 'The Dead One'.

Born under the sign of Mars

This is what Paraguayans say of their country and, after Francia, it is not far wrong. The next Dictator, Lopez, got into conflict with Argentina, the USA, France and Great Britain. But it was his son Lopez who really went to town. Educated in Paris, he was another one who thought he was Napoleon. He proceeded to defeat Brazil and Argentina but when Uruguay joined in against him in 1868 Lopez's army was exterminated. He raised another which he ruthlessly led into battle, killing the faint-hearted and even beating his own mother for expressing reservation about his judgment. The result? When Lopez was killed the population had halved to a quarter of a million — with only 29,000 men.

A poem captures the country's mood at this difficult time:

Weep weep weep
In the branches of the yatay
No more is there a Paraguay
Where I was born like you
Weep weep weep.

The Chaco war

100,000 Bolivian and Paraguayan soldiers lost their lives fighting for oil on disputed territory. One of the most senseless wars in history, it was won by Paraguay — but there was no oil. 1924-1935.

Modern Paraguay

In 1943 the dictator Moringo rejected democracy and defended totalitarianism before the US Congress — who applauded. One man has ruled since 1954. His name is Stroessner. He is Catholic, Paraguayan and over 40 — as all good dictators in Paraguay must be. There are parties but they can be prohibited. The president can be overruled by a two-thirds majority. But the party in power (the president's) automatically gets two-thirds of the seats. Nevertheless, Stroessner is not elephantine in his approach. His favourite method of passing laws is to begin, *"Wouldn't it be a good idea if. . ."* — and then to leave it to the imagination of the council.

Population: 3 million

Size: One and three quarters that of Britain, 160,000 sq. miles

Government: Republic

Language: Guarani, Spanish

Religion: Roman Catholic

Capital: Asuncion

Currency: Guarani

Tips for tourists

Drink the national drink, maté. It is narcotic and has done much to cure Paraguay of a large native population.

Taste the unlikely-sounding elixir, *yerba de urina*.

Feel secure. One-third of the country's budget goes on defence.

Peru
Republica del Peru

Population, Size, Government, Language, Religion, Capital, Currency

Population: 18 and a half million

Size: Five and a half times that of Britain, 496,000 sq. miles

Government: Republic

Language: Spanish, Quechua

Religion: Roman Catholic

Capital: Lima

Currency: Sol

Tips for tourists

Ride on the highest standard gauge railway line in the world, at 15,801 ft.

See Pisarro's mummified remains in the Cathedral at Lima — his body has the texture of dried locusts.

Avoid the Amazon jungle — it contains tribes of cannibals, head-shrinkers, and some missionaries. Also professors of philosophy.

Buy alpaca wool in Peru — it is the world's sole producer.

In the Middle Ages the legendary Incas lived in Peru. They were sun-worshippers. This did not mean that they went to the Costa Brava every year on holiday, but that they worshipped the sun god. Their civilisation ended when the Costa Brava, in the shape of the Spanish, came to them.

'Civilisation'

For 300 years the Incas ruled an area which included Peru, Ecuador, Bolivia, Chile, and parts of Colombia and Argentina. They enjoyed what was, for the time, one of the world's most advanced civilisations. Based on a combination of slavery, patriarchal rule and primitive communalism, their society had eliminated poverty. There was no money — gold and silver were purely decorative. The Incas had a genius for administration and for engineering. They built very sophisticated irrigation systems, reservoirs, and buildings that could withstand earthquakes. They invented the suspension bridge and the hammock. Today, Peru is the world's leading producer of fishmeal.

This Indian hat proves that the Incas did discover the slide carousel.

Short and curlies

When the Spanish general, Pisarro, arrived in Peru in 1531, he had only 183 men with him. But he succeeded in conquering 14 million Incas. The secret was hair. Indians, like some Asians, were beardless, with little hair on their bodies. So when the Inca ruler, Atahualpa, heard that a 'white god with a beard' had landed in Peru, he was anxious to meet him. Pisarro, on whom there was hair but no flies, took this opportunity to capture the Inca and hold him ransom for a roomful of gold

and silver. Although the ransom was paid, Atahualpa was not released but garrotted. Perhaps there was a misunderstanding over the ransom note for, despite their sophisticated society, the Incas were unable to read or write. The Inca Empire, totally dependent on its ruler, collapsed. In the first 50 years of Spanish rule 10 million Inca Indians died.

Future shock

The Incas did nothing of importance without first consulting various signs. Some of the portents which fortold the future were:

The pattern of coca leaves in a shallow dish.

The arrangement of the veins in the lungs (inflated) of a sacrificed white llama.

The meanderings of spiders.

Such methods were used to diagnose illness, to predict the outcome of battles and to ferret out crimes — for example that they were being murdered by the Spanish.

Politics

Independence from Spain in 1823 was achieved with the help of Simon Bolivar, who seems to have liberated South America in a job lot. Politics was dominated by dictators and intervention by the armed forces, interspersed by occasional outbreaks of democracy. In an odd twist, the military junta that took power in 1968 began a series of reforms designed to give real economic power to the people. But today the gap between rich and poor is still vast — 10 per cent of the landowners own 93 per cent of the land and there is 70 per cent illiteracy.

Guerilla philosophy

The present civilian government, under President Fernando Belaunde Terry, is right-wing and unpopular. It faces increasing problems from the Shining Path (*Sendero Luminoso*) guerilla movement, whose leader, Abimael Guzman, is probably the only guerilla leader in the world who is a former professor of philosophy. Presumably he does not rely solely on Socratic dialogue to win new followers:
Abimael Guzman: "Do you support the Shining Path?"
Peasant: "What exactly do you mean by 'path'?"
Abimael Guzman (to aide): "Kill him, Sancho".

Philippines

Republica de Filipinas/Republika ng Pilipinas

From coconuts to donuts

'We spent 300 years in a Spanish convent followed by 50 years in Hollywood'. A popular Filipino saying which helps explain why *MacDonald's* and *Dunkin' Donuts* thrive alongside numerous Catholic churches and thriving coconut and abaca industries. Converted to Islam by the Arabs, then predominantly reconverted to Roman Catholicism, then converted to Coca-Cola by the Americans, having been occupied en route by the English, the Dutch and the Japanese, the Philippines is not surprisingly the least oriental country in the Orient.

The intrepid Portuguese Ferdinand Magellan claimed the archipelago for the Spanish crown in 1521. His personal gain in the affair was, however, minimal as he was killed shortly afterwards in a skirmish with petty chieftain Lapulapu. His leaderless band of 22 men returned pronto to Spain, thereby completing the first circumnavigation of the globe.

The 7,107 islands which comprise the Philippines became a dependency of the United States in 1900 and after a brief and unpleasant period of Japanese occupation attained independence on July 4th, 1944. A legacy of these assorted visitors is three official languages with English as the 'lingua franca'.

The Philippines is numerically the world's third largest English speaking nation and the largest Tagalog speaking one.

Sin

90 per cent of the population is Christian and the country is the only Catholic one in Asia. Religion is taken seriously, and the longest Christmas in

New uniforms have made the Filipino police the least respected force in the world.

the world is celebrated here. Holy Week is taken yet more extremely as serious zealots take to the streets as *'flaggellantes'*, their backs bleeding from numerous whippings, and walk into the sea. Very serious zealots are actually crucified at high noon surrounded by friends dressed up as Roman soldiers.

Their spiritual leader — and an outspoken opponent of the government's human rights record and the pornographic nature of films chosen by the president's wife, Mrs. Marcos, for the Manila Film Festival — is the Archbishop of Manila, Cardinal Sin.

Sinners

Sin is an important concept to the incumbent President, Mr. Marcos. When his political opposition asked the population to boycott voting in the suspect 1981 presidential elections, Marcos denounced this action as a 'moral sin', reinforcing his stance legally by decreeing that abstention was made punishable by imprisonment. He is a shrewd politician and it is not to be assumed that his declaration of martial law in 1972 was unrelated to the fact that the old war hero's second and constitutionally final term in office was shortly due to expire.

He replaced constitutionalism with personal dictatorship to counteract the ills of a society which boasts more guns and more shoot-ups per capita than any other.

On a recent visit to Manila, Vice President Bush congratulated Marcos on his 'respect for principles and for the democratic process'.

What's new?

In 1971 the Tasaday tribe, numbering 27 persons in leaves and bark, were discovered preserved in a Stone Age time-warp, their diet ranging from wild flowers to tadpoles. Their eating habits are more adventurous than most of their compatriots. Rice is the staple diet of 70 per cent of the population. The country is the world's largest producer of coconuts, and the 'Tree of Life' provides mainly a meal and export credit.

Another recent 'export' commodity proudly announced by the Government was half a million workers to oil-producing countries. Presumably this will be a growing trade until living conditions are improved in the 'new republic', Marcos's 1981 replacement for his 'new society'.

Population: 48 million

Size: Half that of Texas, 115,000 sq. miles

Government: Republic

Languages: Tagalog, English, Spanish

Main religion: Roman Catholic

Capital: Manila (Quezon City)

Currency: Peso

Tips for tourists

Although head-hunting is believed to be a dying pursuit, avoid the Ifuagao tribe just in case.

Manila is a cultural melting pot and a carnal fleshpot. Scrutinize your hotel bill to ensure you haven't been charged for 'overnight guests'.

If you think the bidding is busy and bizarre at the Chicago Soya Bean Market, witness a local cockfight, the country's unofficial religion.

Study carefully how to get on a jeepney, and take a joy ride.

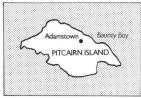

Population: 65

Size: 1.75 sq. miles

Government: Colony

Language: English

Religion: Christianity

Capital: Adamstown

Currency: £ sterling

Tips for tourists

Don't join the navy.

It is a barren place and there are no streams.

Main attraction: carved stone pillars similar to those on Easter Island.

It is unlikely that bounty will ever come to this island again.

Pitcairn Island

Safe haven

Fletcher Christian cast Captain (in fact Lieutenant) Bligh adrift in a small boat in 1790, after the most famous mutiny in history (the Bounty). Bligh made it back to England and is buried in Lambeth. Christian, on the other hand, could not have picked a better place than Pitcairn to conceal his collective guilt. Pitcairn was totally uninhabited and nothing was known of the mutineers' whereabouts until 1808. It is in the Pacific, slap-bang between Panama and New Zealand. It rises from the sea a solid rock, with none of the charming coral reefs associated with the area. It is inaccessible from the sea except from Bounty Bay — and then only in whaling boats.

Mutineer's legacy

Eight Britons, 6 Polynesian men and 12 Polynesian women from Tahiti settled here. They burnt the Bounty to cut themselves off from the outside world. But are their descendants grateful to be bereft of their only contact with the outside world? Fewer and fewer ships call at Pitcairn as the years go by. One day the population may regret its ancestors' impetuosity.

Today the main transport on the island is a specially designed wheelbarrow. The only revenue is stamps and the sale of woodcarvings to the dwindling number of passing ships. Sounds like a place you might want to get off in a hurry.

Trying to get off

By 1800 all the mutineers were dead, except Alexander Smith — known as John Adams, who no doubt changed his name just in case Bligh should one day come crawling out of the rocks. He died in 1829. The previous year George

Nobbs had settled there as pastor and chief magistrate. He persuaded the population to emigrate to Tahiti. Ironically, bad morals in Tahiti made the uncertain band of mutineers' children return to Pitcairn. This must have been a difficult decision. By 1838 the British, to prove to the population that the evil of the fathers would not be visited on the sons, drove out the tyrant Joshua Hill, who had set himself up on the island.

In 1856 all (194) of the population upped and went to Norfolk Island. Two years later 43 of them returned. By the end of the 19th Century, the inability to get off Pitcairn and stay off had led to imbecility — brought on by inter-marriage, which caused deterioration of the intellect and moral energy. Bligh must have laughed in his grave. They spoke an English/Tahitian patois. In 1982 the population was 65 — all still descended from the same crew and Polynesian mixture.

Pitcairn today

The Chairman of the Island Council is called I. Christian. Other names from the famous Bounty crew remain as well, but it's nice to know the Christians haven't lost their touch. They are Seventh Day Adventists. Presumably the Church of England feels remote in the middle of the Pacific. Christian runs a council of ten — four of whom are elected. There is one nurse and one teacher on the island. (Perhaps the best record in the world).

Included in the Pitcairn group are the islands Oeno, Henderson and Ducie. An American hill-billy millionaire is trying to buy Henderson from the British Foreign Office. Pitcairn itself is named after a midshipman who first saw it.

Years of interbreeding have produced dramatic genetic mutation.

Poland

Polska Rzeczpospolita Ludowa

966 and all that

This is the sad story of a once-grand nation which fell on hard times and harder rulers, and has kept on falling. From the year 966 AD, when Poland became a united state, it grew in power and influence (under *Boleslaw the Wry-mouthed* and *Wladyslaw the Short*, among others) until it was almost an empire, dominating Europe with its ideas, culture and science.

Then it was invaded and divided between Russia, Austria and Prussia. Not until the end of World War One did Poland achieve independence again — only to be picked by Hitler's Germany as a prime target for invasion.

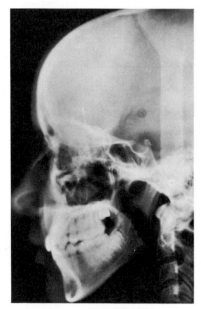

Exclusive! The only known picture of General Jaruzelski smiling.

And now all this

At the end of World War Two (in which a fifth of its population had been killed) Poland was 'liberated' by Russia. A few years later, the people voted for communist rule. Since then, they have been trying sporadically, and unsuccessfully, to liberate themselves from Russia.

After being legalised in 1980, the independent trade union *Solidarity* rapidly became the world's biggest, with 9 and a half million members. It is now the world's biggest banned union. The Poles are reduced to drowning their sorrows in drink (see *Tips for tourists*).

Famous Poles

The astronomer Copernicus, the composer Chopin, the discoverer of radioactivity Marie Curie, Karol Wojtyla, better known as Pope John Paul II (93 per cent of Poles are Roman Catholics), Lech Walesa.

Less-famous Poles

The Barbara Cartland of Poland was Maria Wirtemberg, daughter of Princess Izabela. She wrote the country's first romantic novel, *Malvina, or the Perspicacity of the Heart*.

Food and drink

Poles like food and love drink (see *Tips for tourists*). They consider beer to be low class and stick to spirits. They delight in eating meat three times a day. Unfortunately, there is a chronic meat shortage in their country now, causing many of them to spend hours each day queueing outside the butcher's.

Up the poles

Poland is the second biggest country in Europe (after Russia) in both size and population. It is Eastern Europe's largest producer of food and the world's second biggest potato producer. It is also Eastern Europe's biggest tractor and truck producer, which is a major honour in the communist world.

Slippery pole

Poland is in as much of a mess economically as it is politically. It owes Western banks 30 billion dollars, which it can't repay. And the 'longest line in Europe' is how Poles describe the waiting list for their home-produced cars. Some customers have to wait up to ten years. And when the car arrives, it will almost certainly be in rust-prone white and full of faults. However, most new-car faults can be put right by bribing the factory's warehouse assistants.

Proverb

It doesn't take a Cracow rabbi to see that.

Population: 36 million	
Size: One and a third times that of Britain, 120,000 sq. miles	
Government: Communist	
Language: Polish	
Religion: Roman Catholic	
Capital: Warsaw	
Currency: Zloty, groszy	

Tips for tourists

Don't be fooled by 'cocktail bars'. They sell fruit-and-milk drinks only.

Be ostentatious — spend money. Tourists to Poland spend less than those who visit any other country.

Be ostentatious — stay sober. Poles are the world's greatest spirit drinkers.

Population: 10 million

Size: A third that of Britain, 34,000 sq. miles

Government: Republic

Language: Portuguese

Religion: Roman Catholic

Capital: Lisbon

Currency: Escudo, centavo

Tips for tourists

Read *The Letters from a Portuguese Nun, 1669* — precursor of the 'Confessions of a Window Cleaner' series.

Don't believe anyone who says Columbus discovered America — or that the Irish or Vikings did for that matter. Ten years before Columbus, a Portuguese fisherman, Sanchez, is believed to have reached it.

The British have always supported the port industry — imaginatively named after the port they imported it from — Oporto.

Cork is the chief product (two thirds of the world supply), and cork, eucalyptus and pine forests cover 20 per cent of the country.

Portugal has the largest collection of vintage cars in the world.

Portugal
Republica Portuguesa

A circular tale

Portugal is one of the oldest countries in Europe. Her boundaries were set in 1139. Before then, the Romans were the first to settle there, calling their port of call *Portus Cale*, hence the country's name. After them the place was overrun by Visigoths, Berbers and Moors. By the 10th Century one area decided this wasn't very moorish and started to call itself Portugal. Alfonso the Fat extended the country's powers between 1211 and 1223 and King Dinis (1279-1325) set the ball rolling for the next 700 years by building a navy. This conquered the world and Portugal only returned to its borders of the 14th Century in 1974. A long and exhausting journey.

World-beaters

One of the secrets of the great Portuguese navy was a new ship called the caravel. Portugal's position — so influenced by the sea — was a help. Also Spain was on its other flank and going

On being told in 1974 that they now had the vote.

to Spain for fun is a modern phenomenon. This provided the incentive to set sail. Henry the Navigator, in tandem with John the Perfect and Manuel the Fortunate, laid the bedrock of conquest overseas. Under the house of Aviz, India, Brazil, Greenland, California, China, Japan, Ethiopia and Molucca were all discovered and colonised.

Magellan was the first to sail around the world, Bartholomew Diaz sailed round the Cape of Good Hope and Columbus and Cabral filled in the bits in between. Under the Portuguese, Luanda in Angola became the first African city south of the equator. 1415 began 'the Great Age'. All the new world was divided in half between Portugal and Spain.

But then disaster struck. Overstretched by its mighty empire overseas Portugal proved easy meat for the Spanish who stepped in and annexed it. This was the greatest annexation in history and Spain became the most powerful country in the world.

Home sweet home

The Portuguese on home territory were and are considerably quieter than their overseas adventures suggest. In spite of the fact that they produce the stuff, they hardly ever drink port, nearly all of which is exported abroad — mainly to Great Britain. In fact they are a morose people. The two Portuguese words which capture the country's mood are *saudade* — meaning 'yearning' — and *fado*. Fado is unique to Portugal and is a plaintive ballad, wailed rather than sung, of unrequited love, passion and despair. The cafes of major cities contain *fadista* — the wailers — and performers begin after 11pm, presumably when resistance to extreme sentimentality is lowest. The most famous fadista in Portugal is Amalia Rodrigues.

Their other hobby is bullfighting. But this, too, is toned down compared to the Spanish variety. They never kill the bull but vault over its horns in much the same way as the ancient Minoans.

They have saints for everything. Santa Quiteira protects the unwary against mad dogs. In the most remote city in Portugal, Miranda, they speak their own language and dance the stick dance. Men hold sticks in either hand and tap them to the rhythm of the music.

They now have a democracy and a minister for the quality of life.

Qatar

The State of Qatar

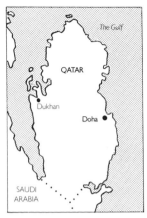

Geography

Qatar sticks out like a sore thumb from the Arabian Peninsula into the Persian Gulf. It is thumb-sized (a large thumb — 125 miles long by no more than 55 wide) and, like a thumb, the join is hard to see: the border with Saudi Arabia has never been defined.

From the ground it resembles a stale pancake, dry and flat. Its highest point is not much over 50 feet above sea level. It has no rivers.

An ancient sundial shows why the Islamic calendar is over 600 years out of date.

History

The Al Khalifah tribesmen moved into this area in the 18th Century and showed their toughness by beating off a Persian invasion and then overthrowing their absentee rulers.

In 1868, concerned by outbreaks of unrest and piracy, Britain moved in and installed as ruler Muhammad ibn Thani Al-Thani of the leading local family. The Al-Thani dynasty still rules.

In 1916 Qatar became a British protected state after promising to end the slave trade and piracy. When the British left the Persian Gulf, Qatar chose not to join the United Arab Emirates and became an independent state in 1971.

Politics

Executive power is in the hands of a Council of Ministers, most of whom are Al-Thanis. This is not always to the ruler's advantage. Sheikh Abdullah was forced to abdicate in 1951 by his brother, Ali. And Ali's son, Ahmad, was deposed (while on a hunting trip in Iran) by his cousin Khalifa. His first act as

ruler was the smart one of raising the army's pay. This was also a cheap move — there are only 9,000 soldiers.

People

Three out of four of the people who live in Qatar are immigrant workers from Europe, Iran, Pakistan and India. They have come to share the oil wealth.

More than half the population lives in Doha, the capital. In school, the pupil-teacher ratio is twelve to one for boys and seven to one for girls.

Industry

For the first half of this century the economy depended on pearl diving (half the world's pearls came from here), fishing and camel breeding. Qatar was a poor and semi-feudal society. Then oil was discovered. Now it is a very rich semi-feudal society with a welfare state. It has the highest public expenditure per capita in the world.

Ninety per cent of the national income comes from oil and there is lots more where that comes from. The North West Dome field contains one-eighth of the world's known gas reserves.

What do they do with all that money? Much of it has gone on developing an agricultural industry (not easy — or cheap — in a country without water). Some goes on their wonderful health and social services. But most goes on armaments — about 1,000 million dollars a year. The country also has modern roads, hotels, government buildings and a national TV network.

Qatar is also becoming important in the world of finance and banking. There is no income tax.

Population:	A quarter of a million
Size:	4,400 sq. miles
Government:	Sheikdom
Language:	Arabic
Religion:	Islam
Capital:	Doha
Currency:	Qatar riyal

Tips for tourists

Fall ill. The free medical service is one of the best in the world.

If you are female and want to meet local women, join the Red Crescent Society (the Moslem equivalent of the Red Cross). It is the only chance for educated Qatari women to gather freely outside their homes.

Romania
Republica Socialista Romania

Population: 22 and a quarter million

Size: Same as that of Britain, 92,000 sq. miles

Government: Communist

Language: Romanian

Main religion: Romanian Orthodox

Capital: Bucharest

Currency: Leu, bani

Tips for tourists

Don't attempt an illegal border crossing unless you can swim. Two-thirds of the borders are liquid — rivers, seas and lakes.

Eat caviar. Ninety per cent of the sturgeon catch comes from the Danube.

Romanian communism doesn't eradicate class differences. Address someone of superior status *Dumnia-voastra* but someone of inferior status *Dumnia-ta*.

Drink plum brandy. It is the national beverage.

Don't talk on public transport. Romanians don't.

Discord

Romania is a maverick country which reinforces the prejudices of both East and West. To the East, its enormous industrial growth during the 1970's (the world's second fastest) proves that communism works. To the West, the fact that it is still one of Europe's least developed countries proves that it doesn't.

Romania has by far the highest suicide rate in the world and 4 million illiterates, although one in five Romanians is a pupil or student.

Out of tune

Romania was just one of the Balkan states until the early part of the last century, when the idea of Romanian national unity arose, fostered by the radical Philharmonic Society. This led to several uprisings, including one by 40,000 peasants in Transylvania, who presumably felt that if they weren't scared of Dracula, they needn't be scared of anything. The new nation of Romania was formed in 1861. After World War Two, it threw out its king and became a communist state.

Soloists

Romania refuses to be a tame Soviet satellite and has been taking an increasingly independent line in foreign affairs. The people work long hours (44 a week, every alternate Saturday off) and spend most of their free time at the movies (they have more cinemas than any country apart from Russia and the US).

Upbeat

The country pays for its idiosyncracy with oil, of which it is Europe's second largest producer. There is enough salt in Romania to satisfy the world's requirements for 13,000 years. It would last even longer if everyone cooked like Romanians — they don't use salt.

Culture

Favourite traditional song: *The walling-in sacrifice*. Favourite traditional story: *The tale of Fat-Frumos* (Prince Charming). Best-known writer: Carmen Sylva, which was the pen name of Queen Elizabeth, wife of King Carol I. Unluckiest architect: the one who designed the Curtes de Arges monastery and was then forced to commit suicide by the ruling prince so that he could never design anything as beautiful again. Most common subject in current

Romanian art: tractors. Ritual to avoid: in parts of Transylvania, the song of the hen forms part of the wedding fertility rites.

Uncultured

Idiots are treated with special kindness in Romania. Many districts have a 'Fools' Week' when lunatics are allowed to run through the streets beating whoever they meet. Romanians are extremely superstitious, especially in the Wallach area. Women there insist on washing on Wednesdays, spinning on Saturdays and doing nothing on Tuesdays.

For expressing anti-state views these women are forced to walk around with gigantic toilet rolls on their heads.

Language

Romanian consists of 3,800 words of Slavonic origin, 2,600 from Latin, 700 Turkish, 650 Greek, 500 Hungarian and 50 from Albanian. A useful Romanian phrase is: *Va rog sa ma spalati pe cap si sa-mi faceti un mis en plis.* This means: 'Shampoo and set, please.'

Geography

Romania is 31 per cent mountains, 36 per cent hills and 33 per cent floodlands.

Rwanda

Tiny Tutsi

Between the 14th Century and 1959, the Tutsi ruled in what is now Rwanda, although they were only 16 per cent of the population. The Hutu, on the other hand, made up 83 per cent. The trick was that, small in numbers though they were, the Tutsi were very tall. Quite often over 7 feet. After a few centuries the Hutu got used to being ruled.

Tutsi rule

Hereditary kings reigned and were divided into three types. If the king was called *Mutara* or *Cyirima* he was 'king of the cows' and peaceful. If he was called *Kigeri* or *Mibambwe*, he was warlike. If he was called *Yuhi* he was 'king of fire' and denoted prosperity for the country. This was an early form of astrology.

King of the cows

Cows were very important to the Tutsi. They didn't even let their women look after them. They used them (the cows) for milk but never meat. Because women were not allowed to look after the cows they (the women) were very political and took a great part in ruling the country. The only time women got near a cow was when they were married. A common brideprice was one cow and beer for the relatives.

Kigeri or Mibambwe

The warlike kings could be very warlike indeed. As a symbol of victory, the genitals of foreign kings and warriors would be attached to the royal drums

which communicated with god. There were essentially three types of god:
Imaana — generally good
Abazumu — spirits of the dead and therefore unpleasant
Imandwa – a heroes' cult group. Initiation consisted of being insulted, buried in excrement and committing incest.
In 1910 and 1928 the British had a lot of trouble with The Mumbo Cult.

King Leopold

Not another type of Tutsi king but the owner of the Belgian Congo of which Rwanda was, for a time, part. The Belgian Congo was 80 times the size of Belgium leading to Stanley's remark; *Leopold's enormous voracity to swallow a million square miles with a gullet that will not take a herring.*

Tutsi goodbye

Because of Rwanda's central position in Africa — it separates the Nile and the Congo — it wasn't until the 18th Century that traders got to it. Even then, the population carried on under the footsi of the Tutsi. But in 1959, goaded by a weak king who was controlled by the chiefs, there were uprisings amongst the Hutu. The reason the Hutu had always been subservient was that the Tutsi king had given them protection. This had been taken away by the chiefs. The Hutu revolution was over by 1960. The Tutsi complacency was shown by their formation of only one political party to the Hutu's two. In a referendum in 1961 the monarchy was rejected and the king went into exile with 120,000 of his closest friends. Mr. Kayibanda was president until 1973 when he was overthrown by Major General Juvenal Habyorimana.

Population: 5 million

Size: 10,000 sq. miles

Government: Republic

Main language: Kinyarwanda (Bantu)

Main religion: Roman Catholic

Capital: Kigali

Currency: Rwanda franc

Tips for tourists

Visit Allert Park — the first National Park in Africa, where the rare David Attenborough has been seen hiding behind bushes.

Rarer are the gorillas which he brought to our screens. They are killed for their head and hands. Attenborough's gorilla, *Digit*, went this way in 1976.

Don't get sick pining for trains. There is no railway and only one doctor for every 60,000 people.

The country exports the most charming of all exports — extract of pyrethrum flowers. And quinine.

The National Theatre of Rwanda's production of Isherwood's *I am a Camera*.

141

Jamestown
Longwood
ST. HELENA

Population: 6,600

Size: 162 sq. miles (including dependencies)

Government: UK colony

Language: English

Religion: Christianity

Capital: Jamestown

Currency: St. Helena pound

Tips for tourists

Visit the youth club run by the police, called the *Blue Lamp*.

Listen to Radio St. Helena — all transmissions are preceded by *A Life on the Ocean Wave*.

Spot the wire-bird, which prefers walking to flying. It is the sole surviving member of the indigenous fauna and is only found on St. Helena.

See the tortoise which was a contemporary of Napoleon.

Don't worry if you get sick — St. Helena has more hospital beds for the size of population than anywhere in the world.

Visit the islands of Ascension and Tristan da Cunha — dependencies of St. Helena. But allow plenty of time — Ascension is 700 miles north of St. Helena, and Tristan da Cunha 1400 miles south.

St. Helena

The only reason anyone has heard of St. Helena is because it is the place of Napoleon's final exile. It is difficult enough to escape from now — there are no air services — but in 1815 it was even more so. Napoleon failed and died there in 1821.

Napoleon

The Emperor lived here with a faithful retinue of 30. His arrival brought brief interest and prosperity to the islanders. Despite the limitations imposed on his freedom, his household continued to address him as 'Emperor' and scorned frugality.

The 30 people consumed daily more than 75lbs of beef and mutton and 7 chickens. Monthly supplies included 22 roasting joints, nine hams, nine salted tongues, 45lbs of bacon, 210 bottles of Bordeaux, 26 of Champagne, 23 of Madeira, 60 of Graves, and 11 of other wines.

The cause of Napoleon's illness and decline was something of a mystery since the British appointed a doctor whose medical experience was confined to performing autopsies. On Napoleon's death the doctor came into his own and diagnosed cancer of the stomach.

Temporary exile

In 1890 the Zulu chief Dinizulu was exiled on the island. He lived quietly here for seven years, a model prisoner who took to European ways and dress, and learned to play the piano.

History

This volcanic island was discovered in 1502 by the Portuguese who managed to keep its existence a secret until 1588. It was uninhabited and thickly wooded. St. Helena is considered by some to be the oldest land in the world.

Self-imposed exile

The first settler on St. Helena had no nose, no right hand and only four fingers on his left hand. He was Don Fernando Lopez, a renegade Portuguese officer who had been horribly mutilated by his army for deserting to the enemy in Goa. Lopez lived here alone for thirty years.

The island was seized by the British East India Company in 1659. Some colonisation was encouraged and slaves were imported from Africa. By 1737 the islanders had managed to find a governor in keeping with the island's traditions — Captain Robert Jenkins, who had only one ear.

Decline

The opening of the Suez Canal in 1869 dealt a death blow to the island's economy, and poverty became a permanent state. The problems were exacerbated by a series of incompetent governors, the introduction of goats (which, destroyed two-thirds of the islands trees) and the arrival by ship of the white ant, which had the power to reduce anything wooden to sawdust overnight.

Today

A brief flirtation with flax rescued the island's economy until 1965, when the market collapsed. Now most of the island's revenue consists of grants from the British government plus sales of postage stamps. But frugality is a way of life. The government printing office still uses a linotype machine which the foreman mechanic of the government garage assembled from a handbook in 1958.

People

There is a high illegitimate birth rate. Many young couples have gone elsewhere to seek their fortune, leaving their children in the care of grandparents. Thus a large part of the population is either over 50 or under 16.

Many islanders have strange speech patterns. For example, there is a frequent interchange of 'v' and 'w' in the manner of Dickens' Londoners. A tape recording of an islander intended for British radio listeners was scrapped when he repeated several times that he was the island's *wet*.

Making Coca-Cola bottles has reached cottage industry stage on St. Helena.

St. Kitts-Nevis

St. Christopher-Nevis

Laborious union

In 1493 Columbus discovered St. Kitts. He loved it and in place of the Indian Carib name *Liaguiga* — meaning fertile land — he named it after himself — St. Christopher. He somehow failed to discover Nevis, two miles away, until five years later. Presumably he had eyes only for 'his' island. Nevis reminded him of the Pyrenees back home and the Spanish *nieves* means 'snow'.

For all his discovering, it was the British who took the islands in 1628 and, mocking Columbus, called St. Christopher St. Kitts. British cartography eventually prevailed and St. Kitts it has remained.

Then the British united St. Kitts, Nevis and Anguilla, nearly 100 miles away, into one administrative area. Anguilla got out of that at independence by choosing to remain British.

Rivalry

In spite of the fact that the two islands are physically close they are miles apart in other ways. For instance, the journey between them by ferry is 11 miles. Perhaps the reason for Nevis' feeling of inferiority — apart from being inferior — is that St. Kitts became such a popular British colony. Called *Queen of the Caribbees* and *Cradle of the Caribbean*, St. Kitts sent out expeditionary forces to mother the rest of the British possessions in the Caribbean. It was Britains oldest possession in the West Indies. Nevis was not so charming to Englishmen. The reason they first set foot on the island was to hang a Captain John Smith. After an argument, he was let off. It never has been a swinging place.

Healthy rivalry

St. Kitts' popularity was partly due to the huge profits it made from sugar but mainly to its healthy spa waters at Bath — the namesake of the spa in England. Tourists, an unusual phenomenon in the early 18th Century, flocked there. Today there are 29,000 a year. This popularity led to 'some of the finest examples of architecture in the Caribbean' on the island.

Frog sandwich

The British and French shared the island of St. Kitts with equanimity. But not for long. They worked out an arrangement whereby France took the two ends and England had the middle — hardly a recipe for success. Sure enough Britain began to build a fort on Brimstone Hill, 750 feet high, 'The Gibraltar of the Caribbean'. It took 100 years to build. The French captured it. You can visit the old border between France and Britain at Half Way Tree village. Finally the British drove out the French and made the island a crown colony in 1823.

Nevis say die

Not to be outdone by all the action on the mother island, Nevis had its own successes. Admiral Nelson married Frances Nisbet here at Fig Tree Church. His best man was the future King William IV of England.

Alexander Hamilton was born here. He was famous for writing, among other things:
"A national debt, if it be not excessive, will be to us a national blessing".

Otherwise Nevis produces sea island cotton and has a governor called Sir Clement Athelston Arrindell. In 1980, after 30 years, the Nevis Labour Party was ousted by the Peoples Action Party.

Population: 44,300

Size: 101 sq. miles

Government: Associated state of the UK

Language: English

Religion: Christianity

Capital: Basseterre

Currency: East Caribbean dollar

Tips for tourists

For all its health-giving climate, the highest mountain on St. Kitts is mysteriously called Mt. Misery. It also has black sand beaches. Perhaps this is the reason.

It is difficult to control cheating in the annual Tug of War between the two islands.

143

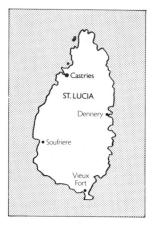

Population: 120,000

Size: 238 sq. miles

Government: Independent Commonwealth member

Main language: English

Main religion: Roman Catholic

Capital: Castries

Currency: East Caribbean dollar

Tips for tourists

Go mad. A quarter of the island's hospital beds are for mental patients.

Beware holiday romance. St. Lucia has the world's worst rate for deaths from syphilis.

Want to boil an egg? Visit the volcano at Soufriere, the world's only drive-in volcano. You can drive right up to the lip of the smouldering crater — then boil your egg in the nearby stream.

If you don't want to go anywhere, visit the Valley of Cul-de-Sac.

St. Lucia

One guide book describes St. Lucia as *a tropical quilt of coconut palms, bananas and exotic tropical blooms.*

History

December 13th is celebrated as Discovery Day — but they haven't yet discovered the year the island was found. The discoverer, one Juan de la Cosa, called the island *El Falcon*. It was inhabited then by Carib Indians who had driven out the earlier population, Arawaks. The English came next on a ship which they had, with enormous foresight, named *Olive Branch*.

Presumably the Caribs could not read. They massacred all but 19 of the party of 63.

Fifteen years later a much larger party of Frenchmen fared no better. It wasn't until 1651 that the French managed to settle on the island — and even then the governor was murdered in his bed soon afterwards by rebellious Caribs.

In 1764 the British seized the island. While engaged in a long struggle with the French for its ownership, they proceeded to wipe out virtually the whole native population and replace it with African slaves.

A form of representative government was allowed by the British in 1924. The representation was limited to the people being allowed to choose three of the 13 members of their parliament. St. Lucia became self-governing in 1967 and independent in 1979.

Politics

There has been trouble between the Prime Minister and his Deputy, both of whom want to be top dog. This has led to the Deputy going off in a sulk and forming his own party.

In 1982 the government fell after it tried to introduce a bill into parliament which would have condoned corruption.

Industry

St. Lucia was a pretty prosperous place in the last century thanks mainly to the sugar industry. Since then the sweet life has turned rather bitter, due not only to the decline in the sugar industry, but to wars, epidemics and hurricanes.

The main export now is bananas. Production was halved by Hurricane Allen in 1980, but there are still 10,000 growers on the island. Other products are the usual West Indian standbys of cocoa, copra and coconut oil. The second biggest industry is tourism.

A large government erection demonstrates the loop method.

There is a thriving charcoal trade with Barbados — not all of which can be caused by the demand for barbecues by rich tourists.

The people

Three quarters of the people are under 20 and a third of the adult population is unemployed. Paying old age pensions is not a problem, though — only 1 per cent of the people are over 65. Education does not cause much trouble, either. Primary schooling is compulsory by law — but the law is not enforced.

The only remnants of the days of French rule are the religion (Roman Catholicism) and a dying French dialect. Defence is in the hands of a small number of soldiers. Shopping is on the heads of a large number of women, who keep it there with banana fibre rings.

Communication

St. Lucians have a choice of nine cinemas to visit (one of the highest per head of population in the world) and of three newspapers to read — the *Voice of Saint Lucia*, the *Crusader* and the *Catholic Chronicle*.

St. Vincent

St. Vincent and the Grenadines

From outer space

St. Vincent looks like a coal scuttle that has dropped bits of coal southwards. The bits are the Grenadines. Half of the island and its dependencies are covered in forest. The Grenadines dependent on St. Vincent are Bequia, Canouan, Mayreau, Mustique, Union Island and Petit St. Vincent.

Indian reservation

Apart from Dominica, St. Vincent is the only island in the Caribbean where the original Carib Indians are still alive. They lasted longer originally because they teamed up with shipwrecked negro slaves and formed a united front. Until 1762 they controlled most of the territory. Between then and 1783 wars between the French and the British prevented either side disposing of the Indians. But then a rising in 1795 led to them being temporarily deported by the British to Rattan. The Caribs called the island *Haroun* meaning 'Land of the Blessed'. St. Vincent replaced it because the island was discovered by Columbus on St. Vincent's Day 1498.

Land of the blessed

With a temperature that rarely sinks below 64 degrees fahrenheit or above 90 degrees fahrenheit it is not surprising the Indians liked it. The Earl of Carlisle

was certainly blessed when Charles I gave it to him in 1627. The difference between Carlisle and St. Vincent must have been overwhelming. Now the group is most famous for Mustique — a partly private island where Princess Margaret lets her hair down. Anyone she invites there would have to be blessed.

Government

Since 1960 the island has held its own parliament consisting of the Queen (of England), a 12-strong House of Assembly and a Governor General currently called Sir Sydney Douglas Gun-Monro. The Prime Minister combines two literary geniuses in his name — Milton Cato.

The special arrangement means that internal government is entirely the responsibility of parliament. Great Britain is responsible only for external relations and defence. For instance, defending the royal family from photographers on Mustique.

Paradise regained

It hasn't needed Milton to bring a reminder of paradise here. The Cannon Ball Tree grows next to the Sealing Wax Tree. The island's products are largely bananas and arrowroot, and the only factories produce rum and cigarettes.

Population: 120,000

Size: 150 sq. miles

Government: Independent Commonwealth member

Language: English

Main religion: Christianity

Capital: Kingstown

Currency: East Caribbean dollar

Tips for tourists

Visit the oldest Breadfruit Tree. It was grown from a seed Captain Bligh brought from Tahiti.

Avoid Mount Soufriere — a volcano that killed 2,000 in 1902 and last exploded in 1979.

The public school soundalike *The Vincentian* is the only paper.

St. Vincent only has one hospital bed

ITALY

SAN
MARINO
• San Marino

Population: 24,000

Size: 24 sq. miles

Government: Republic

Language: Italian

Religion: Roman Catholic

Capital: San Marino

Currency: Lira, centesimi

Tips for tourists

If you want to live dangerously, try the favourite spectator sport — the Crossbowmen's Contest.

Marriage on the rocks? San Marino has the lowest proportion of divorcees in the world.

San Marino

Repubblica di San Marino

Little things

San Marino is the smallest independent republic in the world and the smallest independent state in Europe after the Vatican and Monaco. It perches on the slopes of Monte Titano, completely surrounded by Italy. From the top of the mountain the residents of this landlocked country — which has a maximum length of eight miles — can look thirstily towards the Adriatic a mere 20 miles away.

Small beginnings

San Marino is the second oldest country in the world. More than 1,600 years ago Saint Marinus, a Dalmatian stonecutter, settled here with a group of Christians to escape persecution. By the 12th Century San Marino had developed into a commune with its own laws and consuls. It has remained independent largely due to its isolation and mountain fortresses which stand on top of the three peaks of Monte Titano.

During the 19th Century movement for Italian unification San Marino gave asylum to several revolutionaries. These included Garibaldi.

When Napoleon invaded Italy he respected the independence of this republic and even offered to extend its territories. Perhaps this was to be expected — Napoleon had a soft spot for small things.

Industry

San Marino uses both Italian and Vatican currencies but it issues its own stamps and coins. Indeed, stamps are one of its main foreign currency earners.

There is a flourishing tourist industry but most of the visitors only come on day trips.

The people

Abraham Lincoln said of San Marino: *Your country is one of the most honoured in all history.* It is not a message that seems to be appreciated by the present citizens. Almost as many of them live abroad as stay at home. They match this low opinion of their country with an equally low one of each other: San Marino citizens are not allowed to be judges in their own country.

Politics

Laws are made by the Great and General Council, which is more general than great. It has 60 members and every six months two of them are appointed to act as regents, called *Capitani reggenti.*

One of the reasons no-one has ever invaded San Marino.

Even this geographical backwater cannot avoid political crises. After the last election a 'government of democratic collaboration' had to be formed to break the deadlock.

Those who do best are the prospective unemployed. The state is committed to finding work for those who can't get a job with private industry.

Fighting

San Marino has no army but it is proud of its three military corps which serve on parades during official ceremonies. They are called the *Great and General Council Guard*, the *Uniformed Militia* and the *Fort Guard.* If the country needs defending it can call up all able-bodied citizens between 16 and 55 except teachers and students.

Travel

There are 137 miles of road, most of them uphill. A bus service connects San Marino to Rimini on the coast and there is also a helicopter service in the summer.

Sao Tome
Sao Tome e Principe

Innovation

For years, these islands were just a dropping off place for slaves being taken to America from Africa. So, when slavery was abolished, the dire warnings about the collapse of the Sao Tome economy can only be imagined. But what happened to it was a lesson to all those who fight against the introduction of new technologies. The new technology in Sao Tome's case was the cocoa bean. In 1822 it was brought over from Brazil to these islands — the first place in Africa to grow it. By the start of the 20th Century, Sao Tome was the world's biggest producer of cocoa.

Unfortunately, this economic success went to the heads of the plantation bosses. They decided to go back to their bad old ways and re-introduced slavery. In 1909, British and German chocolate makers boycotted Sao Tome cocoa because it was being produced with slave labour. The islands' cocoa industry has never regained its foremost position, although cocoa is still grown on 93 per cent of cultivable land and provides most of the export trade. The rest comes from coconuts.

Information

Sao Tome consists of a number of islands in the Bight of Biafra, 125 miles off the west coast of Africa. As it is the second smallest African state (after the Seychelles) it would more accurately be described as a nibble than a bight.

The main island is Sao Tome, a looming mass which looks like a whale floating on the sea. Its lower areas are crammed with cocoa plantations, its upper reaches are dense with forests. Its mountains are extinct volcanoes, many of which look like fingers, pointing accusingly at the sky.

The other islands include Principe (population: 5,000) where, in 1977, there was an attempt to break away from Sao Tome and establish a monarchy. Fortunately this failed before the troops had to be called in — Sao Tome has only 160 soldiers.

Exploitation

As well as keeping slaves here, the Portuguese who colonised this previously uninhabited island in the 15th Century used it as a camp for convicts and Jews. In the early 1970's, as Portugal struggled to hang on to its African empire, it turned Sao Tome into a vast concentration camp once again, with prisoners from Angola,

Mozambique and Guinea-Bissau. It must have been just like old times.

Even since independence in 1975, the new rulers haven't been exactly gentle with dissidents. In 1978, the former Minister of Health led an attempted coup. This was decidedly unhealthy for the conspirators, all of whom are still rotting in jail.

Education

School elections are more interesting than national ones. In all schools, pupils elect a teachers' council which then chooses a head teacher.

Sao Tome is a socialist republic which has nationalised most of the land. This was a popular thing to do. Before independence, a couple of dozen Portuguese companies owned all of the estates, one of which covered a tenth of the main island.

In the toiletless waste of Sao Tome, you go out prepared for an emergency.

Population: 87,000

Size: 372 sq. miles

Government: Republic

Main Language: Creole

Main Religion: Roman Catholic

Capital: Sao Tome

Currency: Dobra, centavos

Tips for tourists

Drink the water. It is reputedly the purest in the world.

Don't go to the movies. There is only one cinema.

Don't mind being called a bastard. 82 per cent of the births are illegitimate.

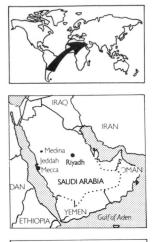

Population: About 8 and three quarter million

Size: Ten times that of Britain, 865,000 sq. miles

Government: Absolute monarchy

Language: Arabic

Religion: Islam

Capital: Riyadh

Currency: Riyal, qurush

Tips for tourists

If you want to get married, remember that a bride costs £5,100 if she is a virgin and £3,400 if she isn't.

When eating in a Saudi home:
Eat only with your right hand.
Do not sit with the soles of your feet facing anyone.
Do not suggest that an Arab man removes his head dress.
Do not ask for alcohol or pork (Porc au vin blanc is definitely out).
Do not panic if your host keeps tapping your knee or shoulder — that is how they like to punctuate discussions.
Never ask after the health of an Arab's wife or female family member.

Saudi Arabia
al-Mamlaka al-'Arabiya as-Sa'udiya

Counting

Saudi Arabia is living proof that even the rich have problems. This is the richest country on earth, for the size of population, but it still has problems counting. It isn't easy to count the fortune it makes from oil. It isn't any simpler to count the population. Half of them are Bedouin nomads wandering from oasis to oasis (using trucks now rather than camels) and another quarter are foreigners attracted by the demand for labour. And counting women is not allowed. (In any case they don't count.)

Most difficult of all is counting the grains of sand. Saudi Arabia is a vast desert, the biggest country in the Middle East. It contains Rub'al-Khali (the Empty Quarter), the world's largest continuous sand area. It would make a wonderful beach if only there was some water with it. Unfortunately this is another of the country's problems — there isn't any water.

Who counts

Politics is very simple here. People just do what the king says. The alternative is doing what the Prime Minister says, but as he is the king, it doesn't make any difference. Most government posts are held by members of the royal family. There are 5,000 of them to choose from, but the good jobs usually go to some of the 250 princes, who are educated at the best schools and casinos of Europe.

Even in a royal family there are bound to be squabbles. King Feisal was assassinated in 1975 by one of his relatives. There was no political significance — it was just a family row.

What counts

Saudi Arabia produces one sixth of the world's output of oil and has a quarter of the world's reserves. It provides 90 per cent of the country's income. Before the discovery of oil the only industry of note was dates (which are still the main food) and pilgrims (who are still the main import — 2 million of them a year, coming to be entertained at Mecca). There has been a less pleasant import recently — Idi Amin, the butcher of Uganda.

The largest airport in the world is here — King Abdul-Aziz airport, near Jeddah. The Hajj terminal is the world's largest roofed structure. The country had 20 doctors in 1950 and more than 12,000 by 1980.

Holy one

The history of Saudi Arabia is bound up with the story of Islam. It was founded by Mahomet in the year 610 and quickly became a powerful political force. Its followers conquered large parts of Africa and Asia. Then in the 14th Century the Turks began to over-run the Arabian conquests and eventually took over Arabia itself.

It was only in the early years of this century that the Arabs fought back. Under their great leader Ibn Saud they eventually won their land back and the modern state of Saudi Arabia was formed in 1927. Just in time for the discovery of oil seven years later.

999

Justice is swift and savage. The laws are based on Islamic tradition and the punishments on bestiality. They include beheading, and cutting off fingers and hands for less serious offences. Sadly, Islam didn't lay down laws to govern things like parking offences, speeding and industrial troubles, so the king has had to invent a few new ones.

Zero

There are two radio and two TV stations. Their output is almost entirely religious programmes. There are five daily papers, 21 weeklies and five monthlies but only one women's magazine (called *New Eve*). This is hardly surprising as women are not encouraged to read — or do much else. Girls were not allowed to go to school until 1960. Slavery was officially abolished in 1962 but it still goes on.

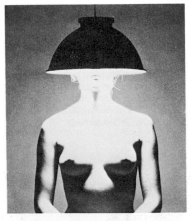

Increasingly westernised, Saudi Arabia has largely replaced stoning, as a punishment for adultery, by microwaving.

Senegal
Republique du Senegal

Slave society

More than one million people in Senegal are members of the Mouride brotherhood or other similar brotherhoods. The Mourides were formed at the end of the 19th Century. The leaders ruthlessly exploit the religious credulity of the population. The disciples are totally devoted to these hereditary leaders and work unpaid, unclothed, unfed — and celibate. They produce one-quarter of the country's groundnuts. In return, the masters convince their servants that they are chosen by God. There is a holy man, for instance, who regularly conducts telephone calls over his unconnected telephone in front of admiring followers in which he talks directly to heaven. *("Hallo. Is that you Gabriel? Could you put me through to God?")* The leaders also avoid the Moslem disapproval of alcohol by claiming that they can turn it into milk before it reaches the stomach.

High society

The Mourides become very rich doing this sort of thing. Some lords earn well over £10,000 in a country where the average income is £25. Part of the job though is to be seen to spend vast amounts. They drive along the mud tracks in Cadillacs and build huge houses. Because of their economic power and sheer numbers, they are a real political force.

Free society

President Leopold Sedar Senghor believes in a world state. His national anthem sums up his world view, it begins, *'The Bantu is a brother and the Arab and the white man'*. His ambition is to be 'a teaching priest to work towards the intellectual emancipation of my race'. And he has the credentials to do it. He was a classmate of President Pompidou at the Sorbonne, and subsequently taught French to the French. He then spent two years in a Nazi concentration camp. Perhaps his greatest achievement, however, is to be a Catholic leader of a predominantly Moslem state.

Less free society

To achieve his high-minded ambitions, Senghor has had to take one or two short cuts of the authoritarian kind. Senegal became independent in 1960 under the banner of parliamentary democracy — but there was only one party. First Senghor attempted a

You can wait up to two years for a taxi in Senegal.

federation with Mali. This broke up after two months when they couldn't work out a constitution. In 1974 another party declared itself democratic and described itself as 'a party of contribution not opposition'. In 1975 they were apparently contributing the wrong thing and 13 people were jailed for belonging to an illegal political party. In 1976 Senghor decided there should be three political parties each one contributing to one aspect of political life. He laid down strict lines within which they were to work. One was to be communist, one liberal — one socialist democratic (his government). Otherwise he keeps an eye on things via French troops stationed at the airport. Senegalese forces are kept out of the way at the borders.

Urban society

Senegal is the most urban country in West Africa. Senghor's policies mean that by the year 2,000, 40 per cent of the population will be living in cities. His education policy (one-third of the budget goes on education and culture) has resulted in a state of over-qualification. You now need an 'O' level to run a bread stall. But there is a huge difference between city and country life. Life expectancy in Dakar is 60 — in the country, 38. This emphasis on sophisticated life has been called by Senghor, 'negritude'.

Otherwise it is peanuts all the way. Senegal is one of the most prolific producers and they have a saying: *When peanuts do well, we all do well.*

Population: 5 and a half million

Size: A quarter that of Texas, 76,000 sq. miles

Government: Republic

Language: French

Religion: Islam

Capital: Dakar

Currency: CFA franc

Tips for tourists

To reach the National Park you have to go to Tumbacounda which cannot be reached by road, rail or air.

See the most famous film director in Africa — or his films. Sembene Ouseman.

See the national sport, wrestling. The 1975 champion was called Double Less.

Careful with your money. The Mouride slaves are very good beggars. In the 19th Century they collected 6 million francs in a single session.

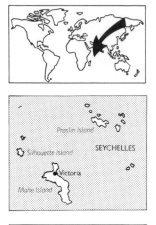

Seychelles

Population: 65,000

Size: 156 sq. miles

Government: Republic

Main language: Creole

Main religion: Roman Catholic

Capital: Victoria

Currency: Seychelles rupee, cent

Tips for tourists

Don't worry about going swimming. Crocodiles, which used to abound, are now extinct.

Don't agitate. The Seychelles have the world's lowest strike rate — 3 days a year lost by industrial action.

Try treasure hunting. The treasure buried 200 years ago by pirates has never been found.

History

These 92 islands form Africa's smallest state. Portuguese navigators jotted down their position around 1500 but it was another hundred years before the first recorded landing. Most of the people who dropped anchor in the following years were pirates, hiding their ships in the coves while they buried their treasure.

In the mid 18th Century a few French settlers arrived. They died out but the cinnamon they planted thrived. They named the islands after Louis XV's treasurer, Compte Sechelles. When the British took the islands over they renamed them Seychelles. They then tried to swap them for some of France's Indian possessions. The French refused, so Britain was lumbered (much of the islands are covered with forests).

Industry

When slavery was abolished in 1838, estate owners had to grow something that was not labour intensive. They chose coconuts. Today copra (dried coconut) and cinnamon bark are still the major exports (90 per cent of them). But major development has followed the building of an international airport (reclaimed from the sea) in 1971. The coconut trees have been cut down to make way for tourists.

Barkers and biters

In 1975 James Mancham was the Prime Minister but was studying law in England. One day the British Prime Minister, Harold Wilson, called him in to discuss the Seychelles' future. Mancham said he wanted the islands to be part of Britain and asked for a knighthood. Wilson refused both requests. Mancham promptly declared the Seychelles independent. Instead of becoming Sir James, he consoled himself with the title of President. He appears to have been impressed by the main landowners, who all lived abroad. He became an absentee president. In his first year in office, he was only in the Seychelles for four days. He travelled extensively in Europe and the USA and although travel may have broadened *his* mind, it didn't do much for his people. They suffered from hunger, unemployment and lack of medical care. In 1977 there was a coup and F. Albert Rene, the leader of the People's United Party, became top dog.

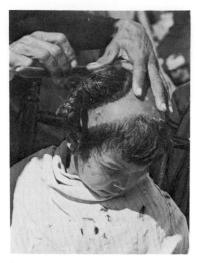

Since the attempted coup, Customs checks into the Seychelles have been rigorous.

Crime and punishment

One in 100 Seychelle islanders is a policeman — there are 500 of them. On average one in five of the adult population commits a crime every year (including those who are policeman).

Crime isn't the only problem. Although the official languages are French and English, 94 per cent of the people speak Creole, the dialect based on the language of the French Indian Ocean slave trade. Witchcraft and voodoo are still practised by some islanders.

Life

Of 500 plant species found here, 80 are found nowhere else. Among the amazing plants are the coco de mer, the screwpine, the pitcher plant and the jelly fish plant. The world's longest-living animals are found here — tortoises who live for 150 years. There is no old age pension.

Sierra Leone

Proverbs

I am not vomiting it. I have not eaten my second wife's fish.
A buttock here, a buttock there, everything goes out between...
To eat an alligator is not gluttony. It is simply a matter of tit for tat.
You should not say to a man who is carrying you on his shoulders that his head smells.

Colonial rivalry

The Portuguese Pedro de Cintra discovered *Serra Lyoa* or Lion Mountains. There probably were no lions in the mountains by the coast and the name either comes from their leonine shape or the imposing nature of the clouds around them. In 1580 Francis Drake visited the place and, like a good tourist, carved his name on a rock. Not to be outdone, the Dutch Admiral de Ruiter carved *his* name on the same rock in 1664 after he had defeated the British fleet.

African lions

Before the colonialists came, Sierra Leone was a highly developed country. In the 18th Century there were schools and a thriving trade. In 1769 the son of a Bullom chief was sent to England to be educated. Although slaving was the reason Europeans took an interest in the country, they could never be as good at it as the locals. Tribes warred and feuded almost incessantly and sold as many as 1,000 slaves per month — in one market place. The Mandingos were so well organised that they heard of the Spanish defeat at Gibraltar within 40 days — before any European.

British lion

But the state of Sierra Leone was the brainchild of an Englishman, Granville Sharp. When slavery was frowned on at the end of the 18th Century in England, he decided to set up a 'Province of Freedom' for liberated slaves in the country. Slaves from England were offered a free trip back to Africa. The capital, Freetown, echoes the pioneering spirit of the Sierra Leone Company. But the task was too great for one company and eventually Britain had to take responsibility for the settlement herself.

Language

Civilised in other ways too, the script of Sierra Leone — called Vai — is one of the few indigenous written languages in Africa. This perhaps explains why black Africa's first institute of higher learning is at Freetown. Sierra Leone contains the rivers *Big Bum, Small Bum, Cess* and *Sewa*. There is the *Rio Pongo* where there used to be a great trading post for slaves. In 1880 the unforgettable *Dungpot War* was fought on local soil. And the powerful Susu tribe hailed from a town called *Wongapong*.

But every cloud has a silver lining. King Jay of Bumpe rivals King Tom for the most pleasant sounding King. The sedentary-sounding Sofa tribe invaded from the north in the 19th Century. And the Loko Tribe held sway until the 1840's. Much of the population picked up European surnames like Caulker, Roger and Tucker. Chief Madam Yoko, however, never gave peace a chance.

The 20th Century

British influence started to be challenged at the end of the last century when a misguided administrator tried to impose a hut-tax on the natives. It was vigorously opposed but the local chiefs suffered considerably under native frontier tax-collectors with names like Dareo Gbo (which means *I will flog you until you cover your feet*) and Jeheh Gutu (*Short talk under torture*). Siaka Stevens, the worlds first rock and roll president, is in power today. The country's founder Dr. Margai was the first black African head of state to die in bed (peacefully).

Population: 3 and a half million

Size: A third that of Britain, 28,000 sq. miles

Government: Republic

Language: English

Religion: Traditional beliefs

Capital: Freetown

Currency: Leone

Tips for tourists

Do not challenge authority: there have been two unsuccessful coups since independence. The first was led by Brigadier David Lansoma. The second by Ex-Brigadier David Lansoma. The Ex-Brigadier is no longer available for comment on the prospects for a third.

Sheri is a tribe.

Bees are used by the locals to release on an enemy before attacking.

The undertaker.

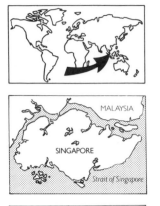

Singapore
Republic of Singapore

This diamond-shaped island is one of the jewels in the crown of the free-enterprise system. It is a small island (26 miles by 14) which consists of almost nothing outside the city of Singapore but jungle. The city itself is a jungle of a different kind. It has been a key trading centre for almost 200 years and now is one of the world's new bustling industrial hubs, relying on cheap labour and laissez-faire capitalism to pump out cut-price goods.

History

Singapore gets its name from a Sumatran prince who landed on the island and saw a strange animal which he took to be a lion (Singapore means 'City of the Lion'). The date of the landing is placed anywhere between the 6th and 14th Centuries, which makes the people's sense of time as poor as the prince's eyesight.

The Portuguese and Dutch dropped in from time to time after the 16th Century but it took a Briton to really make the place's fortune. He was Sir Stamford Raffles who arrived in 1819 and immediately saw that Singapore's strategic position could make it invaluable. It is the central point on the commercial route linking Africa, Asia, Europe and Australasia.

As well as making money from commerce, Singapore did all right out of the military. A major British naval base was established there between the two world wars. This did not help Singapore much in World War Two. The defence of the islands had been based on resistance to a sea attack and the cunning Japanese came in by land. Singapore became independent in 1965.

The people

Singapore has been called 'Instant Asia' because so many cultures intermingle there. It is an enormous mish-mash of races, all united by their devotion to work. More than a third are employed in manufacturing industry and about the same number in commerce. Only 2 per cent work in agriculture. Not much land is available for farming, and not much for people. Singapore is the third most densely populated country in the world.

For their hard work, the people enjoy one of the highest incomes of any Asian country. Their children are now able to share this. A recent law allows 14-16 year olds to work and 12-14 year olds to become apprentices.

All homes are now equipped with outside toilets.

Life expectancy is 68, one of Asia's highest. It has the highest newspaper readership in Asia.

Industry

Singapore has the world's fourth biggest port and is the third largest petrol refiner, although it has no oil of its own. It has more than 3,000 factories and huge shipbuilding, textile and electronic industries.

Politics

The result of the last election was:
People's Action Party — 74 seats
Worker's Party — one seat
Other parties — no seats.
This was the worst result the People's Action Party had experienced. At all other elections since independence, it had won every seat. Its leader, Lee Kuan Yew, has been prime minister since 1959 and is the real power in Singapore, although officially he is appointed by the Head of State, the *Yang di-Pertuan Negara*.

Between 1971 and 81 the Yang was a gynaecologist called Dr. Benjamin Sheares. He had found fame by being advisor to the Family Planning Association at a time when the birth rate was cut by a quarter, making it one of the lowest in the world. But Singapore is still getting more crowded (not enough people are dying).

Population: 2 and a half million

Size: 238 sq. miles

Government: Republic

Official languages: Malay, Chinese, Tamil, English

Main religion: Confucianism, Taoism, Buddhism

Capital: City of Singapore

Currency: Singapore dollar, cents

Tips for tourists

Don't visit 13 Muhammed Ali Lane. It is Singapore's haunted house, where a family of 22 was massacred by the Japanese during World War Two.

Don't visit a reptile butcher. Even if you say you don't want to buy a skinned snake, they will press a flying fox bat on you. They believe them to be excellent for making soup.

Don't admit you've got an ulcer. The local cure is to eat four live mice.

Solomon Islands

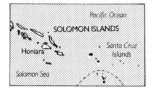

Brain drain

All the rumours that early explorers heard about the Solomon Islands were true. One of the islands, New Georgia, contained 'the most treacherous and bloodthirsty race in the Pacific' — before this century there was hardly an island you stepped on without the risk of becoming a tasty morsel.

The Portuguese first came 'to bring the heathen into the vineyard of the Lord'. But they stepped right into the frying pan of the pagan. The first Portuguese, Gallego, was presented with a quarter of a boy as a gift — including an arm and hand. A favourite trick of the locals was to entertain a visitor lavishly, fatten him up, then chop off his head and suck the brains out. The rest of the flesh was mixed with wine and drunk.

Self abuse

But they didn't only reserve this treatment for foreigners. There were professional murderers on the islands who killed more than 100 people to be eaten by their employers. Pig and little boy was a favourite dish. A child would be seized from its mother and carried round in a circle three times ducking it in the sea until it was so exhausted it hung upside down. Then its head would be chopped off. It would be run around more times until the bleeding stopped and then cooked. Quite often the flesh would just be warmed, not properly cooked. When the Spaniards came they wanted to eat pig rather than boy and so kidnapped the locals intending to swop them for pigs — on a one boy:three pigs basis. The natives were too clever for that and insisted on one boy:one pig. Their chief was called Meta.

Tastier topics

The Solomons were so called because the Spanish wanted their own people to settle there. They therefore pretended that all the gold which King Solomon got to build his palaces in Jerusalem came from there. It didn't work against strong local opposition.

After New Zealand and New Guinea, the Solomons are the biggest land mass in the western Pacific and are largely covered with rain forests and beautiful beaches. Only 12,000 tourists a year are allowed to visit — not because the islanders *literally* can't stomach them, but because they can't metaphorically (there is no longer cannibalism).

Language

When the Portuguese came, they encountered a fleet of canoes from Guadalcanal sent out to meet them. The occupants shouted *"mate, mate"*. But their intention was far from friendly. They were going for the kill.

There are many dialects — and, as you would expect, many words which in English have no equivalent. The most traumatic experience for the islanders was the arrival of firearms. In the Gela language *Kukoro* means to die of fright, an eclipse of the sun, anything terrible — and gun. In keeping with other abrupt characteristics, the Bugotu have no word for 'please'.

Scapegoats

As in every country, the Solomon islanders had a minority section of the population who were the butt of constant jokes. These were the Masi. Stories tell of them cutting down trees on top of themselves, climbing trees and when their head hit a branch thinking it was the sky, and making a wooden platform on which they lit a fire thus burning themselves to death.

Industry

Today the main exports from these thickly forested mountainous islands are copra, fish, timber amd palm oil. Minerals are being kept under wraps. The Solomons do possess, however, a diced shark fin processor. The newspapers are the *Solomon News Drum* and *Solomon Toktok*.

Solomon lavatories are the largest the world has ever known.

Population: 235,000

Size: 11,500 sq. miles

Government: Independent Commonwealth member

Language: Arosi

Religion: Christianity and traditional beliefs

Capital: Honiara

Currency: Solomon Island dollar, cents

Tips for tourists

Visit Iron Bottom Bay. It is the sight of the largest graveyard of Second World War ships.

Be open with the population. They will be open with you. They have one of the highest population growths in the world, doubling in 20 years.

Don't take your dog. In the past they have been used for currency. A dog would be buried up to its neck and have its teeth extracted for money.

Another currency was sticks. In 1900, a week's work was worth two sticks.

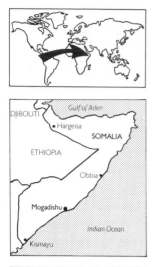

Population: About 5 million

Size: Three times that of Britain, a quarter of a million sq. miles

Government: Republic

Language: Somali

Religion: Islam

Capital: Mogadishu

Currency: Somali shilling, centisimis

Tips for tourists

The most useful thing in Somalia is the galol, a gum tree. Its roots are used as a framework for huts, its bark for making ropes and mats, its leaves to feed animals and its fruit is eaten.

Somalia

Al-Jumhouriya As-Somaliya Al-Domocradia

Geography

Somalia — or, to give it its full name, the Somali Democratic Republic — is the sheath on the horniest bit of the horn of Africa. It doesn't have much else going for it. Much of the country is desert, most of the western boundary is in dispute and the people are indisputably among the poorest in the world.

The people

More than three-quarters of the population are nomads, mainly wandering herdsmen. They are outnumbered by their goats (16 million), sheep (10 million), camels (5 and a half million) and cattle (4 million).

The only fun the nomads have is feuding with each other over water and grazing lands. When they really want to have a good time, they steal each other's camels and cattle and start a tribal punch-up.

History

This area was originally countless small tribal Kingdoms. Unusually for Africa, the first people to try to colonise it were the Chinese, in 1560. The natives sent them packing and did the same to the Persians when they landed a few years later. It wasn't until the end of the 19th Century that Europeans moved in. Britain took over part of the land and the Italians the rest. It became independent in 1960, since when it has never looked forward.

Politics

Appropriately for a young country, the first elections were won by the Somali Youth League. The next was contested by 80 political parties. This was followed by a coup and a Supreme Revolutionary Council took power. All its members were army officers.

The new government got a lot of help from Communist countries. Then the Communists supported neighbouring Ethiopia, with which Somalia had been having an endless border war, so the Somalians decided to have nothing more to do with them. Now most of Somalia's help comes from the United States.

The economy

Somalia has large reserves of iron, gypsum, beryl and columbite but all of them are just being left in the ground. The main exports are fruit, livestock, hides and skins. The skin of the Somali leopard is the most valuable on the world market. This does not do much for the economy.

Language

The main language is Somali but until 1973 it had no written form. This has not stopped poetry becoming one of the nation's favourite cultural forms. Its main themes are war, peace, women, horses and camels, although not necessarily in that order.

Method of execution: sawing through a block of wood which falls on the victim's head.

South Africa
Republiek van Suid-Afrika

History

South Africa used to be little more than the 17th Century equivalent of a motorway service station. Being a convenient stopping-off place on the route from Europe to the East Indies, the Dutch opened a 'refreshment post' there.

Over the years, more settlers came out from Holland and moved further inland. They were known as Boers — from the Dutch meaning 'husbandman' or 'farmer'. They became extremely bored with the hard work, considering menial tasks below them. Conveniently, there were many Africans around (they had been there for thousands of years) — so they were enslaved. Three hundred years later, not much has changed, although South Africa became a British colony in 1806 and a republic in 1961.

Apartheid

Mixed marriages were banned in 1949 but it wasn't until the following year that sex between whites and non-whites was made illegal. The Immorality (Amendment) Act declared this to be *irregular carnal intercourse*. The notorious Terrorism Act enables people to be thrown in jail for almost anything, including 'attempting to embarrass the state' (although embarrassing the South African government is as difficult as making Genghis Khan blush). If you want to please the Africans, call them Bantus, *not* blacks.

Industry

South Africa provides about two thirds of the world's supply of gold. Most of it comes from a huge seam in the Rand, which is five miles deep, 12 feet thick and stretches for 60 miles. Nearly half a million people work in the gold industry and another 750,000 in other mining enterprises. Freelance mining is not allowed — if you stumble across a diamond, you must hand it to the police (but you will get half of its value).

Farming

There are 31 and a half million sheep. Black ones are not discriminated against. Ostrich farming is thriving at Oudtshoorn, where there are 40,000 humans and 90,000 ostriches. Ostrich feathers are used in the hat trade, the skins for exotic leather goods and the meat as steaks. An ostrich egg makes an omelette that will feed 12 people.

A simple police demonstration of what a man suspected of committing a crime should look like.

Language

Most whites speak Afrikaans, which originates from Dutch. Although they pride themselves on their holiness (for 200 years they have considered themselves 'God's chosen race') the Bible was not translated into Afrikaans until 1933. South Africa's greatest linguistic contribution to the world came in the Boer War (Britain v the Boers) at the turn of the century. They invented the words *camouflage* and *commando*.

Sport

South Africans are crazy about sport although they have been boycotted by so many other nations that their international competition is almost masturbatory (they can only play with themselves).

Population: 25 and a half million

Size: Five times that of Britain, 440,000 sq. miles

Government: Republic

Official languages: English, Afrikaans

Main religion: Christianity

Capital: Pretoria

Currency: Rand, cent

Tips for tourists

Visit the shop of Mr. Lister Hunter in Umtata. There you can see a two-hour colour movie of the circumcision ceremony and buy colour slides of the tribal initiation into womanhood. This is as close as you will get to pornography in South Africa.

See the Gumboot Dance at the inter-tribal dancing ceremonies.

To avoid a slow death, don't swim in the rivers. These are often infected with bilharzia, a disease carried by water snails.

155

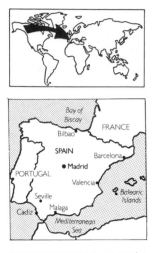

Spain
Estado Espanol

Spain's history since 1479 has been one huge gamble, symbolised by its quest for El Dorado in the 15th Century. Consecutive monarchs bled the gold seams of South America to finance their own luxuries and their country's military designs on the rest of Europe. Even with the wealth of the New World in its grasp, Spain's ambitions have kept it in constant — and massive — debt.

Extreme activity

After eight centuries of Arab rule, the Spanish took to Christianity with astonishing alacrity. In Central America alone they killed over 20 million Indians converting them. At home, palaces were built to house statues too heavy to be supported. The walls of the lavatory at the Palace of Aranjuez were lined with gold and aluminium.

Philip II tried to defeat England, France, Netherlands and Portugal. No wonder the Spanish had an obsession with El Dorado. They needed the money. In the 80 years to 1680, one and a half million Spaniards died trying to lord it over Europe.

The Spaniard monarchy resembled *'a great colossus that during an earthquake had collapsed in a few moments while everyone hurried to enrich himself with the fragments'*. Incredibly by 1680 they were *still* the greatest power in Europe and could justly claim the word 'macho' as their own.

Extreme inactivity

While the Spanish have the word 'macho' they also possess 'siesta' and 'manana'. As the crazed adventurers abroad went about their business, at home things were quieter. Today Spain is still 25 per cent agricultural and produces the heat-loving fruits: olives, oranges, lemons, pomegranates and apricots, and of course, sherry.

In the summer 37 million visitors lie on Spain's beaches — a 40 per cent increase in the Spanish population. Their main effect is to pollute the rivers and the sea. But Spain is not on holiday only in the summer. A proverb has it: *Spanish holidays number 365 exclusive of Sundays.* These are mostly religious and the irony in the Spanish character is perhaps that religion has been the chief force behind their energy and their relaxation. In one fiesta — bull-fighting — they have managed to combine the two.

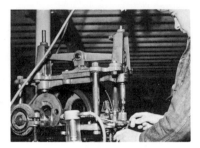

Special machinery ensures that Spain produces more foul wine than anywhere in the world.

Most personal battle

Between Wilfred the Hairy of Catalonia and Charles the Bald of Germany in 878 AD.

Spanish justice

In 1972 Gabriel Grandos, aged 22, was sentenced to 384,912 years in gaol for failing to deliver 42,768 letters.

Modern excitability

Since the 1820's and the collapse of Spain's American empire, the country has been racked by civil wars between the military and the liberals — with the military coming out firmly on top. The wars were continuous until the generals took control in 1868, and in 1874 reinstated the monarchy. In 1936 a counter-revolution led by General Franco caused the three-year Spanish Civil War which cost the lives of over one million people.

The alliance of communists, socialists and foreign elements of the international brigades were defeated by Franco with help from Nazi Germany. The Spanish love of formality was reintroduced when Franco set up the pompous-sounding party: Falange Espanola Tradicionalista y de las Juntas Ofensivas Nacional-Syndicalistas.

In 1975, on Franco's death, 'democracy' was restored with King Juan Carlos de Borbon y Borbon in the chair. But since the 1981 failed coup under General Armada, who sank without trace, the Left in Spain is kept firmly under control and the traditional 'real powers' — the church, the army and the employers — exercise invisible authority.

Other excitable people must include the nation's artists: Salvador Dali describes himself as 'the world's greatest painter'.

Population: 37 and three quarter million

Size: Twice that of Britain, 195,000 sq. miles

Government: Constitutional monarchy

Language: Spanish

Religion: Roman Catholic

Capital: Madrid

Currency: Peseta

Tips for tourists

Visit Franco's tomb — 1,000 feet of rock surmounted with a 430 foot re-inforced concrete cross.

Be careful of affairs of the heart: Portugal has a saying that Spain is *the only country in the world where a man's mistress is uglier than his wife.*

The Spasse is the best retirement spot in Europe. Keep clear.

Spain suffers from the over-production of bad wine.

Don't go. Spain is the leading tourist country in the world.

Don't go. Spain is the leading country for civil disorders.

Sri Lanka
Ceylon

Population

Sri Lanka has been the butt of invasions from India from time immemorial. Most of the population consists of Sinhalese, who are Buddhists. According to the Mahavamsa tradition, Buddhism arrived here by air in 250 BC. There are also one and a quarter million Tamils, who are Hindus and who have no legal rights. They are gradually being removed to India but still tensions between them and the Sinhalese bedevil political life.

There are a further one million Muslims, some Moors and Malays — and some Burghers who are descended from Dutch Calvinists. Ex-Portuguese Catholics crop up here and there too. The Hindus are divided into castes — some very specialised — one exists purely to peel cinnamon.

Over-population

In the last 25 years the population has doubled, causing food shortages, unemployment and unrest. Appropriately for a rubber-producing country, family planning has been high on the list of priorities. But it hasn't yet achieved the success the country needs.

In 1982 a World Health Organisation team went to Sri Lanka to teach the tribes of the interior some rudimentary facts of life. They demonstrated the use

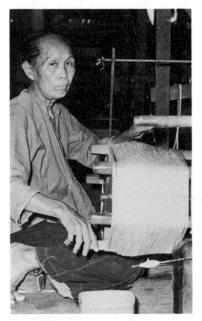

Contraceptive-weaving has proved disastrous.

of a condom by placing it on top of a bamboo pole in the middle of the village, and made eating motions to show how to use the Pill. Returning six months later, they were met by an angry — and pregnant — female population. Inside the village huts the men had placed condoms on bamboo poles, and the women were stirring cauldrons of steaming contraceptive pills.

Origins

Sri Lanka is not the new name for Ceylon but the old one. In Sanskrit *Simhaladripa* means 'Islands of the Sinhalese' but the Sinhalese have always referred to the place as Lanka or Laka and the full version means 'splendid land'. It is indeed splendid and is described as a pear, a pearl and even as 'the tear of India'.

Sweet-toothed

After endless invasions the population ended up in an impregnable fortress called the Kingdom of Kandy, built out of solid rock which, tradition said, would have to be tunnelled before anyone could capture it. In this city, in the Temple of the Sacred Tooth, was placed the most holy Buddhist symbol on the island. The tooth was laid on a lotus leaf of pure gold and surrounded by seven consecutive gold bells encrusted with gems. In fact, both the Indians and the Portuguese say they took the tooth long before it got to Kandy but the Buddhist priests say they got the wrong one. Today it has probably the most impressive religious ceremony in the world in which over 60 elephants take part.

Other sweet things include the fairy tale, *The Three Princes of Serendip*, which has given the English language the word 'serendipity' — meaning 'the gift of finding valuable and agreeable things without looking for them.'

The modern state

The Portuguese bequeathed Catholicism, the Dutch canals and Calvinism. The British left language, administration, clubs and Ceylon Breakfast Tea. After independence in 1948 the UNP (United National Party) was elected to power. Its English-educated style of rule led to the formation of other, nationalist, parties. Their nepotism led to the nickname 'Uncle-Nephew Party'. In 1960, in a new government, Mrs. Bandaranaike became the first female prime-minister in the world.

Population: 15 and a half million

Size: A quarter that of Britain, 25,000 sq. miles

Government: Republic

Official language: Sinhala

Main Religion: Buddhism

Capital: Colombo

Currency: Rupee

Tips for tourists

A nod of the head means *no*. A shake means yes.

Be careful of the Cinnamon Gardens in Colombo. There are no gardens and no cinnamon.

Decorative art is a speciality and Sri Lankans do it everywhere. There is an entire museum devoted to 6th Century decorated bidets, urinals and squatting plates.

Hindu edifices are largely made up of female and male sexual organs.

Drink *toddy* a powerful alcoholic coconut drink.

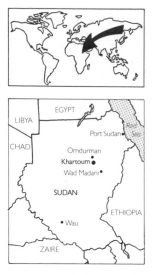

Sudan

Jamhuryat es-Sudan Al Democratia

Tips for tourists

Be careful of the Dinka tribesmen in the south. They have a custom when they marry of killing a man and cutting off his testicles to prove to their future wife that a) they are a man, and b) they have killed a man.

Also watch out for *watania*. It is Sudanese sherry — but tastes nothing at all like sherry.

The beer is grey

To get rid of malaria go to the *Umm Ingleless* — a pot-bellied tree whose bark is said to cure it.

Visit the towns of Boing and Tonge. In the latter the locals try to get put in gaol because the food is better. Dope is illegal — but is on sale at Tonge police station.

Water is stored in the hollow trunk of a baobab tree.

Big waste

Sudan is the largest African country. It is larger, too, than the whole of the EEC with Norway and Sweden added on. It is almost half as big as the United States. But unlike the US its huge plain contains none of the fertile land that would make it a wealthy country. It is mostly desert in the north and the population huddles along the banks of the Nile to keep cool and fed. In the south appear tall grasses, thick woods and, on the border with Uganda, jungle. In this region the inhabitants have an inexplicable habit of standing on one leg.

This bank robber has overlooked one vital clue to her identity.

Life on the Nile

The Nile Basin is one-tenth of Africa and is Sudan's life-blood. It flows into the country passing through the Sudd Swamp to Lake No and on to the capital Khartoum, before heading for Egypt. The surrounding land is so dry that the Nile flows further than any other river in the world without tributaries entering it. Within the Sudan it passes through five cataracts and its flow is determined by the season. Between July and September, half the volume passes through. At one point the maximum amount of water is 11,180 cubic metres per second, the minimum 44 cubic metres.

History

Sudan is a mixture of caucasian — mainly in the north — and black — in the south. The caucasians are Arabs who invaded in the 7th Century AD. Belad es-Sudan means, in Arabic, 'Country of the Blacks'.

Before the Arabs the Kerma Kingdom lorded it. They lived in small huts plastered with animal dung and held together by a rope. The masters were buried in bed, with their slaves accompanying them alive. Often their favourite wives would join them, also alive.

The old Kingdoms of Cush were replaced by Ethiopian invaders of the Pankhi and by the 17th Century Christianity, cut off from the outside world, died out.

Then the British took an interest, via Egypt, because of their stake in the Suez Canal. General 'Chinese' Gordon wasn't so inscrutable however when the 'Mad' Mahdi (madder than Gordon was Chinese) killed him at Khartoum — which means *elephant's trunk*.

Landless

With so much space, it is unfortunate for the country that it is possible to cultivate only one-third. But it is unforgivable that only one-quarter of *this* area is used. They grow cotton and oil-seed and, at Gezira, there is the largest farm in the world — with over 97,000 workers. They produce one-third of the world's gum arabic. But their economic record is bad. One of the reasons must be communications. The roads to Egypt, Libya, Chad, Uganda and Ethiopa are mud tracks.

Comments

The Sudanese are conscious of their backwardness, particularly in the south. There are signs on the banks of the Nile which read,
'Please respect our feelings that we resent showing our primitive habits and tribal customs to the outside world'.
It is an exhortation to tourists not to take photographs of naked people. Rudyard Kipling, however, is complimentary of the locals:
'So 'ere's to you Fuzzy Wuzzy, in your 'ome in the Soudan, You're a pore benighted 'eathen, but a first class fighting man'.
When you travel through the Sudd, beware of extreme boredom. Churchill (Winston) considered that, *'To travel through the Sudd is to hate it forever more'.* The Sudd is indeed *'an immense sponge'*, but the government is trying to rectify this. It is building the Jonglei Canal with the largest excavator on earth. The canal will be longer than the Panama and Suez together and will drain the Sudd marsh to provide irrigation for 400,000 acres in the desert north.

Suriname

Recipe

First take your country: in this case, a small one on the north coast of South America. To the native Indians, add two colonial powers (Britain and Holland) fighting for possession. When the Dutch have control (1815) throw in some slaves from Africa and mix with various refugees who have fled there. When slavery is abolished and there is a shortage of ingredients to work on the plantations, add contract labourers from Asia, China and Indonesia. Stir well, then withdraw the colonial power (1975).

If that sounds like a recipe for disaster, the extraordinary thing about Surinam is that it isn't. The mix has worked remarkably well for a country that has as many as 20 different races all living their own lives in perfect harmony (well, almost). It has earned Surinam the title 'Little United Nations'.

Language

The official languages are Dutch and English. But people speak their own languages in their own regions. For inter-group communication, English, Hindi, Javanese and Chinese are spoken. There is also a language called Surinamese (or *Sranan Tongo* or *Taki-Taki*) which is widely spoken. It is a mixture of West African dialects, Dutch, English, Spanish, French and Hebrew. To make communication still more complicated, the government has decreed that the main working tongue should be Spanish, a language which almost no one speaks.

Mixed-up kid

The Bouterse family seems to have been rather confused when their son was born. They called him Daisy. He grew up to become a sergeant in the army, but the ribbing he must have got in the barracks gnawed at him. In 1980 he led a coup that overturned nearly two centuries of peace. The reasons for the coup, he said, were that the streets were untidy and the dirt paths needed raking.

Daisy's first act on becoming head of government was to promote himself to the rank of colonel, although he kept the officers in the government as NCOs. He turned really nasty when a group was formed to ask for a return to democracy. Its leaders were murdered. Daisy has also closed or burned down all the radio and TV stations and newpapers (except for the ones owned by the government). Daisy chains led the Dutch to suspend a one and a half billion dollar aid programme.

Mixed up people

There are no problems with ethnic minorities. In Surinam, everyone is a member of an ethnic minority. The native Indians still carry on life pretty much untouched by the outside world. The Bush Negroes live like their ancestors did in Africa. The Chinese have become shopkeepers and the Asians small farmers.

If they have any sense of national identity, it appears to be with the Dutch. In the five years before independence, 40 per cent of the population emigrated to Holland.

The Surinamese belong to almost every religion. There are even 80 Confucians. The first synagogue in the Western Hemisphere was built here in 1665 by Jews fleeing from persecution in Brazil.

Mixed up

The Surinam toad incubates its eggs on the back of the female. As each egg is released the male fertilises it under water and then presses it on the back of the female. Sex isn't much fun for a Surinam toad.

Population: Half a million

Size: Three quarters that of Britain, 63,000 sq. miles

Government: Republic

Official languages: Dutch, English

Main religions: Hinduism, Islam, Christianity

Capital: Paramaribo

Currency: Surinam guilders

Tips for tourists

Don't bother going for a train ride. There are only 55 miles of track and 20 of them have been removed.

Watch the time. The Surinam clock setting is half an hour different from neighbouring countries.

For a relaxing sport, join in the favourite local competition — a warbling contest between trained songbirds.

There are people like this all over Surinam waiting for the president.

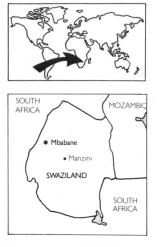

Population: 600,000	

Size: One twelfth that of Britain, 6,700 sq. miles

Government: Monarchy

Languages: English and Siswati

Religions: Christianity and traditional beliefs

Capital: Mbabane

Currency: Emalangeni

Tips for tourists

If you are lucky enough to be granted an audience with the king, remember to crawl out backwards.

If sexism upsets you, avoid the two main festivals:

Incwala: This hails the king as a source of fertility and symbol of power.

Reed dance: This encourages girls to work hard, accept discipline and preserve their virginity.

Swaziland

King and country

Externally, this small country is almost entirely surrounded by South Africa. Internally, it is entirely encompassed by the king and his family.

The Swazi tribe first moved here in the late 18th Century. Their great chief who settled the area was called Sobhuza. Since then there have been only five kings, giving the expression *Long live the king* a special meaning. But it doesn't apply to non-royals. They can only expect to live to the age of 44. The last king was Sobhuza II. He died in 1982 aged 83.

Right royal

Sobhuza II came to the throne in 1921. He was still there in 1968 when Swaziland got its independence from Britain. In the first election for the National Assembly, the royal Imbokoduo party won all the seats. That was OK by Sobhuza. When the next elections were held opposition parties won two seats. That was not OK.

Sobhuza suspended the constitution (which he said was 'un-Swazi') and assumed supreme power. There is now a new constitution, although no one outside royalty seems to have seen it. The government consists of a prime minister, who is one of the king's sons, and a cabinet, most of whom are related to the king. (This is not as bad as it sounds — a fifth of the population is supposed to be related to him.)

Warriors in Swaziland never shave their spears.

Among the titles by which Sobhuza was known were: the Great Mountain, the Bull, the Son of the She-Elephant, Inexplicable, the Mouth that Tells no Lies, the Sun and the Milky Way.

End of the line

One day in 1982, King Sobhuza was attending a meeting of his ministers when he suddenly asked them all to leave except his white Minister of Health, Dr. Samuel Hynd. The king then said to him: *"I am going."* The doctor replied: *"Where are you going?"* With that, the king smiled, raised his hand in farewell, and died.

While he was still wrapped in the traditional skins of freshly slaughtered oxen, the battle for the succession began. He had left more than 500 children by his 100 wives but none of them were eligible to succeed. Swazi custom decrees that the king must be an only child.

The problem was left in the capable hands of Sobhuza's senior wife, who is known as the Great She Elephant.

Rotten Swazi

Swaziland is the brothel of South Africa. The moralistic white men over the border don't like to soil their land with unpleasant things like whorehouses or even night clubs, so they have established them in the neighbouring country and pop over the border for relief.

King Sobhuza was quite happy with this. He worked closely with the South Africans and his country depended entirely on them for transport, banking and postal services.

Mother and law

In the Swazi culture, all power is shared between a hereditary male ruler and his mother. This creates problems when the ruler is 83. Each village is run by a headman, but his mother is the one who really has the power.

The central points of Swaziland's political life are the royal villages of the king at Lozita (population 50) and of the queen mother at Lobamba (population 75). Swazi law and custom is made by the National Council which consists of the king, his mother and all adult males.

Getting away from mother

Nearly all schools are still run by missionaries. There are only 600 men in the army.

Sweden

Konungariket Sverige

In Sweden the social worker is king. More money is spent on social welfare than in any other country in the world, and inevitably Swedes pay some of the highest income tax rates anywhere. But this concern for welfare was not shared by Sweden in times past. The Vikings, for example, believed in family rather than state responsibility when it came to taking care of their old folk. In 1862 Horace Marryat, in *One Year in Sweden*, described how the Vikings discharged this duty:

Filial piety was not then the fashion, and when a man became no longer good for anything, his children and descendants, dancing in a ring, banged him to a jelly with huge weapons called 'family clubs'.

In areas where this service was not available, old people had to make do with casting themselves off cliffs.

High jinks

The desire to throw things off high places is deeply ingrained in the Swedish character. In the early 19th Century, the King of Sweden, out of curiosity, ordered 2 pigs, a house and 2 geese to be sent down the mile-long Trollhattan Falls, one of Europe's greatest. The pigs went first, landed safely, and returned quietly to their sty. The house followed. It was dashed to pieces. The geese shared the same fate. The owner of the pigs then sold them for a vast amount of money because they had been down a waterfall.

Health

Sweden has a very high number of hospital beds for the size of population. Presumably it is trying to clear the backlog produced by 19th Century medical treatment. Mr. L. Lloyd gives a few examples in *Peasant Life in Sweden*, written in 1870.

Loss of appetite. If, when a person is afflicted with this malady, a slice of bread and butter is held for a while down the seat of the privy, and subsequently eaten by him, the administration of the delicate morsel will be attended with beneficial effects.

Toothache — It is said of this ailment, that if on the first occasion of a person being troubled with it, someone — his mother in preference — gives him a smart blow on the mouth, it will never return again.

Lumbago — This malady is cured by a woman that has had twins trampling on the back of the sick man, who in the while lies with his face to the ground. Whilst in this position he inquires three several times of the woman, *"Why dost thou trample on me?"*. Lumbago may also be cured by a smart blow with a broom on the part affected.

Associations

To most people Sweden is blonde au pairs, Volvos and Abba. Surprisingly the Swedes are also great readers. They buy nearly ten times more books than the British. Sweden is also the largest exporter of paper in the world, as over half the country is covered in forest. A further ten per cent is lakes — over 96,000 of them.

Population: 8 and a half million

Size: About twice that of Britain, 173,700 sq. miles

Government: Constitutional monarchy

Language: Swedish

Religion: Lutheran Protestant

Capital: Stockholm

Currency: Kroner

Tips for tourists

Be prepared for anything — Sweden has some of the highest rates in the world for crime, abortion, divorce and suicide.

Avoid men in white coats — Sweden also has the third highest number of mental hospital admissions in the world.

A tough measure against Soviet submarines. Hundreds of *No entry* signs are to be submerged in Swedish waters.

Population: Six and a half million

Size: A seventeenth that of Texas, 16,000 sq. miles

Government: Republic

Languages: French, German and Italian

Religion: Christianity

Capital: Bern

Currency: Swiss franc

Tips for tourists

Be careful who you call *cretin*. It is a Swiss word meaning someone who lives in the valleys interbreeding and deprived of sunshine.

Be trusting. All Swiss men are soldiers and take their guns and ammunition home with them — a unique 'privilege'.

At the other end of the scale from cretins are the Nobel Prize winners — more of whom come from the Zurich Institute than anywhere else.

Feel safe. Every house must have a nuclear shelter by law.

Switzerland
Schweiz/Suisse/Svizzera

The public face

Nestle, Lindt, Tobler chocolates — cuckoo clocks, Gruyère cheese, fondue, Alpine meadows — the Red Cross, the World Health Organisation, the High Commission for Refugees, the League of Nations — precision watches, neutrality, no generals, skiing — prosperity, democracy, unity...these are a few of my favourite things.

The world's first hang glider taxi service, horse racing on ice, the Cresta Run — the world's longest narrow guage railway, apres ski, golf on frozen lakes — 73 per cent mountain, the highest dams in Europe, the first cog-wheel railway, the largest railway tunnel, the atomic clock...these are a few of my favourite things.

The world's oldest democracy, the highest standard of living in the world, the world's top savers with average individual deposits of £5,000 — half the population owning cars, half working in service industries, no strikes...these are a few of my favourite things.

The private reality

Democracy — 30 per cent of the population vote in elections. The government discourages voting because the Swiss have a natural scepticism for authority. A justice Ministry official puts it, *"The citizen has the right not to vote"*. 26.7 per cent is the average turnout for referendums. Of 554 referendums thoughout the world between 1973 and 78 over half were in Switzerland. On the surface this is very democratic. But you can hardly talk about majority decisions on a 30 per cent vote. Women did not get the vote until 1971.

Sitting on the fence

Switzerland's power and influence in other countries lies in its unique economic superiority. Switzerland is the fence for the rest of the world. It is the only country in Europe whose trade with the poorer nations is constantly in surplus. They are the chief lenders to South Africa and 80 per cent of South African gold passes through Zurich.

There are 442 multinationals in Switzerland and out of 1,000 American holding companies, 600 are in Switzerland. Swiss multinationals, including Nestle — possibly the most cosmopolitan multinational in the world — are believed to have exerted sufficient pressure economically to topple governments — particularly that of Allende in Chile.

Switzerland is the largest manufacturer of anti-personnel bombs in the world. Of course, no country is neutral. If it were, it would endorse the remark, *Switzerland does not exist.*

Prosperity

Voltaire quipped, *"If you see a Swiss banker jumping out of the window, jump after him"*. The Swiss are rich — and famous for their banks. Or, at least, some of the Swiss are very, very rich. 3.3 per cent of the population control more than half of the reputed 226 billion francs, and the top 5 Swiss banks have the same turnover as the entire national GNP. The reason for their wealth is their secrecy — which attracts investment, fraud, smuggling, hot money and dirty money for laundering. One tenth of French wealth is invested in Switzerland. Since 1972 the Swiss franc has risen 74 per cent against the pound. The Swiss have justly earned the title *The silent strong-box.*

In 1983 the Swiss government unveiled its new, ideal, prototype citizen.

Syria
al-Jamhouriya al Arabia as-Souriya

First things first

After being invaded by about every possible nation over a period of 4,000 years (see *Israel*) in 1946 Syria became the first Arab country to win independence. In March 1949 it was the first Arab country to have a coup. In August that year it became the first to have two coups. And in December, the first to have three.

Another coup two years later was followed by another first — the first Arabian president to be driven out of his country. Another coup followed. In 1963 there was yet another first — the first time an attempted coup had failed. By this time the Ba'ath Party was in power, which led to two more firsts. In 1964 Syria became the first Arab country to nationalise its oil industry, and in 1966 there was the first coup within the Ba'ath Party.

Front line

The Arab-Israeli conflict has been mainly responsible for Syria's political instability. It is also responsible for something else — the huge part of the national budget that Syria spends on its armed forces.

The army is 200,000 strong, with 2,000 tanks. There are 32 missile batteries, 50,000 men in the air force, with 450 jet fighters and bombers. Military service is compulsory for all males aged over 18 — except for only sons.

Back of beyond

Most of the country consists of the Syrian desert. This is not composed of sand, but of rock and gravel. There is plenty of sand around though — in the sky. It is carried by high winds in 5,000 ft. blankets which darken the sky.

Damascus, the capital, is in an oasis. Average temperatures there are just under 100 degrees Fahrenheit. In 1967 Syria lost part of its territory, the Golan Heights, which Israel grabbed during the six-day war.

Front page

There are four daily newspapers with a total sale of 85,000. This is not just because half the population is illiterate. The papers are not worth reading, all being heavily censored. So you won't be able to read about the major activity of the government — corruption.

Back to basics

The most important inhabitants are sheep. There are 7 and a half million of them. Wool and woollen things are the country's main products. Syria also produces 3 and three quarter million pairs of shoes a year, 50,000 fridges, half a million tons of tomatoes, a third of a million tons of oranges and 300,000 tons of olives.

There are 7 million goats and 8 and three quarter million hens which, despite the socialist nature of the government, have failed to throw off the yoke of oppression — they lay 700 million eggs a year on poultry farms built with Hungarian aid. Syrians, however, eat fewer fish than any other peoples. Syria's main trading partner is the European Common Market.

Population: 9 million

Size: Four-fifths that of Britain, 72,000 sq. miles

Government: Socialist republic

Main religion: Islam

Language: Arabic

Capital: Damascus

Currency: Pound, piastre

Tips for tourists

Feel safe. Syria claims to have the world's lowest crime rate.

Travel: use mules in the mountains and camels in the desert.

This Olympic village design failed to make Syria host for the 1988 Games.

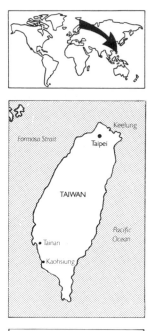

Taiwan
Republic of China

Population: 18 and a half million

Size: A seventh that of Britain, 14,000 sq. miles

Government: Republic

Language: Mandarin Chinese and dialects

Main religion: Confucianism

Capital: Taipei

Currency: Taiwan dollar

Tips for tourists

Jump from the highest cliffs in the world — 6,000 feet.

Enjoy rice. One eighth of the island is covered by it.

Stay in the hotel with the largest lobby in the world — the Grand Hotel Taipei.

Expect turbulence apart from the daily earth tremors. A Chinese historian describes the country, *'There is a rising every 5 years, a rebellion every 3'.*

There are 4 and a half million motorcycles.

Fraud

Pirates infested the island for centuries. But their modest pickings are overshadowed today. A forerunner of modern Taiwanese frauds was a man named Balmasanar. In one of the greatest literary cons ever, he wrote a book on Formosa in 1704 in which he claimed to have been born there and to speak the language. As a result he gained a Chair at Oxford University teaching Formosan. In fact, he couldn't speak a word of it and gave the game away by claiming that Ancient Greek was taught in the University of Formosa — two chapters after his assertion that the entire populaton lived underground, his explanation for his western pale skin.

In modern Taiwan no copyright is safe from rip-off. There are genuine underground operators — producing anything, as long as it isn't genuine. The saying goes, *'If you don't get copied in Taiwan, you're no good'.* From Levis to Revlon, its impossible to tell the real from the imitated.

Creation

The Chinese believe Taiwan was created by two dragons swimming from the mainland 100 miles away. They stopped to frolic and the turbulence caused the rise of the island. Even today there are earth tremors daily. The Portuguese called the island Formosa which means 'beautiful'.

In the 17th Century a mainland general, Koxinga, fled the advancing Manchus who were to overthrow the Ming Dynasty. He conquered the island and cleared it of the Dutch who had previously colonised it. Today Koxinga is the national hero (after Chiang Kai Shek) and has 29 temples dedicated to him.

The Chinese in 1895 gave Taiwan to the Japanese, who brutalised the country, putting electric fences around the jungle to keep in the natives.

Confusion

In 1949 two million Chinese forces under Chiang Kai Shek arrived, driven off mainland China by Mao Tse Tung's Communists. The civil war had been going on since 1945. They declared themselves the Republic of China. Mao declared the mainland China proper but Taiwan held the Chinese seat at the U.N. until 1971. Until then the United States recognised only Taiwan, perpetuating the myth that one day Taiwan would

For fear of China, it is an offence for citizens to travel without their cruise missiles.

conquer the mainland. For this purpose it maintains the world's second highest proportion of soldiers. Today the nationalists hold most of the government posts although 90 per cent of the population is Taiwanese.

Confucian

There are many thousands of temples in Taiwan. But the Confucians win the day with 5,000. Taoism comes second with 2,745 and Buddhism third with 2,520. Otherwise there are Protestants, Catholics and Shintos. Recently there has been a purge of Chinese Gods and Goddesses — because there are too many and nobody knows who they are anymore.

The god of money

Taiwan has the highest standard of living in Asia apart fom Japan and the world's fastest growing labour force. And one of the highest rates of growth in the world. Money is one of the gods which has avoided the purge. The island is a model of capitalism. Everyone works hard, most for low wages. Because money is new to most of the population there is a very high savings rate. Money is earned in one of three ways — hard work, sugar cane (Taiwan is one of the highest exporters) and fraud.

Tanzania

Julius Caesar

This is the land of Julius Nyere. He has been president since independence in 1962 and is chairman of the only political party and head of the armed forces. He has also translated the works of Shakespeare into Swahili.

Much azoo about nothing

Tanzania is one of the biggest countries in Africa and is the world's largest zoo. There are seven wild life preserves, teeming with elephants, rhinos, buffalo, lions, leopards, zebras, giraffes and antelopes. An unwelcome inhabitant is the tsetse fly, which makes 70 per cent of the land uninhabitable.

The country consists of Tanganyika on the mainland with the islands of Zanzibar, Pemba and Mafia. The capital, Dar es Salaam is due to be replaced in a few years by the new town of Dodoma. Mount Kilimanjaro is the highest in Africa.

All's well that ends well

Three hundred years ago the people of Zanzibar drove the Portuguese out of their island with the aid of the Arabs of Oman. The Arabs ruled until the Germans moved in last century. After World War One the British took over, but they gave far more aid to the neighbouring states of Kenya and Uganda, thus making Tanganyika a backward backward country. After independence, Tanganyika and Zanzibar joined in the new state of Tanzania.

As Jule likes it

This is a one-party state, the party being the revolutionary Chama Cha Mapinduzi. It grew from the Tanganyika African Association, of which young Julius Nyere became chairman in 1953. He turned it into a political party. In the country's first elections Julius was elected president (he was the only candidate). Elections are now more democratic. Voters can choose between two candidates, both of whom belong to the same party.

Zanzibar produces most of the world's supply of cloves. There are one and a half million clove trees, providing more than half the island's exports. The unopened flower buds are used not only in apple pies but also in medicine.

To counteract the high illiteracy rate five million adults are being taught to read in a novel way. Books are related to their work. Special ones have been written for fishermen, rice-growers, cattle rearers and peasants growing bananas.

Taming of the few

Until recently Tanzania had the world's most useless air force. It was unarmed, consisting of ten transport planes and seven trainers. Now the Chinese are providing jet fighters.

The navy has four small patrol boats and 100 sailors. The army claims to have a mere 13,000 men. However, it has more than this number in Uganda, where the Tanzanians helped to overthrow Idi Amin in 1971 and stayed on.

Alas, poor nutcracker

The oldest human skull was discovered here. It belongs to *Nutcracker Man* and can be seen in the Dar es Salaam museum. It is one and three quarter million years old. Tanzania also has the earliest known human structure, a rough circle of loosely piled lava blocks at Olduvai Gorge, dating from about the same time as old Nutcracker. In fact, he probably knew it well.

In the wide open spaces of Tanzania a flasher can wait a long time for an approach like this.

Population: 19 million

Size: Four times that of Britain, 365,000 sq. miles

Government: Socialist republic

Language: Swahili

Religion: Traditional beliefs, Christianity, Islam

Capital: Dodoma

Currency: Tanzanian shilling, cent

Tips for tourists

Don't bother getting a holiday job. Less than one in ten of the workforce receives wages.

If you fancy a holiday romance, choose the area you visit carefully. On the mainland there are more women than men. On Zanzibar, far more men than women.

Tanzania has the second highest proportion of divorcees in the world.

Take your flute: *'When you play the flute at Zanzibar, all Africa, as far as the lakes, dances'.*

Thailand

Prathes Thai *or* Muang-Thai

The rudest country in the world. The brothel of Asia. And anywhere else which wants to send its annual conventions there. Millions of naive Westerners refuse to believe this. They have seen *The King and I* and think Thailand is still called Siam (which it hasn't been since 1939) and is full of polite, bowing Yul Brynners whose only fault is that they can't sing.

The truth is very different (except the Thais can't sing). Thailand is obsessed with rudery:

The capital is called *Bangkok*
The king is called *Bhumibol*
The main tourist resort is called *Phuket*
The national spicy condiment is called *nam prik*
Thai for 'hello' is *sawadee-krap*
The biggest selling record recently was *I'm vasectomised*

To celebrate the king's birthday, hundreds of men had vasectomies. Almost the last clean-living thing the Thais did was in 1839 when the country's first printed work was issued. It was a royal proclamation banning opium smoking.

Silly business

Thailand used to have the world's biggest silk industry. It had collapsed by the end of World War Two. Then an American CIA agent called Jim Thompson parachuted into Thailand and set about rebuilding the industry. After 20 years, his company was the world's top silk business. One day, Jim Thompson went out for a walk. He has not been seen since.

Two Thai statues reach a simultaneous orgasm in the world's rudest country.

Silliest law

The Military Service Act of 1954 says every man must serve 25 years in the Army between the ages of 21 and 30.

Silliest name

The full name for Bangkok is *Krungthep Mahanakhon Bovorn Ratanakosin Mahin tharayutthayaan Mahadilok pop Noparatratchathani Burirom Udomratchanivetmahasan Amornpiman Avatarnsathit Sakkathattiyavisnukarmprasit.*

Population: 47 million

Size: Twice that of Britain, 200,000 sq. miles

Government: Constitutional monarchy

Language: Thai

Main religion: Buddhism

Capital: Bangkok

Currency: Baht and satang

Tips for tourists

Don't miss: The annual River Kwai Festival Week. This celebrates and recreates the building of the bridge over the River Kwai by prisoners of war in 1943:
Visit the graves of thousands who perished
Listen to the sound of Allied bombers blowing up the bridge
See the fires on the river-bank recalling the burning of cholera victims
Witness the collapse of mock rails into the river below
Book your seat now on the air-conditioned buses from nearby Kanchanaburi. And pop into the nearby caves to see the world's smallest mammal, Kitti's hog-nosed bat, which weighs less than a tenth of an ounce.

Large female breasts fail to attract the attention of the jaded local population.

Togo
Republique Togolaise

Position:

Togo is a big long country wedged in the armpit of Africa between Benin and Ghana. The reason for its odd shape is that half the country is believed to be in Ghana — but the Ghanaians are unable to find it.

Membership

To become a member of a tribe was a painful experience. The ceremony involved the voluntary death of the individual so that he could be reborn into the tribe. This was circumcision. The circumciser dressed up as a leopard and would pounce unexpectedly on the victim from the bush. The foreskin was whipped off suddenly with a red-hot knife.

Women had to go through female circumcision too. The main reason was to enhance aesthetic and sexual pleasure for the man.

The split

Before 1914 Togo, or Togoland as it was then called, lay under German control. Uncharacteristically, the Germans gave it some element of national pride. Togolese were allowed to run their own plantations and the country had the highest educational record in Africa. In 1914 when the French and British 'rescued' it from Germany, they divided the Ewe tribe, who were the main group, in two. Half of them were in Ghana and half in Togo. This has caused problems ever since. Under French/British rule no other 'development' took place.

Independence

This occurred in 1960 under President Olympio. Not Olympian in anything other than name, he was murdered in 1963 in what was the first coup d'etat in black Africa. More Olympian was Sergeant Eyadema who put Olympio's brother-in-law Grunitzky in power.

Dependence

In 1967 the, by now, Colonel Etienne Eyadema, took the 'In' out of 'Independence' in a bloodless coup which simply made Grunitzky redundant.

He called his party 'The Togolese People's Rally' so there would be no confusion. In 1969 he pretended to release the reins of power and two massive 'popular' demonstrations persuaded him that the country was rallying to the Rally.

Eyadema comes from the Kabre tribe in the north of the country, coincidentally the home of the army. Flushed with his 'popularity' he organised a third popular demonstration. It failed and resulted in the torture and death of opponents. Those remaining had a wage increase.

Promotion

In the 1972 election there was a 99 per cent turnout which returned the colonel with 867,941 ayes against 878 noes. Eyadema, for services to his country and general popularity, promoted himself to General. To confuse his opponents and make plotting more difficult, he banned foreign names, changing his own to Gnassingbe. By 1979 the population had got used to it sufficiently to vote him in for another seven-year term.

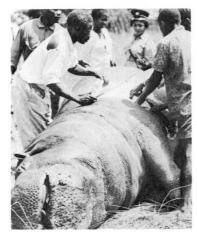

Locals come to the aid of an injured Belgian tourist.

General rule

Togo is a poor country. Its only wealth lies in deposits of phosphate — it is the world's fifth largest producer. The country has virtually no industry apart from a tapioca mill and a match factory. The second export is cocoa and constitutes one of the most harmless smuggling activities in the world — cocoa to Ghana.

Women do all the work in Togo. They are called 'revendeuses' and they sell the major domestic source of Togolese income — cloth, cigarettes and alcohol — in the markets of Lome.

Population: Two and three quarter million

Size: A fifth that of Britain, 22,000 sq. miles

Government: Republic

Language: Officially French, and many African dialects

Religion: Christianity and Islam

Capital: Lome

Currency: CFA franc

Tips for tourists

To go or not to go:
Go to the south for conversation. 99 per cent are educated compared to 28 per cent in the north.

Go to Togo if you don't like dentists. There are only five of them.

Be a slow reader. There is only one paper and no TV.

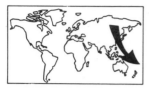

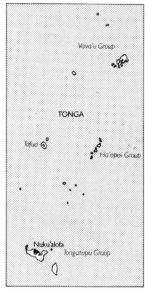

Tonga
Friendly Islands

It is said that during a State visit to England, Queen Elizabeth and the King of Tonga were travelling together in an open horse-drawn carriage, when one of the horses farted. *"I'm so sorry"*, said the Queen. *"That's all right"*, replied the King of Tonga. *"I thought it was one of the horses."*

History

The history of modern Tonga owes everything to the missionary position. Before Wesleyan missionaries converted the islanders to Christianity, a variety of other, clearly untenable positions had produced many years of civil war between the 150 Tongan islands. But in 1883, under the influence of the Reverend Shirley Baker, Chief Taufa'ahau embraced the faith, and changed his name to George. The people followed suit shortly after and a united Tonga was born under King George Tupou I. Today Tonga has the lowest birthrate in the world.

Monarchs

The present King is Tupou IV. His younger brother — HRH Prince Fatafelui Tu'ipele Lake, CBE — is Prime Minister. He is also Minister for Foreign Affairs, Minister of Agriculture and Chairman of the Tonga Commodities Board (Copra, Banana and Construction Divisions). Their mother, Queen Salote, reigned for 47 years before her death in 1965. She is best remembered for her refusal to shelter from a sudden rainstorm at Queen Elizabeth's Coronation in London in 1953. Tongans believe that rain is lucky, and as Queen Salote was over 6 feet tall, no-one wanted to press the point.

Economy

This is an agricultural country where the chief exports are copra and bananas. The main problems are banana scab, coconut pest and rhinoceros beetle — together with occasional hurricanes, like the one in 1973 which left 80 per cent of the population homeless.

Population

Every male Tongan, when he becomes a tax payer at the age of 16, is entitled to 8 and a quarter acres of land for the cultivation of crops. However, the growing population (Tongans have the second largest average family size in the world — 6.9 people) has created land shortage problems.

Population: 101,000

Size: 270 sq. miles

Government: Constitutional monarchy

Language: English and Tongan

Main Religion: Wesleyan

Capital: Nuku'alofa

Currency: Pa'anga, seniti

Tips for tourists

Pregnant? *Puke lelei* means morning sickness.

See the *ma'ulu'ulu* — the world's only sitting dance.

See the *me'etu'upaki* — a paddle dance performed by a large group of men with a slit-gong.

See the *me'elanfola* — a dance with long bamboo stamping tubes and percussion sticks.

Lovely teeth — his ancestors once ate your's.

White magic

Tongans firmly believe that white men rarely work and that the possession of an unending supply of money is a natural state with them.

Radio

The Tongan radio station is called *The Call of the Friendly Islands*, after the name given to the islands by Captain Cook when he came here in 1773. This proved to be a less than completely accurate title since misunderstandings about language and customs resulted in a few fatalities for both Tongans and early explorers. Captain Bligh might also have disputed the title, since the famous mutiny on the 'Bounty' took place in Tongan waters.

Trinidad and Tobago

Discovery

When Columbus discovered Trinidad he didn't noticed Tobago to the north. He had vowed to call the first land sighted after the Holy Trinity. That and the three hills on the island led to its name. The Spanish didn't return until 1531 when they proceeded to annihilate the local Indians:

The Caribs — who when they came from Florida had killed all the male inhabitants and married their women (Columbus found that men and women spoke different languages).

The Arawaks — who played football. *The Chima.*

This done, the Spanish set out for Peru in pursuit of El Dorado. The Dutch sacked the Spanish settlement and the British had their eye on Tobago. In 1641 Charles the First gave it to the Duke of Courland.

Paradise

Before the colonists really got going, Trinidad and Tobago were truly paradise islands. Tobago was called *Bird of Paradise Island.* And the Arawak name for Trinidad was *Land of the Humming Bird.* The country still supports 400 species of bird and 600 of butterfly. They have a national flower — the wild poinsettia. The trees are more prosaic: crappo, poui and fiddlewood.

Boomtime

In 1783 the Spanish encouraged settlers of Roman Catholic faith. They brought slaves. Between 1783 and 1797 while the Indian population halved, the slaves increased from 310 to 10,000. Sugar, cocoa and tobacco made the French settlers rich. Tobago is thought to be named after *tobaco* — an Indian pipe. Ben Jonson raved about Trinidad's tobacco and it was reputed to be better than Havana's. Coinciding with the boom, the plantation owners banned the use of African drums by the slaves. This was the cause of a different kind of boom — the steel band.

The black economy

Trinidad contains the world's chief source of asphalt. The Pitch Lake was first used by Walter Raleigh to caulk his ships and, perpetually renewing itself, has since covered the roads of the world.

Rum has always been part of life. Blackbeard and *Yo ho ho and a bottle of rum* was an underestimate. Before slavery was abolished, it was forbidden to give a negro less than 5 gallons of rum at a time. Today 20 million litres a year are produced and the Sunday paper is called *Sunday Punch.*

Since independence in 1962, oil has made Trinidad and Tobago one of the most prosperous countries in the Caribbean. Now, apart from oil, the economy is deteriorating. Oil, gas and asphalt make up 90 per cent of exports.

Multi-coloured

Today many nationalities and creeds live here. There are equal numbers of African and East Indian descent, the two main groups. Hindu is second only to the Roman Catholic faith.

Despite the country's motto *'Together we aspire, together we achieve'*, there is not a lot of togetherness except at carnival time. In the general election of 1971 only 28 per cent voted and in 1976, 54 per cent. In 1970 there were riots and an army mutiny and there is high unemployment today. A weekly newspaper is called *The Bomb.*

Special protective headgear must be worn against falling melons.

Population: 1,165,000

Size: 1,980 sq. miles

Government: Republic

Language: English

Religion: Roman Catholic, Hindu

Capital: Port of Spain

Currency: Trinidad and Tobago dollar

Tips for tourists

Visit the most exciting religious figure — The Black Virgin of Siparia, who dressed in leather.

Dance — but not until you drop. Trinidad is the home of the calypso and the limbo, but has one of the lowest doctor/patient ratios in the western hemisphere.

Read *Swiss Family Robinson*, supposed to be set here.

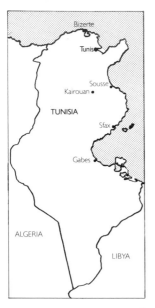

Bizerte
Tunis
Sousse
Kairouan
TUNISIA
Sfax
Gabes
ALGERIA
LIBYA

Population: 6 and a half million

Size: Two-thirds that of Britain, 63,000 sq. miles

Government: Republic

Religion: Islam

Language: Arabic

Capital: Tunis

Currency: Dinar, millimes

Tips for tourists

Travel by camel. There are 205,000 of them in Tunisia and a mere 110,000 cars.

You can easily spot the main street in any Tunisian town. They are nearly all called *Avenue Habib Bourguiba.*

Tunisia is reputedly the favourite gay holiday resort.

See the villa of Georges Sebastian in Hammamet. Frank Lloyd Wright described it as *"the most beautiful house I know".*

Tunisia
Al-Djoumhouria Attunusia

A pantomime

Tunisia is the Cinderella of North Africa, a poor little country surrounded by rich and ugly neighbours. Most of its early life was spent not sitting in the ashes but being reduced to them. This was where the great city of Carthage thrived. It rivalled Rome for a while, before being destroyed.

Pantomime dames

The women of Tunisia are the most liberated in the Muslim world. They have fewer illegitimate births and more abortions than any African women (but they can't legally have abortions until they have five children). The Personal Status Code of 1956 abolished polygamy and decreed a minimum age for marriage, as well as preventing husbands divorcing their wives without a court decision. Some women have responded to their freedom by becoming traffic police in downtown Tunis.

Prince not-so-charming

Since independence in 1956, Habib Bourguiba has been president. He has been made President for Life as 'an honour for the country' (his words). His son, Habib Bourguiba junior, is expected to take over the country when his father, who is now in his 80's, dies.

In 1974, Tunisia announced that it would merge with its neighbour, Libya. This would have been like Cinderella marrying an ugly sister. Fortunately, the plan collapsed.

Charming

This is a beautiful land of splendour in the north and desert in the south. Much of it is lined with olive trees — olive oil is the country's main product and makes up more than half of its exports. If you want a job, there is only one sure way to get it — nepotism. You are unlikely to get one with the charming Habibi. He works in the old part of Tunis, a smile always on his lips, engraving customers' names on the bottoms of copper ashtrays.

Carthage

The people of Carthage used to have some pretty unpleasant habits. They publicly strangled their first-born, then burned them on a sacred pyre as a sacrifice. That didn't save them from the might of the Roman Empire. There are still many Roman remains here. Visit the largest Roman building at Thugga, in the north: it was a brothel. Its trademark — a huge phallus — has been modestly removed and the building is politely described now in guide books as 'a mansion'.

Marriage

A week before his wedding, a Tunisian man sends his bride a basket containing candles in the shape of a hand, red henna to dye her feet and hands, and lumps of harz to dye her hair black. These can all be bought in the souks of old Tunis. Souks are market stalls where tourists get soaked if they can't haggle. When buying something here, the price is irrelevant — all that matters is how well you can bargain.

Language

In Arabic, there are 99 words to describe God.

French attempts to introduce a one-way system in the Tunisian desert were largely unsuccessful.

Turkey
Turkiye Cumhuriyeti

Gift to Europe

Backgammon and bridge were both invented here, called bridge because it was played on the bridge of Galata over the straits. Parchment was invented at Pergamum — after the Alexandrian Library, jealous of the success of the Pergamum Library, cut off supplies of papyrus. Other dubious gifts are doner and shish kebab, redeemed only by the great gift of opium in the 1960's (Turkey has 20 per cent of the world market). The Mongols are thought to have invaded in the first place because of the grass which *fermented, made women fecund and men invincible*. More likely is that it *washed the warriors' hearts of the world's grime* — or they just got stoned.

Hungry for Europe

Only 3 per cent of Turkey is in Europe but, since the revolution, every effort has been made to westernise this Asian country. After Mustapha Kemal — Kemal means perfection — raised the standard of the Republic of Turkey in 1922 he became know as Ataturk — father of the Turks. The 'Turks' themselves originally came from Turkestan in Mongolia and you can't go much further east than that.
Turkey is not:
religious education (Muslim)
oriental headgear
dervishes
polygamy
clerical garb
old style titles
Islamic surnames
the Arabic alphabet
the Hegira Calendar (Muslim)
these were all abolished by Kemal.

Gobble gobble

Turkey controlled one quarter of Europe plus Iraq, Israel, Syria, Egypt, North Africa and Yemen, with the aid of *janissaries*. They were sons of the conquered and the best soldiers in the world. T. E. Lawrence (of Arabia) sees their prowess as a result of *'This quite hopeless lack of initiative...'*.
 Before the Turks, Emperor Constantine of Constantinople was the first Christian Emperor — even though he killed both his wife and son.
 Michael the Drunkard superceded Basil the Macedonian and the Seljuks invaded.
 The Crusaders attacked the Arabs and Genghis Khan and Tamburlaine laid waste.

A routine check for cocaine smugglers on the Turkish border.

The Turks got Constantinople under control at last in 1453 with their emperor, soon to be known as Fatih, in charge. They kept it for exactly 400 years.

Independence

Kemal worked miracles to modernise Turkey much of which, in spite of the Empire, was totally backward. By 1922 the pseudonym *'Sick Man of Europe'* had really stuck. Even today people in the east live in caves and, in the town, a system called *gecekondu* allows a person to build his own house on unowned land as long as it is completed in one night. If the roof is being put on as dawn rises, he must start again.
 Between 1930 and 1970 the population tripled. In undeveloped areas, women of fertile age spend half their lives pregnant. There is only one car per 180 people (Switzerland for example, has one between two) and the economic situation has led to one million Turks working abroad.
 Turkey has one of the world's highest rates of inflation. Democracy tottered on until 1960 when an army coup deposed the president and hanged the prime minister. Civilian government was again suspended after the 1980 coup overthrew the Justice Party.
 There is no free press despite the 2,326 daily papers and periodicals.

Population: 46 and a half million

Size: Three times that of Britain, 300,000 sq. miles

Government: Republic

Language: Turkish

Religion: Islam

Capital: Ankara

Currency: Turkish lira, kuru

Tips for tourists

Visit Mount Ararat — the reputed resting place of Noah's Ark.

The coffee ritual requires guests to drain every last drop of this disgusting brew.

Eat *woman's thigh* — a dish of meat balls and rice.

Nibble *woman's navel* — a dessert.

Don't get roped into any criminal activity. Turkey is the only country in Europe with the death penalty.

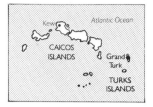

The Turks and Caicos Islands

Question 1

The Turks and Caicos consist of six small islands. One of them (Grand Turk) has an international airport. Another (South Caicos) also has an international airport. A third island (Providenciales) has a population of less than 1,000. What is the last thing in the world it needs?
Clue: They have just built one on it, using £5 million of British foreign aid.

Question 2

You run a multi-national holiday business. You wish to build a huge tourist centre on an idyllic isle in the West Indies. You say one of the main reasons for siting it on the particular island you choose is to help its unemployment problem. These are the unemployment rates on three of the Turks and Caicos islands:
Salt Cay — 8l per cent
Middle Caicos — 68 per cent
Providenciales — 3 per cent
Where will you build your tourist centre?
Answer (if you are Club Mediterranee): Providenciales.

Question 3

A multi-national holiday company agrees to build a huge tourist centre on a tiny island if the government will build a new international airport. The airport is built. Which of these will happen:
1. Millions of dollars worth of property speculation will take place.
2. The drug trade will move in.
3. The holiday company will fail to build the tourist centre when it said it would.
4. All of these.
Clue: The right answer is 4.

Take off

The islands were first spotted by the Spanish explorer Ponce de Leon in 1512 but it was 150 years before anyone settled here — Bermudans who established a salt-panning industry. Things didn't pan out too well for the islands. France and Spain fought over them for years but it was the British who eventually won control. The islands were a Jamaican dependency from 1874 until 1959 and became a Crown Colony in 1962. They became a separate colony in 1973.

There are executive and legislative councils but the governor still has responsibility for external affairs, internal security and defence.

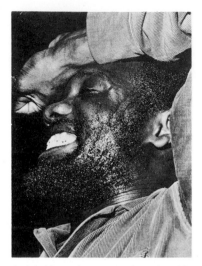

An inhabitant tries to remember where his country is.

Cruising

For centuries the islands survived on two industries — salt and fish. The main exports now are crawfish, shellfish and sunburned tourists. Tourism has been growing fast, although there were still only 11,500 visitors in 1981.

Incoming mail arrives once every three weeks. There is no regular outgoing mail. There are 625 phones, three doctors and 30 hospital beds.

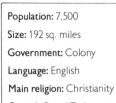

Population: 7,500

Size: 192 sq. miles

Government: Colony

Language: English

Main religion: Christianity

Capital: Grand Turk

Currency: US dollars, cents

Tips for tourists

Don't set up business as an undertaker. There are only about a dozen deaths a year. (But you could wait for a plane crash).

Take bottled water. There are only 21 inches of rain a year, so drinking water is scarce.

Fly there.

Tuvalu

The language

There are only 13 letters in the country's alphabet which accounts for the similarity of most of the words. The atolls are called Nanumea, Nanumanga, Niutao, Niu, Vaitupu, Nakufetau and Funafuti — the capital. The Prime Minister is called Puapua — but what really takes the biscuit for sheer lack of letters is the name of the ambassador to the United States. He is called Ionatana Ionatana. Incidentally, he resides in Tuvalu.

The history

Polynesians first settled here a long time ago. They came from Samoa in hollowed out tree-trunks. There is still an island story that tells of a voyage which set out to sea and never returned. This probably refers to the epic crossing from Samoa to Tuvalu in a small boat. It also perhaps explains why the enormous potential for a fishing industry is ignored. In 1892 the British made what were called the Ellice Islands a British protectorate and lumped them together with the Gilbert Islands, although their peoples were of two different races. The Gilberts are Micronesians. In 1975 the Ellice Islands separated from the Gilberts and in 1978 became independent under the name Tuvalu.

The desperate search for new grazing goes on.

Greatest moment

In World War Two the United States made Tuvalu — the Ellice Islands — its base for the first American attack on the Japanese ring around the Pacific. The Gilbert Islands were the target and their capture was the first major break in the Japanese defences. 5,000 Japanese died to 1,000 Americans — dispelling a belief that the Japanese had spread

about American cowardice. Today the war machines which didn't survive are still visible. Watery graves of hardware litter the islands. The successful operation was called Galvanic.

Customs

The first customs you encounter are of course at the airport. This is at Funafuti and consists of a grass strip from which pigs and chickens have to be chased before the plane lands. Other customs include a traditional punishment husbands inflict on straying wives. They bite off their noses. Male adultery on the other hand is met with a more final penalty. The guilty man is put in a canoe without food or water or a paddle and given a good following wind out into the Pacific.

The land

There isn't much of it. Only 9 and a half square miles. And even then the population is trying to make it smaller. Each island wants self rule.

None of the islands is more than 15 feet above sea level and there is no soil to speak of. Nothing much can grow except coconuts and the limited subsistence farming that is carried out is done by mashing up coconuts and coconut trees and making a light covering of fertile soil from it. But the islanders are hugely proud of their coconuts which, with postage stamps, are the mainstay of the economy. All they eat is coconuts and fish.

Politics

They are a mystery. During the 1981 elections Mr. Lautasi said: *"Politics are new to us"*. And he was a candidate. What western politician would dare canvass on that platform? Of the 7,400 population about 500 have jobs, and a family who is employed might have one member at a desk, one in a service industry and one — the best — at home to look after the coconuts. It is a poor country with average earnings of £250 per year.

Population: 7,900

Size: 9 and a half sq. miles

Government: Independent Commonwealth member

Language: Tuvaluan, English

Religion: Christianity

Capital: Funafuti

Currency: Australian dollar

Tips for tourists

Try palu sami — coconut cream with onion and curry powder wrapped in taro leaves.

No need for waterproof watches. For centuries the inhabitants have made hermetically sealed boxes for their belongings on ocean voyages. These are called *taluma*.

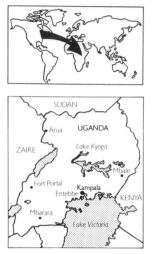

Population: 13 and a quarter million

Size: Same as Britain, 90,000 sq. miles

Government: Republic

Main languages: English, Swahili, Luganda

Main religions: Christianity, traditional beliefs

Capital: Kampala

Currency: Uganda shilling, cents

Tips for tourists

If you want to cash a cheque, take a large sack. The largest denomination banknote is 100 shillings, which will only buy a third of a bottle of beer since inflation soared after the civil war.

Don't bother saving the last dance. Local dances like the *bwola, lunyege* and *jing ding* are only performed by women.

Don't believe anyone who says they used to be married to Amin. He killed most of his ex-wives.

Uganda

Before Amin

This landlocked country full of lakes and rivers had become the kingdom of Buganda by the middle of the last century. Then the British moved in and tried to persuade the Bugandan chiefs to become large landlords and the natives to become serfs. It took them 20 years to realise this wouldn't work.

When Uganda became independent in 1962 the government was led by Dr. Milton Obote. The first president was the former King of Buganda, but Obote quickly accused him of treason and he fled. Obote became president. He appointed a former sergeant called Idi Amin as the army commander.

Idi Amin Dada, VC, DSO, MC

In 1971 Amin led a coup against Obote and established himself as ruler of Uganda. In the next eight years he:
... was responsible for the murder of at least 100,000 people and the torture of another 200,000.
... promoted himself to Field Marshal, awarded himself the VC, DSO and MC, and formed a Navy with himself as Admiral of the Fleet.
... engaged in a wrestling match with a Miss Omona, head of Uganda's Netball Federation. Gallantly, he declared the contest a draw.
... drank the blood of his Minister of Works and ate the liver of his Foreign Minister.
... claimed to have had long conversations with God, to whom he

King Freddy of Uganda acknowledges defeat to the High Commissioner in the annual Liberace lookalike competition.

had 'direct access'. He also had lunch with people risen from the dead.
... kept the severed heads of his victims in his fridge.
... ordered that VD should be called *good hope* so that sufferers would not be embarrassed. Then he decreed that anyone spreading the disease would be jailed.
... announced he would swim across the Suez Canal as a tribute to the Egyptian army (he didn't).
... planned to erect a monument to Hitler and told the UN: *"Germany is the right place where, when Hitler was the Prime Minister, he burnt over 6 million Jews."*
... became Uganda's leading film star and director (making films about himself).
... had a military unit named the *Suicide Revolutionary Mechanised Regiment*. (Their uniform was yellow).
... said *"I have the whole of Britain shaking so much I should qualify for a degree in philosophy."* And: *"Do not reveal the secrets of your lovers to imperialists or Zionists."*
... declared himself head of a Scottish Provisional Government.
... forced prisoners to kill each other in gladiatorial contests — then eat their victims.
... offered to settle a border dispute by having a boxing bout with President Nyere.
... survived 13 assassination attempts.
... killed women who wouldn't sleep with him and ritually sacrificed one of his sons, Moses.

Hello

When Amin became President he was given a lunch of honour by the Queen at Buckingham Palace. British diplomats welcomed him as 'a thoroughly nice man', 'as gentle as a lamb' and 'a burly, genial giant'.

Goodbye

He was eventually thrown out by an army from Tanzania. He now has a new home with the oil sheiks of Saudi Arabia. Obote is once again in control of Uganda — one of the few African leaders who has returned to power after overthrowing the man who overthrew him.

Food

Coffee is the most important crop. Ugandans eat more potatoes and less sugar than any other people.

Union of Soviet Socialist Republics

Soyuz Sovyetskikh Sotsialisticheskikh Respublik

Mental health

Russians drink vodka with everything. So it isn't surprising that half of all their illnesses are alcohol-related and excessive drinking is the third major cause of death. To compensate, revenue from liquor sales is the equivalent of the Soviet military budget.

If the drink doesn't get you, the mental hospitals may. Among their recorded diagnoses are: *'deficient capacity to adjust to his social surroundings', 'overestimation of his own person', 'grandiose ideas of reforming the world', 'extolling the Western way of life', 'an obsessive mania for truth-seeking', 'wears a beard'* and *'putting up an icon and photographs of people like Academician Sakharov and General Grigorenko'*.

Culture

The most popular entertainments in Russia are the ballet, the circus and mushroom-picking (Lenin spent the last year of his life gathering mushrooms). They have more cinemas than any other country and take out more library books.

A Russian proverb: *To live a life is not so simple as crossing a field*.

Painting to avoid: Malevich's *White on white* series, which represents the ultimate rejection of objects in the visible world. Art now: Mukhina's stainless steel group *Worker and Collective Farm Woman*. Rewards: 'People's artists' are entitled to the same special pensions as 'heroes of labour'.

Revolution

Before the revolution in 1917, Russian history was a gory list of Tzars. Many of them were called 'the Great'. This was a self-imposed title. Thus Peter the Great was as bad as Ivan the Terrible (both tortured to death their eldest sons). Catherine the Great was an obscure German princess who murdered her husband so that she could assume the throne. Frederick the Great could not consummate his marriage.

There was nothing very great about the revolution, either. In fact, it was based on a terrible mistake. It is called 'the October Revolution'. Actually, it took place on November 7th — but they were using the wrong calendar when they named it (they were looking at the old Julian calendar).

Beneath the skin

The USSR, the world's biggest country, consists of 15 separate republics. The smallest, Armenia, is the oldest Christian nation (Christianity became its national religion 1,700 years ago).

The biggest is Siberia, which is one and a half times the size of the USA. It contains every known element and could become the world's largest producer of gold and diamonds. However, no one wants to work there. Although they are paid 50 per cent more than in the rest of Russia and get free homes, every year more than a million more people move out of Siberia than move in.

The people of Georgia are said to be the handsomest on earth and they have a higher proportion of centenarians than anywhere. They attribute this to yoghourt and the local brandy.

Red sales

Jeans (nicknamed *Devil's hide*) cost £200 a pair. An album of *Jesus Christ Superstar*, about £60. A 4oz. jar of instant coffee, £10.

The Communist Party has 15 million members and 200,000 full-time officials. There are more doctors than in any other country and four out of five of them are women. Russia is the world's biggest producer of cigars. Its national railway has the biggest payroll of any civilian organisation — 2 million employees.

Population: 270 million

Size: 85 times that of Britain, 8 and a half million sq. miles

Government: Communist

Language: Russian

Main religion: Russian Orthodox church

Capital: Moscow

Currency: Rouble, kopek

Tips for tourists

Don't buy eight pairs of shoes. One in eight pairs made in Russia won't fit anyone because they are so badly made.

On a taxi ride, sit beside the driver, not in the back. This is a symbol of equality (but you'll still have to pay).

Visit the Stalin museum in Gori, where you can see his school report containing high marks for Religious Knowledge. (Forty million people died during Stalin's reign of terror).

Places not to stay:
a) The world's biggest hotel — the 3,200-room *Rossiya* in Moscow
b) The world's largest swamp — covering 18,125 sq. miles of the Pripyat river basin
c) The world's largest labour camp (*Dubrovlag*) or prison (*Kharkov*: population 40,000)
d) The world's largest cemetery (at Leningrad: population 500,000).

Heavy disguise makes verification of Soviet troop movements very difficult.

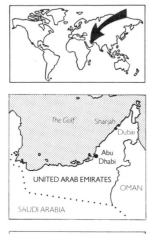

United Arab Emirates

Tips for tourists

Beware of the camel beetle. It first injects anaesthetic into the victim then, at its leisure, chews off, for instance, the top lip (a favourite of his).

Beware of the camels. They are left in the roads at night. If one is killed by a car, the Sheikh awards £500 to the owner. Sometimes the camel is not killed and thrashes its way into the car destroying the driver. Camels have a syphilitic saliva which blinds.

Beware of the locusts. They eat everything in sight except concrete.

Sinbad the sailor

If Sinbad ever existed, it was along this stretch of the Gulf, and it is about this area that the story has been written. Not surprisingly. From the 7th Century, pirates plagued the coasts. At the beginning of the 19th Century they began to get on the nerves of the British and interfere with their trade with India. The area became known as 'The Pirate Coast' and the most famous pirate, Mir Mahanna of Bandar Rig, was described as the 'most execrable tyrant who ever lived'. He killed his father for not liking him enough, followed by his mother for complaining about him killing his father. From this, perhaps, comes the local proverb:
I taught him archery day by day:
When his arm grew strong, he shot me.

A pre-1974 Opec conference.

Other lunatics

Piracy is now a thing of the past, since the British made a treaty — the first in Arabia — *'Thou shall not commit piracy against British shipping'*.
Amazement at the possibility of a truce led these emirates to be known as the Trucial States. But other dangers were to come. The Qawasim, for instance, carried on a war with the local sheikh. They were so fanatical they attacked even those who weren't their enemies. They were defeated in 1819. But still danger lurks in the mountains of the UAE. The Shihuh tribe — who have blue eyes and whose origin is unknown — are not renowned for hospitality. If you approach the mountains where they live, first fire a gun (into the air). An answering shot means welcome — of sorts. No reply means — beat a hasty retreat. Two British tourists, who wandered in recently, were fed on bread and water for three days and then released naked into the desert.

Modern change

The Emirates consist of Abu Dhabi, Dubai, Sharjah, Umm al-Qaiwan, Ras al Khaimah and Fujairah. Five have no oil, one has some — and one has huge reserves. The latter is Abu Dhabi — the richest political unit in the history of mankind. In 1972 a population of 70,000 attracted an export revenue of £210 million. It is not possible to buy land here, though you may be given it. All nationals can have a free house. This is partly to bring in the desert bedouin and partly because the Sheikh can afford it. Sheikh Zayed has a benevolent attitude towards his subjects which perhaps makes him the greatest benefactor the world has ever known. *"Money is of no use unless it is for the benefit of the people"*, he says magnificently.

His great dream is becoming reality. As a young man, he was sick of the sight of desert and wished to make it fertile. Today hundreds of miles of desert roads are lined with trees, watered by underground hosepipes.

To feed the people, 10 tons of eggs are flown in every morning. This makes up for the endless fish which is the only protein here. Even the sheep are fed on fish and taste like it. The other emirates have no such great sheikhs. But some still take an obsessive interest in the running of their land. Sheikh Rashid of Dubai is personally in charge of the telephone and electricity companies.

Other wealth

There is none. There used to be pearl-fishing. Men dived 60 times per day for one and a half minutes, 120 days of the year. The beds are now worn out and so are the divers. In the old days they made their boats from sewing planks together — but this isn't the reason that whaling ships were called *Bum Boats*.

United Kingdom
United Kingdom of Great Britain and Northern Ireland

"England is at last ripe for revolution", said Trotsky in 1925. But in the 1980's there's still no sign of it. The ownership of the land in the UK has changed little since William the Conqueror, the rulers are still toffs predominantly from the private schools and Oxbridge, and the jargon of feudalism is still alive — much of it in daily use. The only revolution here has been in the ownership of video recorders, of which the British own more for the size of their population than anywhere in the world.

Correct form

Debrett's *Correct Form* explains how to address an hereditary knight, of whom there are only two in the country. The explanation is provided appropriately by Sir Iain Moncreiffe of that Ilk: *"I was asked this very question by the barman of one of my clubs which one of the two hereditary knights had just joined. The correct answer is just 'knight'. So if staying at Glin Castle, you will know to say 'Goodnight, Knight".*
There follows four hundred pages of detail on what is, for example, the correct mode of address for a divorced Scottish peeress, or the 'widow of one who would have succeeded to a Peerage had he survived'.

There are so many ballroom dancers, they regularly spill into the streets.

Foreign affairs

'Let's put the 'great' back into Great Britain' has became a fashionable slogan here. It's not hard to discover how it went missing. For years the country has suffered from monarchs who, like George V, 'did nothing for 17 years but kill animals and stick in stamps', and from British diplomats who get by by speaking English very loudly. Sir Neville Henderson, the Ambassador to Germany before the last war, was clearly well-versed in the special art of British diplomacy: *'Goering may be a blackguard, but he's not a dirty blackguard'.*
British military intelligence has been similarly handicapped — by men such as Field Marshall Haig, Commander of the British forces in World War One, who said in 1914: *"Bullets have little stopping power against the horse'.*

Language

Britain's most useful gift to the world has been the English language. Three-quarters of the world's mail is in English, half the world's newspapers and three-fifths of all radio stations. There are almost a million words in the vocabulary but 95 per cent of all usage involves only 3,000 of them. There are 127 different recorded ways to spell 'Raleigh' — as in Sir Walter.

Education:

Generations of British schoolchildren have had to learn that a group of lions is called a 'pride' and several geese a 'gaggle'. A British linguist recently suggested some useful modern groupings: A removal of dentists, a wave of sailors, an invasion of relatives, an apology of telephone operators, a dearth (or a departure) of servants, an offshoot of gardeners, a hail of Nazis, a dawdling of waiters.

United Kingdom?

To call this country 'united' is wishful thinking. The Scots hate the English and everyone hates the Welsh. The Irish are viewed as stupid or dangerous or both, and an embarrassment politically. The policy of most recent governments has been to pretend that Northern Ireland isn't really part of the nation. This tactic has met with limited success.

Population: 56 million	
Size: Slightly larger than Britain, 94,000 sq. miles	
Government: Constitutional monarchy	
Language: English	
Main religion: Church of England	
Capital: London	
Currency: Pounds, pence	

Tips for tourists

Always address the Queen as *Ma'am* — to rhyme with 'Pam'. It is no longer appropriate to say *Ma'am* — to rhyme with 'palm'.

Start sewing on your sequins — Britain has the highest number of ballroom dancers in the world for the size of population.

Red-heads will feel at home in the Highlands of Scotland, where 11 per cent of the population has red hair — the highest concentration in the world.

Keep a check on your money — England has the worst record in the world for counterfeiting.

Tips for tourists

Respect the flag. It must not be left in the dark or get wet or touch the ground. It must be flown everywhere.

Be careful of the phone. Although there are 550 million calls every day, they are all monitored by a defence organisation called NSA which has a 2 million dollar budget a year.

Do not be lured into marriage. There are half as many divorces as marriages.

United States of America

The greatest...

...amount of murders. Over 20,000 per year — more than Europe, Japan and Australia put together.

...living thing in the world. The 280 feet tall Californian sequoia tree.

...whip factory — producing several hundred thousand per year.

...landowner in the world. The US government, owning land the size of India.

...Jewish population — twice as many as Israel.

...donor of pipe organs, Andrew Carnegie who gave 7,000 around the world.

...amount of radio stations — 8,608. The US has only 5 per cent of the world's population but produces over one-quarter of the world's output. They grow 42 per cent of the world's corn and lose more days in strikes than anywhere.

Mediocrity

There are 23 million illiterate adults in the US and 13 per cent of 17-year olds cannot read, write or comprehend anything at all. Perhaps this is understandable in a country whose leaders are unable to get across simple ideas in their native language. Nixon is perhaps the best example: *"I know that you believe you understand what you think I said, but I'm not sure you realise that what you heard is not what I meant."*

It all started with Abraham Lincoln who, in a judgment of a book, said: *"People who like this sort of thing will find this the sort of thing they like".* Presidents of America are a confusing bunch of people. But they are also confused. Nixon again, at the funeral of President Pompidou of France: *"This is a great day for France".* Or Gerald Ford toasting Egyptian President, Anwar Sadat, *"To you and the people you represent, the great people of the government of Israel."*

A British ambassador to Washington once remarked of Teddy Roosevelt, *"You must always remember that the President is about six".*

Language

Although England is now the mother country, every European nation contributed to its formation. Robert Benchley explains: *"We call England the Mother country because most of us come from Poland and Italy".*

Also one-quarter of the Irish population at the time of the famine headed for America. Four and a half million Jews came in the 40 years at the turn of the century, over one million Norwegians, and millions from Austria, Hungary and Russia.

What has emerged from this hotch-potch of languages and cultures is the American language. And American names. They call themselves: Wava White Flagg, Nancy Pigg Bacon, Susan Eatwell Burpitt, Margery Ready First, Mary Hatt Box, John Will Fail, Strange Odor Andrews, Longhorne Bullitt Dick, Herbert Youle Gotobed...

Defence

The first threat to the Americans came from American Indians. They've solved that by putting them in 80,000 sq. miles of reservation. Now it's the Russians. The defence budget is stretched to combat this threat but they still manage to spend half a million dollars per year on mowing the lawns of generals and admirals and 6,000 dollars advising the government how to buy Worcester Sauce.

Government

In 20 states of America, only people who can read can vote. They tend to be the states where people can't read. In Hawaii you are allowed to read in Hawaian. In Alabama each voter must take an anti-Communist oath.

The constitution was drawn up in 1787 and has executive, legislative and judicial branches. The Supreme Court — judicial — has the supreme power to over-rule the entire constitution. Each state can make its own federal laws. So you may find you can smoke dope in one state legally and, by walking 10 yards to the left, receive a 10-year prison sentence. The courts of America have jailed a dog for biting a cat, fined a monkey, hanged a five-ton elephant for treading on its keeper's head and lynched cows, sheep and sows for being sodomised.

The world's first all-gay railway.

Upper Volta
Republique de Haute-Volta

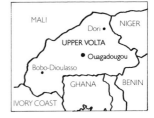

The pits

God wasn't joking when He fitted Upper Volta into the armpit of Africa. That's exactly what it is.

The flattest...

...country in Africa.
...major industry — oil seed crushing.
...economy — almost entirely subsistence farming. The main export is Upper Voltans, half of whom go abroad to find work.

Several obvious fakes have been produced in an attempt to prove that an Upper Voltan was the earliest man.

The lowest...

...proportion of doctors for population. There are only 51 in the whole country, 48 of them in the capital.
...intake of calories.
...life expectancy — men, 27, women, 33.
...proportion of telephones.
...airforce — 50 airmen, no planes.

The poorest...

...country in the world.
...word, *nana* meaning 'to take without paying'.

The least...

...diplomatic wage proposal — when the National Assembly was asked in 1965 to cut the salaries of all government employees. That meant everyone in the capital. Rioting followed.
...significant gesture — when Kwame Nkrumah of Ghana and President

Yameogo of Upper Volta, in an attempt to foster greater African unity, built a wall in a frontier village then knocked it down with axes (to symbolise an open frontier).

Natural disasters

Upper Volta is a landlocked country sweltering near the Sahara. In the summer, temperatures rise to over 100 degrees in the shade (and there isn't much of that). In the rainy season the three huge Voltan rivers overflow, threatening to destroy with floods what the deadly tsetse fly has left unscathed.

Unnatural disasters

It isn't only the tsetse which live off the back of the people. The French did it first after colonising Upper Volta at the end of the last century. Then various neighbouring states grabbed it. And since it became independent in 1960 a few individuals have thrived while the rest of the population suffered.

One such was Maurice Yameogo who made the smart move of founding the country's first political party. This helped him to become a) Prime Minister b) President c) a multi-millionaire, which he did by pocketing public money. He spent a million pounds on his own wedding celebration. That didn't affect the result of the 1965 election — Maurice was the only candidate.

He was deposed the following year in a coup led by the army chief, Colonel Lamizana, who went on to become a) President, b) as corrupt as Yameogo, c) deposed in a coup led by the new army chief.

Politics

Turnout in elections is extremely low. One reason for this could be that although there are eight political parties, the constitution only allows three on the ballot form.

Things may be changing, though. It was recently announced that folklore, improvisation and charlatanism would no longer be accepted as methods of government (other politicians, please note).

Dining out

Ninety five per cent of the population live off the land with a daily calorie intake well below the accepted subsistence level. The crocodiles and herds of hippos which roam the country eat better. The economy is peanuts — literally — that is one of the few crops.

Population: 7 million

Size: A bit bigger than Britain, 105,000 sq. miles

Government: Republic

Religion: Traditional beliefs

Official language: French

Capital: Ouagadougou

Currency: CFA franc, centime

Tips for tourists

Don't bother watching TV. The local station, *Voltavision*, broadcasts three shows a week to the Ouagadougou area.

For a quiet evening out, visit one the *Houses of Youth and Culture* where young people play cards and read. These are never crowded. Ninety per cent of the population is illiterate.

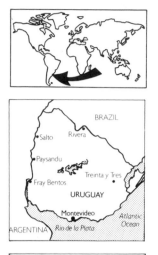

Uruguay
Republica Oriental del Uruguay

This is the smallest independent state in South America. It consists of almost nothing but grazing land on which live the country's most important occupants — cattle. More than half the humans live in the capital, Montevideo.

History

At one time part of Spain, then a province of Brazil, Uruguay gained its freedom in 1828. It didn't use it wisely. There were 12 years of civil war followed by six of war against Paraguay followed by 20 of military rule.

Unlike most other countries, Uruguay seemed to learn from experience. For most of this century it has amazed the rest of the world by being a South American country renowned for its political stability and advanced social laws.

Nowhere is perfect, though. The military took over in 1973.

Industry

The foundation of the economy was laid in 1603 when a far-seeing governor, Hernando Aria de Saavedra, shipped in 100 cattle and 100 horses and left them to get on with it. They went forth and multiplied so abundantly that before long a flourishing trade in hides began. It is still Uruguay's main industry, and they have more cattle for the size of population than anywhere else.

The country's main import is would-be divorcees. It was the first Latin American state to legalise divorce and thousands of divorce-seekers still flock in from Argentina and other less liberal nations. Women may get divorced without giving a reason. A proposal to extend this to men met with violent opposition.

More about animals

In keeping with a nation of horsemen, the army boasts two cavalry regiments. The national slogan is *Como Uruguay, no hay*. This does not refer to a famine of foodstuffs for horses. It means 'There is no country like Uruguay'.

The most common reptile is the *Vibora de la cruz*, a dangerous viper with marks like a cross on its head.

More about reptiles

Although being reasonably advanced politically, the government faced mounting economic problems in the middle of this century. Between 1955 and 1970, inflation increased by 9,000 per cent.

Uruguay's constitution contained careful safeguards to protect the people from dictators. Unfortunately, it did not protect the people from themselves. In 1966 they voted for the adoption of a presidential system of government.

As if all this wasn't bad enough they had to contend with the Tupamaros urban guerrillas, who named themselves after Tupac Amaru, an Inca who led a rebellion against Spanish rule, in the 18th Century. The result was inevitable. The military took over.

It is dangerous for foreigners to bathe in some rivers of the interior.

More about politics

The two main political parties, the Colorado (Red) and the Blanco (White) take their names (and colours) from 150-year-old factions. Before 1958, the Colorado Party had held power for 93 years.

The present military rulers are currently trying to get back to democracy by holding elections in which they put up military candidates. So far, these have been soundly beaten.

More about the population

It consists of 11 million cattle, 20 million sheep, 525,000 horses, 400,000 pigs, 7 and a half million poultry and less than 3 million people.

Population: Three million

Size: Three quarters that of Britain, 70,000 sq. miles

Government: Republic

Language: Spanish

Main religion: Roman Catholic

Capital: Montevideo

Currency: Nuevo peso, centesimo

Tips for tourists

Although Uruguay is known as the Switzerland of South America, don't bother looking for the white-topped mountains.

Don't think you can get away with murder just because the death penalty has been abolished. It was replaced by 40 years' penal servitude.

Men should behave responsibly. Investigation of paternity is compulsory whenever an illegitimate child is born.

Vanuatu
Republic of Vanuatu

Where are you, Vanuatu?

In the Pacific Ocean — a group of green, mountainous islands stretching for 400 miles. The largest is called Espiritu Santo. The others include Epi, Pentecost, Aoba, Efate, Erromanga, Aneityum and Paama.

Who are you, Vanuatu?

A difficult question to answer. These islands have always had an identity crisis.

They were discovered in 1606 by the Portuguese, who promptly lost them again. They were rediscovered by the French in 1768. Six years later the British pretended that *they* had rediscovered them, too. They named them the New Hebrides, after the Scottish Hebrides. The French, with startling originality, renamed them Les Nouvelles-Hebrides.

Naturally there was considerable conflict between the British and French, neither of whom could be satisfied with just dividing the islands between them. At one stage the British tried to show they had the Lord on their side by sending Bishop George Selwyn round the islands pretending that *he* had discovered them.

The problem was solved eventually by a deal in which both countries agreed to administer the islands jointly. During World War Two the Japanese, while invading everywhere else nearby, failed to discover the New Hebrides.

The islands became independent in 1980 and changed their name to Vanuatu — presumably so that *no one* would *ever* find them again.

What do you do, Vanuatu?

Another identity crisis — the place keeps changing its mind.

In the middle of the last century, sandalwooders arrived. They were replaced by cotton planters. Cotton soon gave way to bananas. Bananas were superceded by coffee. And coffee by coconuts. Coconuts were followed by maize. Finally maize was swamped by cheap labour imported from Vietnam. Although they must have been confused about what they were producing, this led to a short-lived boom for the islands.

Now the only industries worth mentioning are basketry, canoe-building and pottery. Profits are low. But the islands are rapidly becoming a tax haven (there is almost no taxation) with banks and companies that need a hidey-hole moving in fast.

Getting through to Vanuatu

The local telephone company is called Vanitel. Radio New Hebrides broadcasts in three languages, English, French and Pidgin.

Saluting you, Vanuatu

The national flag contains a boar's tusk overlaid by two crossed fern leaves.

The Vanuatu police do not carry guns.

Population: 110,000

Size: 5,700 sq. miles

Government: Republic

Religion: Christianity

Language: Bislama

Capital: Vila

Currency: Vatu

Tips for tourists

Be careful if you try to buy a pig. There is a breed of hermaphrodite pig on Espiritu Santo.

Be careful if you try to buy a bride. Bride prices have always been high on these islands. That was one reason given for the population falling last century from 800,000 to 80,000.

If you go mountaineering, beware. Three of the 'mountains' are active volcanoes.

ITALY

VATICAN
CITY

Railway
station

Radio
station

St. Peter's

Vatican museum

St. Peter's
Square

Tips for tourists

Be humble. The smallest state in
the world heads the largest
religion, 700 million people.

Learn Latin — the official
language of this, the true
descendent of Ancient Rome.

Be awed. The pontiffs are the
oldest government in the
western world. Like Julius
Caesar they are still called
Pontifex Maximus.

Be understanding. The Vatican
spends more money on defence
(100 Swiss Guards) than it does
on health and education
together.

Expect only spiritual comfort
nowadays. The Vatican has a
birth rate of nil.

Vatican City State

Stato della Citta del Vaticano

In practice

The Vatican possesses:
the largest collection of antiquities in the
world,
the most beautiful square in the world,
which took the lives of 20 Popes to
complete,
the most magnificent collection of art in
the world,
the largest residential palace in the
world.

The Vatican has risen from the ashes
of ancient Rome. It was on this site that
Nero's Gardens and the Circus stood —
where thousands of Christians were
martyred for their beliefs. St. Peter's
Church stands where St. Peter is buried
and on the Piazza San Pietro stands the
obelisk brought from Egypt by Emperor
Caligula which in 1586 was erected in
its present position by 600 men and 150
horses in a four-month operation.

Now as well as being the centre of the
Roman Catholic church, the Vatican
City is a vast museum of the most
sublime masterpieces in the world of art.

Power failure

In 1859 Vatican territory incorporated
3,124,688 subjects. Now there are
1,000. No existing state has been so
decimated.

The Vatican is the smallest state in
the world. This did not happen without
much unholy haggling. Used to supreme
power since the foundation of the
Christian church, the Vatican didn't like
it when, in 1870, its territory was lost to
a unified Italy. The temporal powers of
the Pope were suspended during a cold
war period in which Popes instructed
Catholics not to vote in elections.

Then in 1929 the Pope signed the
Lateran pact with Mussolini which gave
independent sovereignty to the Holy See
in the Vatican City and one or two small
properties in Rome and the Pope's
Summer Palace.

Italy compensated the Vatican's loss of
power with 750 million lire in cash and
an annual income of one billion lire. The
Vatican's investment programme would
make an interesting read but it is a
secret, being one of the few states in the
world not to publish a budget.

The Lateran pact

This is now largely out of date but no
political party nor the Vatican itself
wants to risk changes. For instance, the
clause which states that an attempt on
the Pope's life should be treated in the
same way as an attempt on the life of the

king would be hard to enforce. There is
no king and no death penalty, (the
penalty for an attempt on the king's
life).

Recently there has been much
argument between the Vatican and Italy
on the subject of divorce. The Italian
government legalised it. The Pope
objected and asked for a referendum.
The government replied that the Pope
needed to raise a half million signatures
by law to get a referendum. The Pope
raised 1,370,134. The referendum
endorsed divorce.

A spiritual city

The Vatican has:
a railway station
a prison
an army barracks (for the world's oldest
army)
a radio station which broadcasts to 6
continents in 14 languages
its own money
its own flag
its own printing press, called *Polyglot*
because it can print in any language
— from old Ecclesiastical Georgian to
India Tamil.
its own law courts where the Pope can
make his own laws.

After the embarrassment of the Turin
Shroud, the Vatican goes for more direct
proof of Christ's existence.

Venezuela
Republica de Venezuela

Starters

The Spanish called this country Venezuela, which means 'Little Venice'. For some extraordinary reason, they were reminded of that beautiful waterbound city by the crude native huts on stilts which they saw when they first arrived here.

This is now the richest country in Latin America. But that is all due to oil. For most of its independent existence, it has been ruled by a series of military dictators, interspersed with civilian strife.

A Venezuelan peasant prepares a line of cocaine on the roof of his home.

Quizlings

Venezuela is now the nearest thing South America has to a democracy. When it holds elections, voting is by means of coloured ballot cards. Each political party has a different colour. There are 11 political parties. Although this is helpful for the illiterate, it does nothing for the colour-blind.

Winners

In 1824, in the town of Angostura, the Prussian doctor Johann Siegert invented the famous bitters which still bear that town's name. Unfortunately, the town no longer bears it — it is called Ciudad Bolivar. And bitters are now made in Trinidad. That doesn't affect Venezuela's wealth, which is due to oil, of which Venezuela is one of the largest producers. It has attracted 2 million illegal immigrants, mainly Colombians, who flock in for the high wages.

Venezuela has been building a wonderful rail network since 1950. Only 100 miles of track have been laid so far.

The quaintest thing about the place is the names of the banks: the Workers' Bank, the Labourers' Bank and the Livestock Bank.

Losers

A quarter of Venezuela is grassy plains but the country has never taken off as a cattle-rearing nation. This is mainly because thousands of cattle drown at flood time when the Orinoco River overflows.

Population: About 14 and a half million

Size: Four times that of Britain, 350,000 sq. miles

Government: Republic

Language: Spanish

Main religion: Roman Catholic

Capital: Caracas

Currency: Bolivar, centimos

Tips for tourists

See the 'pigeon housing estate' at Macuto.

Ride the world's highest cable railway (4,360 yards) to Pico Espejo.

Don't carry a pocket knife. The police are apt to confiscate them as 'concealed weapons' as street crime is reaching epidemic proportions.

See the Caroni waterfall which, at a mile high, is the highest in the world (Niagara falls only 175 feet, but has a larger volume).

Quiz

1. Who was dictator of Venezuela from 1909 to 1935
   Christopher Columbus
   General Juan Gomez
   Shirley Temple?
2. Who was the richest person in Venezuela in 1935
   Mahatma Ghandi
   General Juan Gomez
   Kermit the Frog?
3. Who was the biggest landowner and had more cattle than anyone else in Venezuela in 1935
   Batman
   General Juan Gomez
   Jimmy Carter?
Clue: He died peacefully in his sleep (in 1935).

Vietnam

Cong Hoa Xa Hoi Chu Nghia Viet Nam

Legend

According to mythology Vietnam's history began when King De Minh married an immortal fairy. They begat King Duong Vuong (of the Land of Red Demons) who begat Lac Long Quang (Dragon Lord of the Lac) who married Au Co, an immortal who bore him 100 eggs. From them sprang 100 sons, from whom sprang the Hong Bang dynasty. Their kings each ruled for 150 years. The country was called the Land of the Tattooed Men.

History

When history proper started Vietnam was a backward country — so backward its name was Nam-Viet. The Chinese invaded in 111 BC and ruled for a thousand years. The locals eventually threw them out and then saw off the Mongol hordes of Kublai Khan.

With a record like that, no one else should have bothered trying to invade. But they did. At the end of the 16th Century the French arrived. They behaved in typically gallic fashion, starting with seduction and ending with rape.

Winners

If there were a World Cup for war the Vietnamese would be clear winners. They have taken on all the top war teams and thrashed them (even though they did have home advantage).

The French were beaten between 1946 and 54. Then the Vietnamese faced the might of the United States which at one stage had half a million men in the field. After that, the Chinese moved in, only to be given a sound drubbing. Only the Russians are left. If they play and are beaten the Vietnamese should be allowed to keep the world (or at least their own country). The biggest winner has been Ho Chi Minh, the man who gave his name to a city, a trail and thousands of student demonstrations.

Industry

Nearly three-quarters of the people still work in agriculture. Seventy per cent of the workforce are women. This is because so many men are in the army. Vietnam has one million soldiers, the second biggest army (for size of population) in the world (Cuba has the biggest). Almost everyone over 16 is in the army reserves.

The average wage is 50 dong a month — about £11. Families are grouped in twenties in 'mutual aid and labour

The government have tried everything to get the Vietnamese army to invade the rest of the world.

cells'. The principal farm machinery is still the water buffalo and elephants are used extensively for logging. The main export recently has been Boat People — more than 400,000 of them have fled to other countries.

Politics

In 1975, two years after the American pull-out, the North and South were united. The whole country is now a 'state of the dictatorship of the proletariat based on the alliance of workers and peasants under the leadership of the working class'.

The government has ordered family altars to be taken down. They have usually been replaced with altars dedicated to Ho Chi Minh.

The national anthem is called *Tien quan ca* — 'The troops are advancing'.

Food

After fighting, the main strength of the Vietnamese is cooking. There is a big Chinese influence. They are the only people in the whole Pacific and South-East Asia area who use chopsticks. The most important part of their diet is fish — they eat more than twice as much of it as meat.

Population: 54 million

Size: One and a half times that of Britain, 130,000 sq. miles

Government: Communist

Main religion: Taoism and Buddhism

Language: Vietnamese

Capital: Hanoi

Currency: Dong, hao, xu

Tips for tourists

Wanna see some action? Try a library. The Vietnamese say: *For us a book is a weapon. Every poem, every painting and every songbook must be a bullet shot directly at the enemy.*

Don't bother looking for rhino. They are virtually extinct having been overhunted because the locals think their horns are an aphrodisiac.

Avoid food containing *nuoc mam*, a sauce based on fermented salted fish.

Virgin Islands

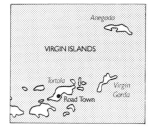

Virginity has as much to do with the Virgin Islands as tree surgery does with the Special Branch. In fact, not so long ago the Virgins had the highest rate of illegitimacy in the world.

Early promiscuity

Christopher Columbus discovered and named the islands in 1493, in memory of St. Ursula's 11,000 virgins who died in an epic defence of their chastity. The Virgin Islands put up no defence against Columbus. And having done it once they obviously felt there was little point in refusing others. So they have since been had by just about everyone — Spanish, British, Dutch — even the French.

The Spanish were into something else beside virginity, over which a veil should perhaps be drawn. Suffice it to say that by the end of the 16th Century it had involved the death of all the natives on the islands.

Other activity

Even today there isn't a lot to do on the islands except lose your virginity. For this purpose there are 44 uninhabited islands (out of a total of 60) and endless stretches of virgin sand. Some of these islands have names such as *Peter*, *Cooper*, *Beef* and *Norman*, suggesting a commemoration of some individual conquests. Of course one of Norman's other conquests has become familiar to generations of schoolchildren.

For those with a different but related activity in mind, there is always the Free Bottom area of the capital, to which, incidentally, there has recently been an extension of sewage services.

Leisure

There is a disco in the islands. And a library. Both in the exotically-named capital, Road Town. Monarchists can always look forward to a visit from the Queen — regularly every ten years or so. She came in 1966 to open a bridge, and again in 1977 to open the islands' parliament. There are fewer cinemas here than anywhere in the world.

Work

This is a place of waiters. In fact the majority of the people work in the tourist industry. The rest work in agriculture or make hollow concrete blocks, and rum. Many of the islanders go to work in the neighbouring US Virgin Islands where the jobs are the same but the wages are higher. The vast majority of islanders are of African descent.

Population:	11,000
Size:	59 sq. miles
Government:	UK colony
Language:	English
Religion:	Christianity
Capital:	Road Town
Currency:	US dollar, cent

Tips for tourists

Don't be alarmed at the colour of the water in the toilets — there is a desperate shortage of fresh water, so salt water is used for sewage removal and fire fighting.

Before you go, read *Cultural Aspects of Delusion: A Psychiatric Study of the Virgin Islands*, for the full flavour of the people.

Visit Norman Island — said to be Robert Louis Stevenson's *Treasure Island*.

Panic — and profound guilt — when the islanders were told the meaning of the word 'virgin'.

Western Samoa

Samoa i Sisifo

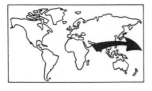

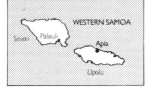

Population: 160,000

Size: 1,000 sq. miles

Government: Constitutional monarchy

Language: English, Samoan

Religion: Christianity

Capital: Apia

Currency: Tala

Tips for tourists

Don't speak to a Samoan while standing. It's bad manners.

Sit with your legs *under* you.

If you pass a meeting in a car, get out and walk.

A curfew is signalled by *a)* a blast on a conch shell, *b)* the striking of a freely suspended oxy-acetylane cylinder.

Take dark glasses. Samoans live in the least private homes in the world.

Early settlers named these three islands Samoa — from Sa, meaning 'sacred' and Moa, meaning 'centre of the earth'. The other Samoa is American Samoa — to the east.

Begorrah

Western Samoa is less commercialised than its American counterpart and has a negligible industrial or commercial output. The islanders, therefore, are fairly relaxed, careless and, above all, unpredictable. It is this trait of unpredictability which has led to the country being called 'The Ireland of the Pacific'.

The national characteristic is not only lack of responsibility. The islanders chew the herb Kava which induces apathy and gets them through the long, hot days. One of this drug's effects is a sudden change of temperament, from natural pleasantness to sullen, unwelcoming hostility. In this case, sit it out. It passes as quickly as it arrives. The Samoans are, by nature, a warm and hospitable race.

Since they gave up eating human beings, Samoans will do anything to attract attention.

Unpredictability

Their national games are cricket and rugby, which they learned from the New Zealand colonists. They are very hard players of both. Cricket — or kirikiti — is played with anything from 50 to 100 players a side and can last several days or weeks since the Samoans don't have anything else to do. Spectators also join in the game at crucial moments. One batsman, caught by a spectator, was given out by the umpire and objected. The umpire was adamant, particularly as the catcher was his own brother.

Unconvinced, the batsman killed the umpire with his bat.

The men wear skirts called lavalava and there is a common acceptance of transvestism which they introduced as a social practice to combat an imbalance in the sexes. So looks can deceive.

One custom which shows their unpredictability most clearly is when, without warning, a whole village descends on another and imposes itself on its hospitality by eating them out of house and home. This behaviour is then reciprocated. It is called malanga.

History

Originally populated by wandering seamen thrown off more crowded islands, Samoa soon became the centre of the Polynesian group. They have the oldest Polynesian language and, in 1962, still led the other islands by becoming the first to achieve independence. The islands Savaii and Upolu are the traditional home of the Maoris. Until World War One, the colonial powers sluggishly fought over Samoa with the Germans gaining the upper hand. Colonial foolishness reached its height in 1889 when eight ships of rival nations refused to be the first to leave harbour as a hurricane approached. Four were sunk and the others damaged. New Zealand then took over the administration. Now H.H. Malietoa Tanumafili II rules — otherwise known as *Ao o le Malo*. He appoints the Prime Minister and the Cabinet.

Culture

This is mainly Scottish due to the residence here of Robert Louis Stevenson who wrote and died on Samoa. He came to the islands to lead a quiet life with plenty of Vitamin C to cure his illness. He died of a fatal brain haemorrhage while helping his wife mix mayonnaise for dinner.

He appeared again in 1939 on a postage stamp. His chief observation of the inhabitants of Samoa was *'Their song is almost ceaseless'.* Rupert Brooke also wrote here and Somerset Maugham found some of his characters in the islanders. Neither stayed to die. One 19th Century writer observed, *'beautiful places...green forever...perfect shapes of man and woman, with red flowers in their hair, nothing to do but study oratory and etiquette, sit in the sun and pick the fruits as they fall'.* Nothing has changed.

Yemen Arab Republic

al Jamhuriya al Arabiya al Yamaniya

A land of opposites

The Yemen Arab Republic is usually referred to as North Yemen although it is situated to the west of the other, communist, Yemen. Called *Felix Arabia* by the Romans because of the prosperity brought by water and spice caravans, the Yemen Arab Republic is now among the world's ten poorest countries, with an annual average income of £60. Yet a family house in the capital costs £500 per month to rent. The explanation is that more than half of the male population works abroad. They return after two or three years and flood the country with foreign currency. There is money everywhere.

Yemen is the most fertile country in Arabia. It is positively green. But the agriculture is a joke — land squandered, less than half used. Rainfall varies from 3 to 40 inches over a terrain which is at the border of two air masses — the northerly winds and southern monsoons.

Politically, the Yemenis are no more consistent. In 1962 there was a civil war between royalists and republicans. They compromised with a republic run by royalists. Nasser called the population *"Republicans in the morning, royalists in the evening".* The blind are called 'clear-sighted'.

Backward of beyond

An English industrialist in San'a recently claimed that he was dragging the Yemen Arab Republic by the scruff of the neck straight into the 15th

Century. This is not far from the truth. The Yemen Arab Republic is the most secluded country in the world. It doesn't even know its own borders. The UK considers the land mass to be 46,160 sq. miles. The government claims 77,200. The whole of the eastern and southern border is a dotted line. It must be a relief to the population that the west is bounded by the Red Sea.

Although the 20th Century is gradually making an impression, bonfires are still lit during an eclipse of the moon to ward off evil spirits. Horns are placed on the sides of houses for the same effect. The houses themselves are left deliberately unfinished since God is the only being who can complete anything and it would be an insult to try.

Economy (of effort)

Industry is non-existent. 4,750 people are employed in purely domestic production. Their three year plan involves an underwear factory and a reprint of the Koran.

What earns them most of their foreign exchange is coffee — the world famous mocha coffee comes from the Yemen Arab Republic (it is exported through Mokha). However, qat, a narcotic shrub, is taking over. This is short-sighted as qat can only be exported without loss of quality to Ethiopia and South Yemen. But then, qat apparently induces short-sightedness.

The Yemenis couldn't even afford to build their own roads. They were built by:
The USSR, from Hodeida to Taiz
China, from Hodeida to San'a
The US, from Mokha to Taiz
West Germany, from San'a to Taiz
Kuwait, from Taiz to Turba.

Politics/history

They are the same really. Nothing has changed except the outside world.

The Imam until 1961 was a morphine addict, a sadist, and had protuberant eyes. He read a poem of his own on San'a Radio which caused a civil war. The 1977 president was assassinated because he fixed the bride price. His successor was killed by a South Yemeni peace envoy — even though he had freed the bride price, causing an inflationary spiral.

Proverb

When the old dog shits biscuits, there will be a change in Yemen.

Islamic law encourages the use of amputated limbs.

Population: 7 and a half million

Size: A quarter that of Texas, 73,000 sq. miles

Government: Republic

Language: Arabic

Religion: Islam

Capital: San'a

Currency: Riyal

Tips for tourists

Eat with the right hand. The left is unclean.

Women eat left-overs.

Take care of the barber. He also performs circumcisions.

Before going, look at the figures. No-one emigrates to Yemen. Millions emigrate from it.

People's Democratic Republic of Yemen

Jumhurijah al-Yemen al Dimuqratiyah al Sha'abijah

Population: 2 million

Size: A bit larger than Britain, 110,000 sq. miles

Government: Socialist republic

Language: Arabic

Main religion: Islam

Capital: Aden

Currency: South Yemen dinar, fils

Tips for tourists

Don't bother with an umbrella. There are only three inches of rain a year.

Don't bother trying to watch TV. There are only four hours of transmission a day — and they're in Arabic. (In any case, there are only 25,000 TV sets).

Geography

The People's Democratic Republic used to be known as Aden. That is like referring to England as London. Aden is just the capital but it was the only bit that mattered to the British when they ruled. Aden was important as a strategically-placed port on the Gulf of Aden near the Red Sea. The rest of the country was sneered at as just a lot of sand and volcanic rock strewn around it. Maybe some of the natives agreed. They called the desert in the north Rub' al-Khali (the Empty Quarter).

Sheep's eyes are not the only Arab delicacy.

History

The British East India Company took over Aden in 1839 as a massive coal bunker for ships steaming back and forth to India. They left the various feudal lords, emirs and sultans who ruled the interior to get on with it, sending in the odd agent to keep them friendly. Some of these agents were attracted to the job by the Bedouin Arab's tolerance of homosexuality in an otherwise intolerant world.

In 1937, the British declared that Aden and its surrounding territory were a colony. This was never more than an uneasy arrangement. In the small area around Aden itself, the British lived a life of fashionable London society, with Christmas pantomimes, cocktail parties and fancy-dress balls. Out in the rest of the harsh country, a hungry, isolated and savage people lived in fortified villages, clutching their daggers and rifles, always guarding their fields and flocks from greedy neighbours.

In 1960, the locals rebelled and the British showed they could be as savage as any natives. There were two liberation movements, the NLF and FLOSY, who agreed only on their hatred of the colonists. The NLF won (what do you expect of a guerilla organisation called FLOSY?). With bad grace, Britain got out.

Life

Yemen has the world's highest birth rate. Around the coasts the seas abound with sardines and sharks. On land the most important animals are the ibex and oryx. Both are faced with extinction.

Politics and industry

In 1970 just about everything except the local handicraft firms were nationalised.

Only people aged between 21 and 23 can be elected to the Provincial People's Committees.

The present Minister of State has the most appropriate name in the world for a politician. He is Abdu Azia Abdul Wali (for short, A. Wali).

Yugoslavia
Socijalisticka Federativna Republika Jogoslavija

One nation

There are
2 alphabets
3 religions
4 (main) languages
5 (principal) nationalities
6 republics
7 border countries

Square one

Serbia, Croatia, Slovenia, Montenegro, Bosnia, Herzegovina and Macedonia used to co-exist in the area. Initial difficulties were caused by the split in the Church of Rome. Serbs took on the Eastern Orthodox faith, Croats Roman Catholicism. Feudal lords fought it out until Turkey captured the lot. They were challenged by a rising led by Black George in Serbia.

More ugly than Ugly George, more unpredictable than Boy George, Black George was thought fit to lead the rebellion. His credentials were impeccable. He had already killed his father and brother. The Turks were driven out of Serbia and appeased by the gift of Black George's head. The area achieved independence in 1878.

World War One

It was Serbia's quarrel with Austria over Bosnia which caused the war. Emperor Franz Joseph was murdered on his way to a dinner where the dessert was *Bombe Surprise*. Austria *was* surprised and spread the war to Europe.

There's only one Josip Tito

Tito was the seventh son of fifteen. He had fought heriocally in World War One, being severely wounded in the back with a bayonet while fighting a Russian with a two-pronged spear. After the war he was sent to gaol for anti-state activity and described it as *'just like being at university'*. In World War Two, Yugoslavia went in under the leadership of Prince Paul. He was not a happy man with Hitler: *"Prince Paul's attitude looks like that of an unfortunate man in a cage with a tiger, hoping not to provoke him, while steadily dinner time approaches."* Tito, on the other hand, was acclaimed by Heinrich Himmler. *"I wish we had a dozen Titos in Germany".* In the war even Tito's dog was on his side, flinging itself across his face, saving his life.

At his death in 1979 a song went further than any of his admirers:
*Comrade Tito our white lily
All the young are greeting you
All the young and all the old
Comrade Tito your people's hope
Comrade Tito to you we swear
From your path never to stray.*

Politics and the state

Yugoslavia is the most truly Communist of the Communist countries. There is genuine worker participation in factories. But 85 per cent of the land is privately owned. In 1968, when the Soviet Union invaded Czechoslovakia, Tito put up posters at all airports which read *'Every country has the right to decide its own affairs'.* Though when Kosovo tried to leave Yugoslavia in 1981, severe repression resulted.

The economy

In 1960 maps of the country marked roads in two categories: one for carts and one for donkeys. Now a system of metalled roads exists. In 1977, 11 times more beer was drunk than in 1952. In the same period, illiteracy slumped from 50 per cent to 15 per cent.

Much of the economic advancement was achieved by very low wages and food rationing. But Yugoslavia has had the highest rate of inflation in Europe since 1965 and high debts. In 1981 prices rose by 40 per cent.

Population: 22 and a half million

Size: Slightly bigger than Britain, 99,000 sq. miles

Government: Communist

Languages: Serbo-Croat, Slovene, Macedonian

Capital: Belgrade

Currency: Dinar, para

Tips for tourists

Maraschino is the national drink.

Wine is also important. Visit Jerusalem, a wine village named by weak-hearted Crusaders fulfilling their oath *'to come to Jerusalem'*.

The sardine season opens in mid-June.

Vegetarians are welcome. In Yugoslavia there are even vegetarian jackals.

Yugoslavian independence. This woman is now spun round at high speed to dry her washing.

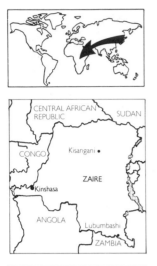

Zaire
Republique du Zaire

Zaire is not only a country. It is also a river. And the name of the currency. The President is called Mobutu Sese Seko ('Mobuto the Redeemer') which is also the name of a lake. There is a port on the coast called Banana.

Zairization

Zaire was called the Belgian Congo — before it went native under President Mobutu in 1973. All the old familiar names were changed — people, towns, rivers, lakes. Nothing was spared. Significantly, the road system collapsed — people were probably too confused to leave home and let it fall into disuse. There are now many abandoned plantations where farmers can no longer get their produce to town (wherever that is).

Old ways

Routes out of Zaire seem to be well-known. Coffee, gold, diamonds and ivory are smuggled out on a massive scale, perhaps along the country's many navigable rivers. Goods are also smuggled in. Fraud and the inadequacy of import controls led the Government to declare in 1979 that *the import figures no longer reflect reality*.

Zaire is so chronically in debt to Western countries that it is effectively run by the IMF. In 1980, the country was reported to be *Africa's worst economic disaster*.

Politics

Zairians don't need to get lost venturing out to join a political party. There is only one — and it comes to them. All Zairians are born members of the Mouvement Populaire de la Revolution (MPR). Those who ask *"What revolution?"* or *"How populaire?"* often find themselves up the Ubangi (a tributary of the River Zaire). Despite all these disincentives to leave home, 98.16 per cent of the population managed to locate a ballot box and re-elect Mobutu (the only candidate) as President in 1977.

The redeemer

President Mobutu is incredibly wealthy. He owns several palaces in Zaire and Europe and appropriated most of the profits from the Ali-Forman fight in Kinshasa in 1974. When he bought a US transport plane he asked that it should arrive filled with $60,000 worth of Coca-cola.

Pygmies with a six-foot white man or Masai with a twelve-foot one.

Dr. Livingstone, probably

It was near Lake Tanganyika (now Mobutu Sese Seko) that the American journalist Stanley found David Livingstone, the legendary Scots explorer, in 1871, and delivered his immortal words of greeting. Suffering from malaria, dysentery and mutiny from his African bearers, Stanley discovered Livingstone in the same state, plus internal bleeding. They broke open a bottle of champagne, the only thing to have survived the trip. Stanley returned to the States four months later to file his story.

Livingstone, who had set out to explore the continent with the words *"I shall open a path to the interior or perish"*, had achieved both goals by 1873.

Little and large

The River Zaire is the fourth longest river in the world. In places it is 10 miles wide. Zaire is the world's largest producer of industrial diamonds — about half the world's total. Zaire has: The largest forest reserves in Africa Half the world's cobalt production One seventh of the world's potential hydro-electric power capacity.

Life

Kinshasa, the capital, is the largest city in black Africa and the second most expensive in the world. Zaire has edible mushrooms the size of umbrellas and people the size of pygmies. In fact, they are pygmies — about 100,000 of them — some of whom are the smallest people in the world, the Mbuti. Average height for a Mbuti man is 4ft 6ins and for a woman 4ft 5ins.

Population: 29 million

Size: Ten times that of Britain, 900,000 sq. miles

Government: Republic

Main language: French, Lingala

Main Religion: Roman Catholic

Capital: Kinshasa

Currency: Zaire, likuta, sengi

Tips for tourists

Confine yourself for a few days in the appropriately named Mama Yemo hospital in Kinshasa — the busiest maternity hospital in the world.

Don't bother looking for a chemist shop. There are fewer of them per head than anywhere in the world.

The Mbuti pygmies make clothing from tree bark hammered with a piece of elephant's tusk.

Zambia

Roads

Zambia is part of the world's largest plateau. In the north the scenery is so monotonous that, in the rainy season, drivers spinning in the mud have travelled back the way they came without realising. Zambians have the highest motor accident rate in the world. This could be due to the lack of traffic lights.

Pre-Rhodes

For a long time after the discovery and exploitation of the rest of Africa, Zambia remained relatively untouched. The Portuguese had settled in Angola on the west coast and Mozambique on the east, and walking from one to the other became an obsession with them. Several intrepid explorers tried — and failed even to reach the borders of what is now Zambia.

It was a long time after the 16th Century Portuguese landings elsewhere that they were able to exploit the interior for slaves. The result was that tribes fled inland from the coast to avoid slavery. Today there are more than 90 different tribes in Zambia.

Once penetration began, however, the natives never stood a chance. In the kingdom of Chief Kangolo from 1550 the man in charge of defence and security was called the 'twite'.

Pre-pre-Rhodes

The earliest evidence of what man's ancestors looked like comes from Zambia (formerly Northern Rhodesia) and is called *Rhodesian Man*. Discovered in the 1950's this skull was used by their British masters to frighten native copper miners. It is 25,000 years old and shows an even smaller brain capacity than post-Rhodes man.

The famous book *King Solomon's Mines* by Rider Haggard is believed to have been inspired by the unknown interior of Zambia. Until the country was explored by Livingstone, rumours persisted about large amounts of treasure waiting to be taken.

Rhodes

The country was first colonised for its copper. Today the Copperbelt region is the third largest copper producer in the world. Cecil Rhodes founded a company to tap the copper seam until he was bought out by the British government. The British suggested making a federation out of Nyasaland and Northern and Southern Rhodesia.

In the teeth of African opposition this was done and a Machiavellian voting system was devised to persuade Africans that they had a vote. Voters had to have: an income of £300 per annum and eight years' education, *or* an income of £420 per annum and primary education, *or* an income of £720 per annum.

Since, even today, the average income is £250 per annum, proportional representation clearly wasn't the aim of the British. Sure enough, numbers of black votes were:
Southern Rhodesia — 420
Northern Rhodesia — 3
Nyasaland — 0
Northern Rhodesia achieved independence in 1963, 17 years before the name Rhodes finally disappeared off the map (being replaced by Zimbabwe).

Post-Rhodes

Today Zambia is ruled by the United National Independence Party under Kenneth Kaunda, who is president for life. The tribes carry on much as before. The Tonga wear sticks through their noses. The Makibi do complicated dances on long poles. The Twa — meaning 'did you see me?' — pride themselves on their invisibility. If you meet a Twa and he says *"Did you see me?"*, an affirmative answer will throw him into a mad rage.

Population: Almost 6 million

Size: Three times that of Britain, 290,000 sq. miles

Government: Republic

Official language: English

Main religion: Christianity

Capital: Lusaka

Currency: Kwacha, ngwee

Tips for tourists

Try the national dish — Lake Tanganyika sardine.

Visit the largest falls in the world, the Victoria Falls. Twice as high as Niagara, 5 million gallons of water per second tip over. The natives call them *'the smoke that thunders"*. Their vapour can be seen 20 miles away.

Visit the Kariba Dam, the largest man-made dam in the world. It is so big that migrating cuckoos once thought it was Lake Victoria and stopped on their journey. The natives killed large numbers and there was a noticeable lack of them in Britain that year.

Bring a good book. There is no television.

Zambia has virtually no traffic lights, but plenty of zebras crossing.

Zimbabwe

Tips for tourists

Lesbians should not be fooled into visiting the Great Dyke — it is only a huge geological split, 8 miles wide and 320 miles long.

Self-abusers should not be fooled into visiting Wankie National Park. It is a massive game park which, although containing many flesh-eating animals, gives little satisfaction.

Heterosexuals should not be fooled into mixing with the natives. Half the adult women and 20 per cent of the total population have or have suffered from VD. In one Harare suburb 99.99 per cent of adults are victims.

White hopes

A thousand years ago, the fabulous city of Zimbabwe stood here. The massive citadel was built of small granite blocks skilfully laid without mortar. Nearby stood the hill where gold was smelted. But by the time the British adventurer David Livingstone travelled up the Zambesi River to have a look around, all that was left were ruins inhabited by leopards, baboons and wild pigs.

So there was only one thing Dr. Livingstone could presume — that this would be a great place for the British to exploit. The exploiter-in-chief was Cecil Rhodes (who had made a fortune from diamonds by the age of 18 and later in life virtually owned and ran the whole of southern Africa). He set up the British South Africa Company which went on to run the country until 1923, when it became a British colony, Southern Rhodesia.

Liberal use of the horn was a hallmark of colonial Rhodesian taxi-drivers.

White mischief

After World War Two there was an influx of whites from Britain — scared at what the socialist government back home would do. Even so, by the early 1960's the whites were still outnumbered by more than 30 to one. To preserve their position, Rhodesia declared itself independent. Sanctions were imposed by a horrified world. This could have been disastrous for smokers, as Rhodesia was the world's biggest tobacco grower. However, nothing very dramatic happened and all the sanction-busting was swept under the bush. In 1979, the blacks got the power they

wanted, since when they have been able to concentrate on fighting each other rather than the whites.

Geography

Zimbabwe is a landlocked country in south-east Africa. It is conveniently situated next to South Africa — convenient during the days of UDI for sanction-busting by South Africa, convenient now for the South Africans to send in undercover squads to destabilise the Zimbabwean government.

Silly names

The president is called Canaan Banana. Cinemas are called bioscopes.

Redundancy

The trouble with having so many guerrilla armies was that the soldiers all had to be found jobs in the new Zimbabwe national army. So the government has set up a special department called the 'Demobilisation directorate' which is doing its best to get people out of the army and rehabilitated into unemployment.